The Rise of New Brokerages and the Restructuring of Real Estate Value Chain

Shusong Ba · Xianling Yang

The Rise of New Brokerages and the Restructuring of Real Estate Value Chain

XIAMEN UNIVERSITY PRESS

Shusong Ba
HKEx
Hong Kong
China

Xianling Yang
Lianjia Real Estate Research Institute
Beijing
China

Translated by Feng Yue, Hanxiong Zhu, Menghan Deng and Chunqiu Xia

ISBN 978-981-10-7714-2   ISBN 978-981-10-7715-9   (eBook)
https://doi.org/10.1007/978-981-10-7715-9

Jointly published with Xiamen University Press, Xiamen, China

The print edition is not for sale in China Mainland. Customers from China Mainland please order the print book from: Xiamen University Press.

Library of Congress Control Number: 2018939012

Printed on acid-free paper

This Springer imprint is published by the registered company Springer Nature Singapore Pte Ltd. part of Springer Nature
The registered company address is: 152 Beach Road, #21-01/04 Gateway East, Singapore 189721, Singapore

Preface: The Redefinition of Intermediaries

At present, China's real estate industry is at the history turning point of transformation. Housing supply as a whole is becoming more balanced, and the time of supply shortage is past. China's housing market is experiencing a transition from incremental development to stock circulation. In 2016, the sales of secondhand houses in a dozen Chinese cities exceeded that of new houses. The sales of secondhand houses in Beijing, Shanghai, and Shenzhen are twice to three times of that of the new houses, respectively, which signifies that China's first-tier cities have entered the stage led by secondhand houses. Some second-tier cities like Hangzhou, Nanjing, and Suzhou also see a rapid rise of the turnover rate. As the rate of urbanization and turnover is rising, more cities will enter the time of housing stoke.

In this day and age, the intermediary industry serves as an important part of housing stock circulation market. The standardization and development of it play a very crucial role in improving the effective housing circulation. Theoretically, the circulation rate not only determines the housing market's supply, it also influences the upgrades of housing demand and finally will make a difference to the effective allocation of housing resource. The nature of circulation lies in the match of supply and demand. The match efficiency fundamentally determines the utility of the supplier and the demander. In principle, if the market is effective enough, each flow of houses represents a Pareto improvement of housing consumption. From these perspectives, the role of intermediary is self-evident. In recent years, the intermediary penetration in the secondhand house trades and circulation continues to improve, and it is almost 90% in Beijing and Shanghai. In the future, with the continuous standardization and service capability improvement, the intermediary industry will have a more and more significant role and outstanding function in the secondhand house circulation.

More importantly, the definition of intermediaries today has experienced fundamental changes. First, the boundary between secondhand house intermediary had new house agent and is becoming more and more vague. The connected effect of new houses and secondhand houses is increasingly obvious. Second, the connection between intermediary and finance is becoming increasingly closer. The circulatory finance development has led to the establishment of more effective links between housing assets and cash flow. It also helps realize a freer flowing of the ownership of houses. Third, the intermediary industry becomes an important transmission channel. Fourth, participants of the intermediary industry are more and more diverse. Developers, agents, Internet companies, and financial institutions have joined the brokerage industry. This complex and diversified industry structure did not exist anywhere in the world before. From this point of view, the standardization and healthy development of the intermediary industry are not only of great interest to the house buyers and sellers, but are also of direct interest to the real estate market's healthy development.

However, the chaotic intermediary industry is also one of the most obvious subdivided trade structures. Though long established, it has a very short history. Many years ago, intermediaries already played a role in housing transactions. However, the housing intermediary industry as a whole still has not had considerably mature basic regulations, rules, or a scientific theoretical system. It also lacks fundamental industry bottom lines. From the point of a broker, the short working years, the high draining rate, and the lack of belonging and security are all prevalent problems.

As a result, the rise of the new intermediary will be an industry mission in the next 5–10 years, whether from the point of real estate industry's transition or from that of the industry's healthy development. There are at least five symbols of the rise of the new intermediary: First, the flow rate of secondhand houses rises to the comparable level of developed countries. Second, there are a great number of professional brokers. Their earnings increase with their working years. There are codes of conduct, sales languages, moral bottom lines, and business ethics for brokers. Their senses of belonging and happiness are enhancing. Their learning materials are constantly being improved. Third, there are a number of comprehensive and vertical listed companies in the housing stock market. Fourth, there is wide attention from the academia.

Of course, the rise of the new intermediary cannot be achieved by itself. We studied and compared the brokerage industry's development in the USA, Japan, Britain, Australia, Hong Kong (China), and Taiwan (China). We summarized successful experience and shortcomings. According to the current development of China's industries, we put forward the following six key pillars of the brokerage industry:

The first pillar is the production, distribution, and matching of information. It is necessary to implement written commission, recognition, and encouragement of exclusive entrustment, and also to apply the "name and shame" system and punish severely those intermediaries that transmit misleading information. These constitute the starting point of establishing industry-wide norms.

The second pillar is the trading system. Force the implementation of property rights verification and capital supervision, and protect the transaction security and consumer rights and interests. It is the core of the realization of transaction security.

The third pillar is the liquidity finance. Clearly distinguish and support the financial innovation of the smooth trading's short-term capital turnover. It is the key to resolve the capital pain point of customer transactions.

The fourth pillar is the mobile Internet. Reshape the process of housing transactions, break the traditional brokerage industry cost structure, and achieve the unity of economies of scale effect and network effect. It is the most important infrastructure of the future real estate brokerage industry.

The fifth pillar is the industry supervision system. Implement parallel management mechanisms of the government and industry self-discipline, and better play the role of industry associations. It is the fundamental support of the brokerage industry standardization and development.

The sixth pillar is the team of professional brokers. Bring in the brokers access mechanism, establish the broker behavior norms and rules of practice such as business ethics, etc. Promote the specialization and professionalization of brokers. This is the core pillar of the brokerage industry norms.

Facing the historic opportunity of industry development and looking at the present situation and the future of the brokerage industry, it is the mission of all industry participants to create a well-regulated and healthy brokerage industry. As researchers, Dr. Yang Xianling and I are honored to observe and witness the development and maturing of the industry and systematically sort out and summarize the process as much as we can. We also carry out initial theoretical discussions to some degree. We also look forward to more scholars to join the research of this industry and bring in more thoughts and changes so as to gradually lead this industry to a healthier future.

Hong Kong, China   Shusong Ba
October 2016

Acknowledgements

Upon completion of the book, we want to thank friends, scholars, and peers who have generously helped us along the way.

To Mr. Li Tongrong from Gigahouse, Taiwan, Dr. Cao Yunzheng from Japanese Real Estate Research Institute, Dr. Xiang Dong from Linajia Research Institute, and friends from Overseas Department of Lianjia, our greatest appreciation for your rich, accurate, and valuable information and suggestions on international experience.

Friends in the real estate industry have offered us selfless help. They are Chris Wang, realtor of Coldwell Banker, USA; Richard Chan from First American Title Insurance Company; Ms. Ichino Miyuki, Japanese Real Estate Notary; realtors, transfer agents, and financial assistants from Lianjia; Dr. Song Jingyu from Beijing Ehomepay Company; Mr. Tian Haitao and Ms. Xu Yan. We are greatly inspired by their profound understanding of and most direct and realistic experience in real estate industry.

We are fully aware that errors and negligence in the book are inevitable due to limited time and knowledge, taking into consideration that basic research in real estate brokerage industry is still weak and study of international experience and best practices is insufficient. We will strive to improve our study continuously and apologize for any mistakes or negligence in the book. We look forward to having more peers and researchers in other fields to join us in the pursuit of valuable research that drives industrial progress.

Contents

Chapter 1
The Six Pillars

- Nowadays, the connotation of brokerage industry has been greatly changed and enriched. The industrial norms today not only refer to those of brokerage firms, but a system that requires multi-side participation as well. Consequently, traditional firms centring merely on brokering would face a phasing out.
- This chapter presents six pillars for the future real estate brokerage industry, namely, the generation, distribution and matching of information, transaction system, circulation finance, mobile internet, supervision system and professional brokers. These six pillars would constitute a key framework in regulating and developing the brokerage industry.

China remains comparatively disordered in the real estate brokerage industry, and compares unfavourably with other countries in the existing home market, with a circulation rate of only about 2%. Low commission rate, vicious competition, repetitive capacity construction and high draining rate of broker sunder a brokerage model are still haunting the whole industry. Concerning the developing trend, the booming mobile internet has significantly changed the way people live and dramatically improved customer experience, yet has made little difference to the real estate, where the impact of the internet remains infant, and has not yet improved the information symmetry. It appears that China has still got a long way to go before entering a new era.

So, what should we do to move into the future, replace disorder with regulation and realize the rise of new brokerages?

1 Indicators of the Present Situation and Existing Problems of Chinese Real Estate Brokerage Industry

Apart from the impression left in our mind, indicators that allow vertical and horizontal comparison could be more reliable when evaluating the development level of the brokerage industry of a country. Generally speaking, the indicators could be

© Xiamen University Press and Springer Nature Singapore Pte Ltd. 2018
S. Ba and X. Yang, *The Rise of New Brokerages and the Restructuring of Real Estate Value Chain*, https://doi.org/10.1007/978-981-10-7715-9_1

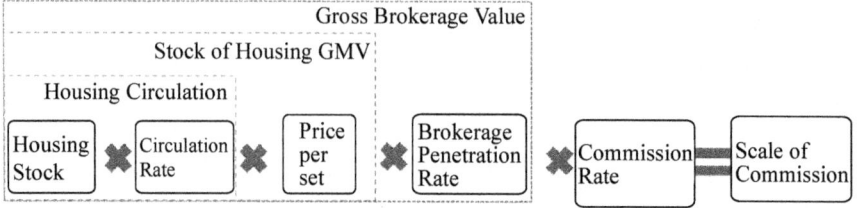

Fig. 1 Multiplier relation among indicators of total amount. *Source* Market Research Centre, Homelink

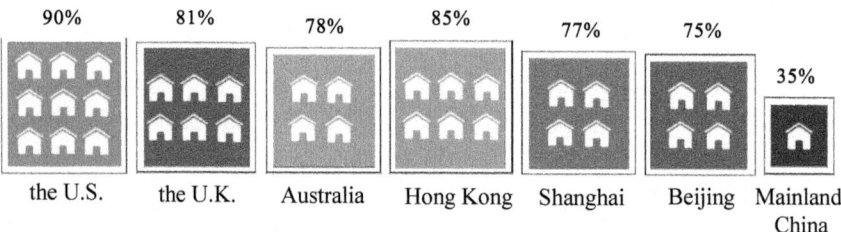

Fig. 2 The percentage of existing home transaction GMV in different countries and regions. *Source* Market Research Centre, Homelink

divided into three categories: indicators of total amount, of distribution and of efficiency. The first kind is mainly composed of circulation rate, brokerage penetration rate and commission rate, which could show the size of the profit pie of the whole brokerage industry in a country. The indicators of distribution include profession concentration ratio, number and scale, relative income level and commission splits, which present the allocation of income among companies and brokers. The indicators of efficiency usually refer to the number of taken orders per capita, capacity per capita as well as capacity per company. By looking into these indicators we can not only conclude the status quo and problems of Chinese brokerage industry throughout history, but make a better choice for where it should lead by comparing the experiences of other countries as well, as shown in Figs. 1 and 2.

1.1 Circulation Rate

Circulation Rate, the crucial factor of the size of a marketplace, measures the activity of a market. By comparison we can draw the following conclusions. From an international perspective, the circulation rate of Chinese brokerage industry remains relatively low and calls for further improvement: the American market has a circulation rate with a historical average of more than 4%, and its peak at 6.6%; the British market once achieved a circulation rate of 5.3%; while in China, by

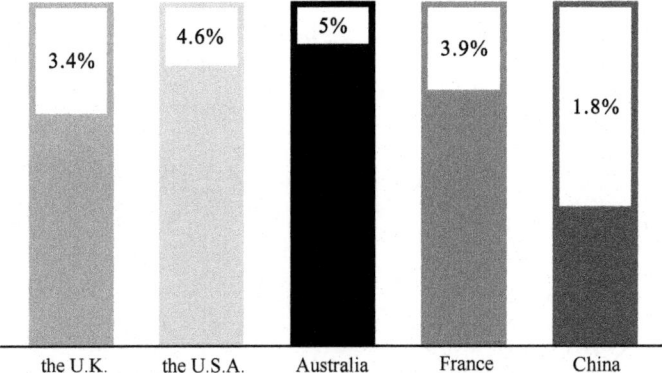

Fig. 3 Average circulation rates of existing home markets in different countries. *Source* Market Research Centre, Homelink

contrast, the circulation rate in 2015 is approximately 1.8% (as shown in Fig. 3). From the level of cities, Chinese cities significantly differentiate in their circulation rates. Statistics show that in 2015, the volume in existing home market and that in new home market showed a ratio of greater than 1:1 in roughly ten cities, and the figures are remarkably notable in Beijing, Shanghai and Shenzhen with a ratio of, respectfully, 1.5:1, 2.4:1 and 2.5:1 (Figs. 4 and 5).

Home transactions in most second-tier cities and almost all third-tier cities remain new-home dominated. In a regional context, the maturity of brokerage industry notably differs among different regions of a city. In Beijing, for example, the 200 thousand existing homes transacted in 2015 are concentrated in approximately 4000 relatively developed communities, with 80% of the transacted houses higher concentrated in 2400 communities—20% among the overall 12 thousand communities in Beijing. In the six urban districts of Beijing, moreover, up to 65%

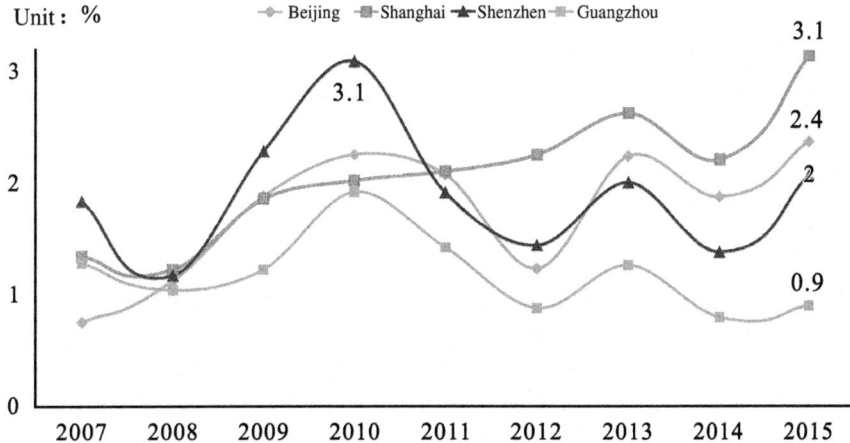

Fig. 4 Circulation rates in different cities in China, from 2007 to 2015. *Source* Market Research Centre, Homelink

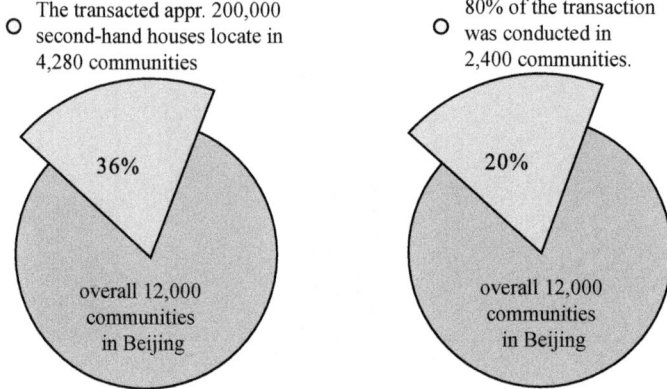

Fig. 5 The distribution of Beijing existing home transactions, 2015. *Source* Market Research Centre, Homelink

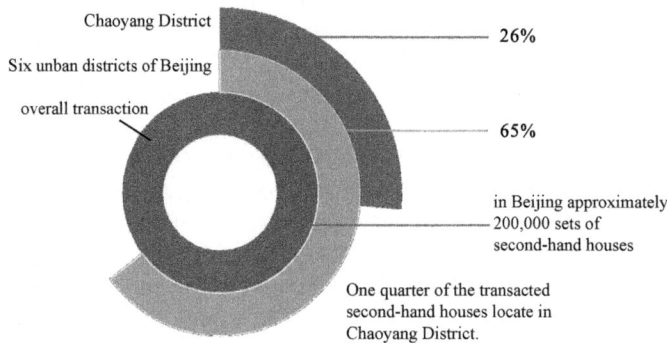

Fig. 6 The concentration of existing home transactions in Beijing city. *Source* Market Research Centre, Homelink

of the transaction volume features existing home market, with Chaoyang District alone accounting for 26% of the volume in the market. (Shown in Fig. 6).

1.2 Brokerage Penetration Rate

In countries and areas where the real estate brokerage industry has been relatively mature, especially where there are strict requests on the procedures of transaction, self-dealing transactions are no longer popular. Developed countries like America, Japan and Britain keep a brokerage penetration rate of more than 90%. In recent years, the industry in first-tier cities has been developed rapidly, and the transaction

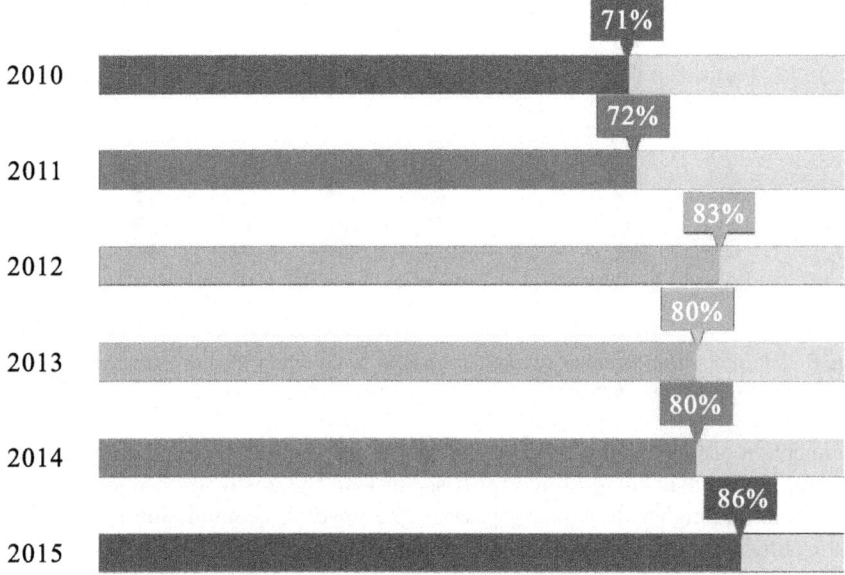

Fig. 7 The brokerage penetration rate in Beijing, from 2010 to 2015. *Source* Market Research Centre, Homelink

conducted with brokers is taking a much larger proportion, though, much more effort is needed.

In a further regulated brokerage industry with an integrated service system, the percentage of transactions conducted with brokerage companies would remarkably rise in the years to come. Nowadays, the existing home markets in first-tier cities in China are relatively regulated, with comparatively high brokerage penetration rates and stable paces of moving ahead. In 2015, the brokerage penetration rate in Beijing achieved 84%, increased by 6% than in early 2014; the rate in Shanghai achieved 85% in 2015, with an increase of nearly 5%. (As is shown in Fig. 7).

1.3 Commission Rate

The commission rate is a consequence, naturally resulting from a series of conditions: (1) the efficiency, ceteris paribus, and the commission rate share a reverse relationship. In principle, with the development of the Internet and technology, the commission rate features a tendency to decline. (2) The threshold of brokerage industry is another decisive factor. Theoretically, if the entry and quit between the brokerage industry and other professions are not seriously hindered or impeded, the income of brokers should remain paralleled with that of the average level of other professions lest a large number of people crowd in, cut-throat inner-industrial

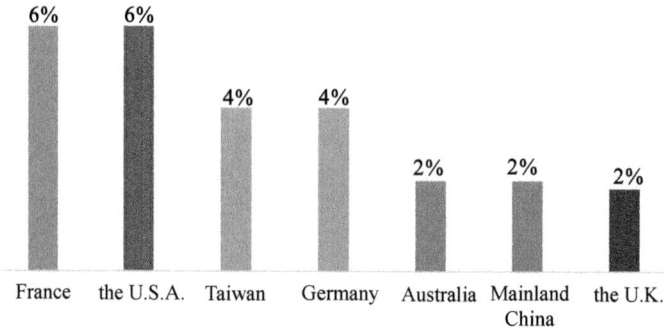

Fig. 8 The commission rates in existing home market in different countries and regions. *Source* Market Research Centre, Homelink

competition occurs and the commission rate be reduced. (3) To a certain extent, the housing price shares a substitute relationship with the commission rate. With the cost fixed, the higher the housing price is, the lower the commission rate will be. For example, the American brokerage industry has its commission rate at 6%, three times that in Britain, while the median housing price in America is only half of that in Britain. That is to say, a comparably much higher commission rate in the US doesn't consequently result in a higher level of income among brokers, and the fact is, on the contrary, that most of them are paid less than the median level of income in America. (4) The model of commissioning is significantly critical to the mechanism and level of the commission rate. By comparing among different countries, we can see that the commission rate is notably higher under the model of trusteeship than of brokerage (as is shown in Fig. 8).

From the analysis above, we can see that the commission rate is influenced by a series of factors, and the influences casted by the factors feature diversity and variety. Practically, we may focus less on the level of commission rate, yet more on whether the fluctuation of the commission rate matches that of efficiency, and that of the service system.

Generally speaking, the commission rate of Chinese brokerage industry remains around 1%, which is comparatively low. And the status quo results from the low threshold of the industry as well as the vicious competition and excess capacity under the brokerage model. To conclude, the low-level price competition together with the problems result from repetitive capacity stings the whole Chinese real estate brokerage industry.

1.4 Commission Splits

Commission splits denotes to the commission split among the participated agents, and that between an agent and the brokerage company he is working with. Practically, the commission splits could work as an essential indicator. For one thing, the commission mechanism of a company directly determines the income of its brokers. Brokers are the breadwinners of the company, and the "super brokers" are even valued as treasures. Thus we say that to attract and keep those brokers, the commission rate plays an important role. For another, the commission split would also affect the brokers' practical performance, which would further influence customer experience.

By adoptingan MLS (Multiple Listing Service) and a mechanism of bilateral entrustment, American brokerage industry features relatively simple commission mechanism and predictability in brokers' incomes. The commission split between a seller's agent and a buyer's agent is at a rate of 50/50. The consequently mutual benefit between agents effectively promotes their cooperation and the sharing of housing resources—buyer-seller match becomes more efficient, and the customer experience gets improved.

However, without such a common code as MLS has, or exclusive entrust and the cooperation mechanism between buying and selling agents, the commission split in China's brokerage industry is much more different. Under a traditional mechanism of commission splits, the major split goes to the companies; while American companies keep a split of less than 20%: a typical case could be RE/MAX, an American real estate company which gets a commission split of approximately 5%. On the other hand, the cooperation among agents is essential for the whole industry, while few China's traditional brokerage companies have clear code for the splits among brokers. This could lead to a vicious competition over customers and housing resources, and further harm the buy-seller match and hinder customer experience from being improved.

2 The Changes that Re-defined the Brokerage Industry

Today, the connotation of brokerage industry has been greatly changed. For further regulation and development, we should first understand and grasp the changes.

2.1 A Housing Environment Centring on Brokerage Starts to Show Itself

Firstly, the overall housing market could be categorized into three markets, namely, primary market, secondary market and aftermarket, respectively corresponds to the generation, circulation and management of properties; among them, the increasingly important role that circulation plays in the whole housing environment accounts for the most significant change in the real estate market nowadays. In China, the most significant change in housing market takes place as a transition:

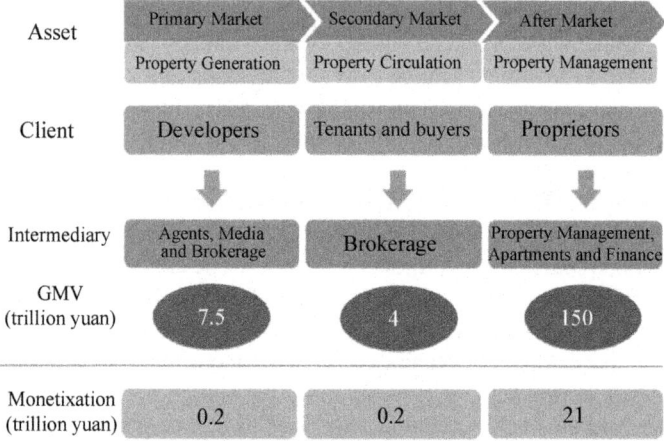

Fig. 9 Levels of China's housing market. *Source* Market Research Centre, Homelink

from a market of the generation of property, to one of property circulation and property management.

Secondly, the brokerage industry, as a critical medium, is being viewed as the core of real estate industry. With the comparative advantage of "being closer to customers", brokers are more and more frequently employed to deal with new-home transactions; the joint brokering service for both new and existing homes prevails, and the boundaries between existing and new home brokerages are blurring. Moreover, with the advantages of being connected with housing resources, and the rich accumulation of property data, the brokerage industry stands a great chance in entering the sphere of housing management and increasing its business scopes. According to statistics, the GMVs of new home and existing home brokerages are respectively about 7.5 and 4 trillion, while the property management is targeted at a housing stock with an asset value of 150 trillion, which is by far larger (As is shown in Fig. 9).

2.2 People from Different Walks of Life are Participating

Participants of brokerage industry now feature diversity, thus are faced with a significantly changed competition. In a foreseeable future, China's brokerage industry will gradually form into a game among several essential systematic forces.

Firstly is the giant brokerage company that started from brokerage businesses and developed into fields of new home agency, youth hostels and property management. These companies, in principle, enjoy advantages as first movers on the basis of their rich housing trade scenarios, and are expected to become the most important participants and tendency drivers.

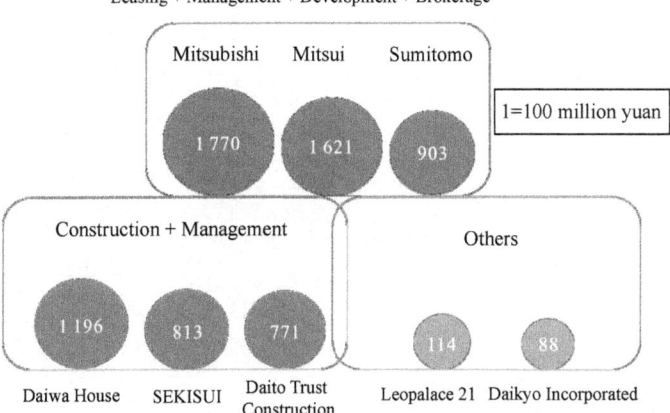

Fig. 10 Market capitalization of several comprehensive developers in Japan, (May, 2016). *Source* Market Research Centre, Homelink

Secondly are the comprehensive developers that started from developing, and horizontally and vertically merged with other spectrums, including youth hostels, property management, real estate finance, architecture design, and so on. The trend is now crystal clear that real estate developers in a transformation period, especially those state-owned and listed enterprises which are rich in fund and resources, rather than just focusing on the developing market, are expanding their effort on the market of property management. Japanese enterprises, for example, Mitsui, Mitsubishi and Sumitomo, are typical cases that have experienced successful transformations from the development toward the management, brokerage and leasing of property. (See Fig. 10).

Thirdly, internet companies are springing up. The internet companies can be categorized into three types. The first type is the real estate media companies which were founded in traditional PC-era and have transformed into brokerage companies providing tradable services. At present, they are in the turning point from off line services to online services, as well as from media to transaction. The second is the start-ups that were born and bred in the era of mobile internet. They entered real estate industry with new home, leasing and youth hostels businesses, and are now expanding into the brokerage industry. This type of companies could practically turn out to be the wing-flapping butterflies of the butterfly effect—though inconspicuous for now, is probable to have a huge influence. With a crystal ball, they are still yet humble; but with an insight, they'll lead us as a trend and direction, and would ultimately act as the core force in the industrial shake-up. The third type denotes to industrial giants like BATJ (Baidu, Alibaba, Tencent and JD) that are penetrating into the brokerage sector. Although the internet giants seem comparatively irrelative with real estate businesses, they would enter the field in the form of capital, by way of scenario docking and exchanging, on the basis of the housing trade scenario valuing more than 10 trillion yuan.

Fig. 11 Multiple participants
of future brokerage industry.
Source Market Research
Centre, Homelink

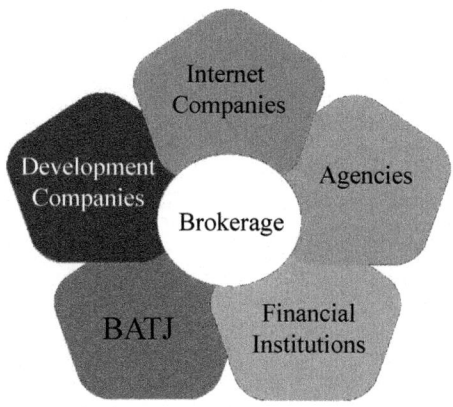

The forth type is financial institutions such as major banks and insurance companies, which would as well expand a deal of effort in real estate market by way of finance. Their central advantage is the access to capital, while the central disadvantage lies in the industrial isolation with trade. Under these circumstances, cooperation with other industries remains the dominant choice. (As is shown in Fig. 11).

2.3 The Transactional and Financial Attributes of Real Estate are Merging

The financial attribute accounts for the core attribute of real estate, while the core of financial attribute lies in an effective linkage between asset value and cash flow, through which the industries of brokerage and finance are well interwoven. From a manager's perspective, it's not advisable to deny or break the link artificially or partially; instead, to promote regulations and development scientifically in the context of market would be wiser, and the details are described as follows.

To start with, the transaction of existing homes represents a circulation between property titles and cash flow. In this process, the combination of finance and brokerage will provide a smooth channel for the circulation of titles, which is why this kind of finance are also named as "circulation finance" or "turnover finance". With the transaction of real estate being increasingly complicated, the transaction cycles being extended, and the transactions being less as stable, to develop circulation finance is not only necessary in the promotion of home circulation and the control of risk, but macro-significant in expanding home supply and stabilizing home price, as well.

Second, existing home leasing, youth hostels and property management stand for the circulation between the right to use the assets and cash flow, involving numerous categories of financial services, including renters' instalment, asset securitization, lease securitization, real estate fund, and so on; these finance services, when compared with circulation financial ones, are more complicated in procedures, more strict with risk control, and thus less combined with the brokerage industry.

2.4   Brokerage Now Plays an Important Role in the Macro-economic Regulation and the Control on Real Estate

Nowadays, the brokerage industry not only is an essential part of the real estate market, but also begins to play as a significant determinant of the real estate and financial policies. In the initial stage of real estate industry, the approach of making policies to affect land purchase, then influence new project investments, and then promote fixed asset investment and economic growth should be logically correct under a transmission mechanism of control and monetary policies. However, when the real estate market has started to develop the transaction of existing homes, the transmission mechanism is less influential, and starts to divide into two cluesinstead. Consequently, the brokerage industry becomes an essential channel for macro-economic regulation and the control of real estate.

Firstly, the changes in policies act as a clue in foreseeing and anticipating. For example, the easing of credit control policy will cast an impact on the sellers' and the buyers' expectations, and practically affect the sellers' new listings and listed prices, as well as the buyers' demand and quoted prices. Under a typical model of C—B—C (Consumer—Business—Consumer) market, pricing mechanism is totally different with that in a B—C market. Generally speaking, the existing home market, where the sellers' and buyers' anticipation plays an increasingly important role, and the "herd-behaviour" is increasingly conspicuous, is more prone to see radical booms and busts, and enter negative circles of bubbles and breakdowns. Thus a healthy and standardized real estate brokerage industry would be utterly essential and desirable in stabilizing the market.

The second clue can be translated into the wealth effect. The price formulated in existing home market would influence the prices in non-transactional stock market, thereby affect the asset value, and consequently affect people's willingness and ability to consume. Again, take Beijing for example: the circulation rate of Beijing existing home stock now is about 3%. That is to say, the price of the active market that accounts for 3% of the existing home market would obviously influence the asset value of the "inactive" housing stock which accounts for 97% of the whole market value, and thereby influence people's feeling of being wealthier or poorer, their willingness and ability to consume, and the growth of economy—the rule that perfectly applies to American and other developed markets, is now prevailing in China.

Fig. 12 The six pillars in the
rise of new brokerages.
Source Market Research
Centre, Homelink

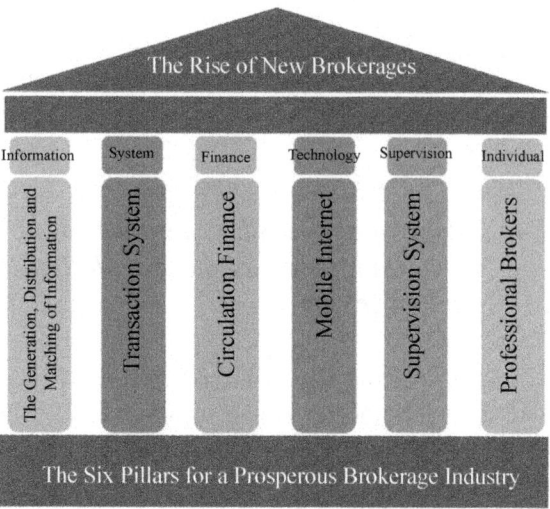

3   The Six Pillars

To regulate and promote the development of brokerage industry and to boost real estate circulation rate and cultivate professional brokers and breathe life into the industry and advance the status of brokerage profession, we put forward the Six Pillars that could constitute a framework in the present context to prop up the prosperity of brokerage industry. (As is shown in Fig. 12).

The generation, distribution and matching of information together form the first pillar, the start-point of a standardized brokerage industry. For the property information to be complete, timely and authentic, and the transactions to be made wittily, transparently and reasonably, the generation and distribution of the information call for fundamental changes: firstly, listings in writing should be implemented. The basic factors in a commission shall be made clear and the commission price and period shall then be confirmed with contracts in writing. Secondly, exclusive right-to-sell listing should be acknowledged and encouraged. Open listing, however, provides no intellectual property protection of the brokers' effort of information generation, so the brokers might be internally stimulated to hide the truth while disseminate false information. In an international context, it's the general trend to replace open listing with exclusive right-to-sell listing. And with the powers of buyers and sellers being balanced, and the market scale being enlarged, Chinese real estate, too, will waltz naturally into the stage of exclusive right-to-sell listing. Thirdly, a "Blacklist System" and a strict punishment system taken against the brokers and Internet companies that disseminate false information should be employed. The status quo, not only lacks a mechanism of punishment, but generally acknowledges the dissemination of false information as a business model. Thus we say that the standardization of information should starts from the very beginning—and it is still a long way to go.

The second pillar, the transaction system is at the heart of the security of transactions. Basically, the risks in asset transaction originate from the temporal or procedural mismatches of contract flow, cash flow as well as title flow, and custody of funds is accounted a most effective way to control the risks. The nature of existing home transaction, different with that of general goods transaction, is a process of dynamic exchange operated with contractual constraints. Accompanied by the flows of information, funds and property titles, the dynamic process is concerned with several timings of fund and title delivery, intricate procedures, multiple participants and the debtors' continuous entering and exiting, and is therefore haunted by unsuitable matches of fund and titles in time, and threatened by uncertain risks lurking in the extended transaction cycles. Moreover, as a kind of non-standard commodities, existing homes feature complex property information, and add to the difficulties and risks of self-dealing transactions—for any rare accidents could result in the buyer's huge loss, which is why compulsory custody of funds is essential and indispensible to guarantee safe transactions and protect the consumers. The story now, though, is quite dissatisfying. The present fund custody, including government supervision, commercial bank custody and four-party (namely, the buyer, the seller, the bank and the broker) custody, are mostly based on banking services. Common drawbacks are seen in custody efficiency, services, and customer experience; worse still, many cities have not yet been equipped with any sort of fund custody.

Circulation finance is the third pillar, and it has two functions. One is to deal with the sore point in transactions for the customers, so as to better meet their needs, and reduce the transactions of uncertainty. The other is to practically constitute smooth transactions by short-term funds. Nowadays, the mounting need for trade-in services only adds to the complexity of the transactions; and more than ever, an existing-home transaction based financial service is desirable and expected. Therefore, to standardize the industry and provide financial support, financial innovations in real estate transactions, especially in existing home transactions, need supporting and encouraging. The present situation reveals that most products of real estate finance, such as the release of mortgage and balance payment, target practical transactions, and could complement the existing banking services. Besides, considering compliance issues, the boundaries of financial policies in real estate market should be drawn clear, and the financial innovations in short-term fund circulation with an aim to smooth transactions, too, should be distinguished and encouraged. As these financial products can play an important role in facilitating transactions, reducing risks, expanding housing supply as well as controlling house prices, they are supposed to be distinguished and separated from leverage products.

The fourth pillar is mobile Internet, which would play as the most important infrastructure in the future real estate brokerage industry—more than a tool, but a necessity, like water and electricity. Several years ago, the internet was nothing but one of the channels for brokers to disseminate information. But today, the Internet has been penetrating into every spectrum, from information to services, of property sector; in the years to come, the Internet would reconstitute the procedures and construction of asset transactions to improve transaction efficiency, and would rebuild the network of brokers' partnership and break the cost structures of traditional brokerage industry, so as to unite the scale effect and the network effect, and disruptively change the whole industry.

The supervision system is counted the fifth pillar, which is the very base that props up a regulated and developing brokerage industry. In America, for example, two parallel supervision systems are employed. One is government supervision, and the other is industrial self-governing. State governments set up real estate associations and bureaus to govern brokerage companies and brokers, in accordance mainly with the Real Estate License Act of each state. In practice, however, industrial associations in America, as a supervisor featuring more severity, more intensity, and closer contact with the industry, play a more significant role. And mainly, there are two reasons. For one, the associations, apart from following the state-made industrial regulations, is neither affiliate with nor subordinate to the government, and is consequently characterized by independency and credibility. The associations are only answerable to the brokerage industry and brokers, thus autonomously safeguard and promote the standardization of industry development. For another, and far more crucially, the industrial associations are guaranteed with independent financial rights and stable revenue. The major revenue streams are association dues paid by brokerage companies and brokers, for in order to join the association, a real estate company or broker must join and pay dues to all three levels of associations, namely, regional association, state association and national association.

The sixth pillar is professional brokers, who play an utterly vital role in a regulated and standardized real estate brokerage industry. In an international context, among more than three-hundred million Americans, there are about one million professional brokers; averagely, in America, there is one broker in every three hundred people. Considering the dense population of China, it's estimated that when an equilibrium state is reached, there will be approximately one million brokers working for 250 million Chinese urban families—with a total family asset worth 15 billion Yuan. (As is shown in Fig. 13) Therefore, it's essential for the service-oriented brokers to be professional, and utterly desirable for integrated professional regulations, including professional norms, professional languages and

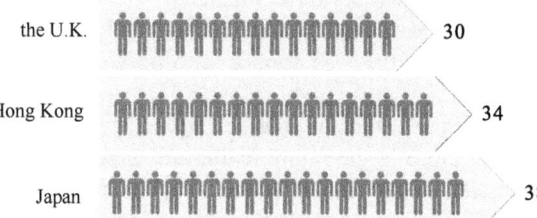

Fig. 13 The number of real estate brokers in every 10,000 people in different regions and countries. *Source* Market Research Centre, Homelink

the U.K.   30

Hong Kong   34

Japan   38

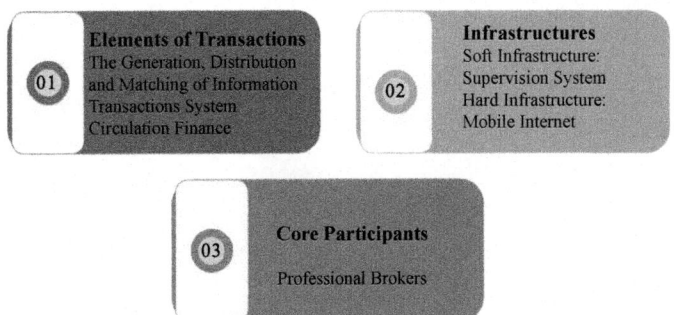

Fig. 14 Categories of the six pillars of a healthy real estate brokerage industry. *Source* Market Research Centre, Homelink

professional ethics, to be established. Additionally, industrial admittance and learning mechanisms are equally demanded, which calls for the teaching materials to be further completed and perfected. For example, American brokers should take comprehensive lessons, including Real Estate Economics, Real Estate Finance, General Accounting, Real Estate Law, Real Estate Asset Management, Property Management and Real Estate Appraisal; Japanese real estate agents, too, are supposed to acquire relative knowledge, including architecture, law, taxes and duties, and appraisal, and pass rigorous examinations before certificated; while Chinese brokerage education is still in an initial stage—with the focus on improving the students' verbal language skills, or, speechcraft.

The six pillars, as a whole, play their respective parts and acting upon one another at the same time, and constitute an integrated framework. The generation, distribution and matching of information is the start point of transactions and a standardized industry; transaction systems are the skeleton of transactions, and circulation finance functions as the lubricant of the system; mobile Internet is the hard technical infrastructure, and supervision system is the soft infrastructure; and professional brokers are the core of the whole industry. Constituted and combined, the six pillars working together will prop up the regulation and standardization of the real estate brokerage industry. (See Fig. 14).

Chapter 2
The Generation, Distribution and Matching of Information

- The information is the start point of existing home transaction, and the generation, distribution and matching of information determines the transaction efficiency.
- In the short run, we need to set up a system of housing resource listing contract in writing, a real-name housing resource information release system, and a deposit mechanism for authentic housing information to regulate the generation of housing information and guarantee the completeness, timeliness and accuracy of the information.

In the long run, with more and more participants from different fields joining the brokerage industry, we should set up a multi-industry and interagency information supervision system which covers multiple participants, so that the release of information could be standardized, and that the supervision of brokerage companies, Internet companies, software companies, brokers and other participants could be incorporated into a unified framework.

Housing transaction is a highly information-intensive process of policy making, requiring accurate information in each session. Housing supply is highly-localized, decentralized and non-standardized, while the market demand is highly differential and individualized, thus the information asymmetry in housing transactions remains a prominent problem. In terms of information, the primal issue for housing brokerage industry would be to obtain sufficient, transparent and prompt information, expose the information at much as possible, improve information matching efficiency, reduce the buyers' home search cost, and create a closed loop of secure, efficient information processing.

© Xiamen University Press and Springer Nature Singapore Pte Ltd. 2018

S. Ba and X. Yang, *The Rise of New Brokerages and the Restructuring of Real Estate Value Chain*, https://doi.org/10.1007/978-981-10-7715-9_2

1   The Connotation and Determinants of the Information in Existing Home Transactions

1.1   The Definition and Connotation of Information

The information in home transactions includes not only the static and the information of physical condition of a house, but also the information generated in transactions that features dynamicity. Particularly, the dynamicity shows it self during the generation, distribution, matching of information and the trading process. (As is shown in Fig. 1).

The information could be further categorized into four parts, namely, the information of listing, the information of physical condition, the information of ownership and the information of matchmaking.

1.1.1   The Information of Listing

The information of listing mainly consists of: the entrusted agent, the listing agreement and the term of listing. Among them, the most complex part is the housing resource information, which is generated in the process of the home-seller's entrusting his for-sale home to agencies. And listing agreement usually comes in three types: exclusive right-to-sell listing, exclusive brokerage listing and open listing. (As is shown in Fig. 2).

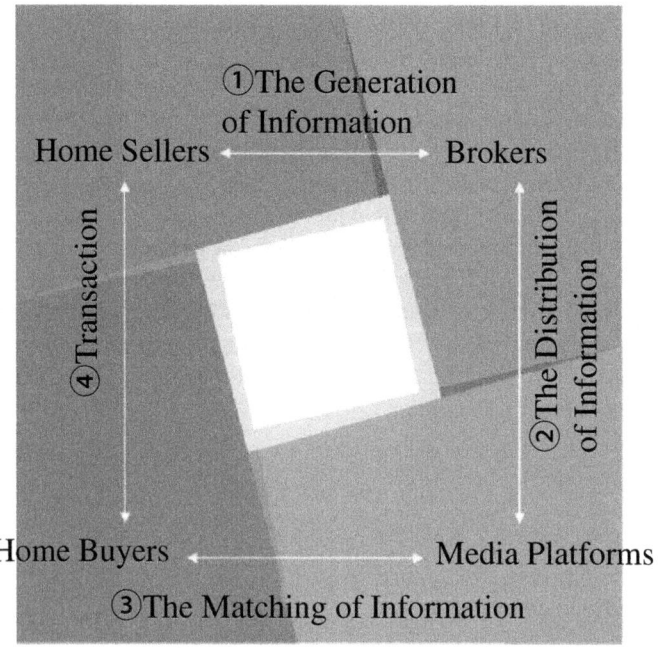

Fig. 1 Transactions and the generation, distribution and matching of housing resource information. *Source* Market Research Centre, Homelink

Fig. 2 The three types of
listings. *Source* Market
Research Centre, Homelink

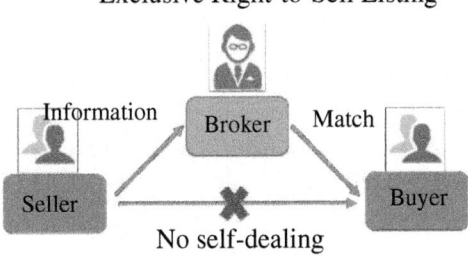

Exclusive Right-to-Sell Listing

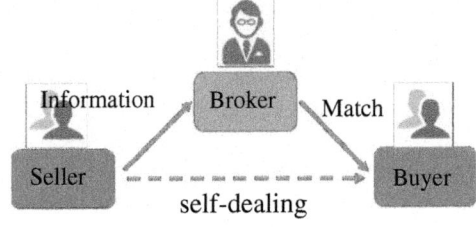

Exclusive Brokerage Listing

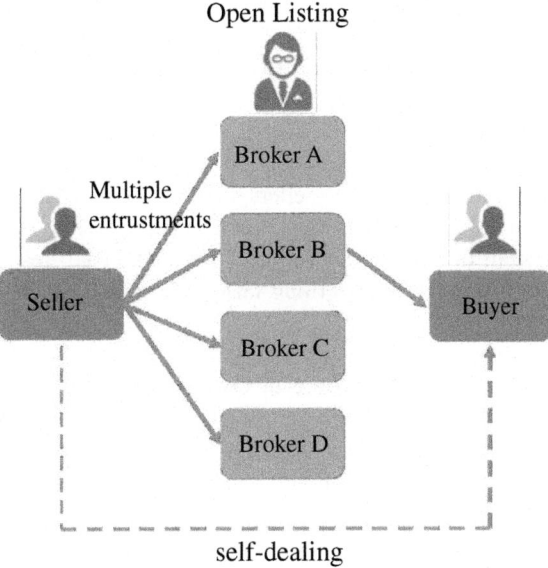

Open Listing

Exclusive right-to-sell listing gives the listing agent an exclusive right to sell the client's property. Listing contracts of this type stipulate that the seller must pay the commission as long as the listing agent finds a buyer who will agree to the selling terms during the terms of the listing contract.

Exclusive brokerage listing contracts only one agent to sell the home. Its difference from exclusive right-to-sell listing is that no sales commission is owed if the home seller finds a buyer by himself.

Open listing allows a home seller using multiple real estate agents to sell his home, but only the one that finds the buyer and eventually helps close the deal could collect the commission. And as with exclusive brokerage listing, if the home seller finds a buyer by himself, no sales commission is owed to the entrusted agents.

1.1.2 The Information of Physical Condition

The Information of physical condition of the real estate consists mainly of the quality, the floor space, structures, defects etc., of a house, as well as the factors that influences the residents' experience, such as neighbourhood, transportation, education resources and medical services. To improve the quality of the information of physical condition, it requires the main body of housing information-holders (including the home sellers, the brokers and the authorities) to disclose the authentic information completely and accurately. In developed countries, legal assurance systems for information of physical condition have been set up, defining the obligation of the home-seller to give accurate account of the home, the duty of the agencies or an independent inspection agency to inspect the entrusted home and disclose the actual information. Additionally, the authorities have built up transparent databases for the public. The information of physical condition of real estate in China's existing home transactions, however, is usually available at the brokerage companies, or acquired through the inspection conducted by the buyers themselves. The home-sellers, holding the most accurate and complete information, though, are not yet obliged to disclose the full information. Plus, the inspection system of housing condition is not completed, resulting in a weak accountability when problems concerning false information occur.

1.1.3 The Information of Ownership

The information of ownership includes the proprietary information, mortgages, property management fees and other debt information, as well as other rights attached to the homes, such as household registration and school district divisions. To clarify the information of ownership is an intricate and complex job, and the potential third-party involved more often than not adds to the difficulty of such management and the risk of disputes over large amounts of money. To prevent such problems, we need a mechanism for pre-transaction interagency information sharing and post-transaction risk sharing and transferring. The primal issue in the information of ownership now lies in the blocked information access, the cumbersome verification and the unavailability of dynamic information such as the recent mortgage or seizing of a house. Thus the risk in a transaction is shared merely by the home-seller and the buyer.

1.1.4   The Information of Matchmaking

The information of matchmaking refers to the dynamic information generated in the matching of housing resources and customers, which includes quantifiable visible information, such as the number of accompanied home viewing trips, received inquiries and the extent and frequency of the price adjustments conducted by the home-seller. It also includes the anticipated changes, the degree of urgency and other information that are unable to quantify. The information of matchmaking affects the final price and timing to cut the deal, works as an important indicator of the direction of a trade, and is also the type of information featuring the weakest shareability. That how much is the information of matchmaking disclosed is directly decided by the regulations set by brokerage companies and the rules of information-sharing platforms, while the hard-to-quantify part is usually kept exclusive by brokers as the fruit earned by in-person investigations in communities and preserving relationships with customers.

1.2   Factors that Influence the Quality of Housing Resource Information

High-quality housing resource information features completeness, authenticity and timeliness.

By completeness, it demands the disclosure of all on-sale housing resources and finesse of the information of each set.

By authenticity, it demands the housing resource information announced by brokerage companies and agents be physically authentic, the seller's intention to sell and willingness to entrust be genuine, and that the announced selling price be the reflection of the seller's true will.

By timeliness, it demands (1) the freshness of the information, i.e. the buyers are presented with real-time housing resource information; (2) the presented information shall reflect its immediate developments during transactions, such as an immediate reflection of the price-adjustment conducted by the seller, or an in-time deletion of the information as soon as the deal has been cut.

Three factors significantly influence the quality of the housing resource information:

The first factor is the agent's exclusive right to sell, i.e. the home for sale being exclusively entrusted to the agent. For its high-production cost and low-reproduction cost, the housing resource information requires being legally protected, to avoid such cases like "hitchhiking", where the information that an agent acquired by hard work could be freely employed by others. The exclusive right-to-sell listing is in fact a protection of the agent's information of property title, with which the agent could expose his listing as much as he could without such kind of worries. Besides, the cooperative relationship among brokers immunes them from the motivation or incentive to expose false listings, thus guarantees the authenticity of the information in traffic. On the contrary, under the model of open listing, the brokers view the information as personal property that should be concealed and hidden from the public; some would even make up fake listings to attract customers, which will affect the accuracy of the ERP (Enterprise Resource Planning) of brokerage companies, and would decrease the authenticity of its disclosed listings.

The second factor is to choose the suitable way to distribute the information: through one or several platforms. To ensure the completeness, authenticity and timeliness of the information, based on the practice of the U.S., a platform that covers all information of the market or takes a monopolizing position in the housing resource market is a must. On the contrary, separate and isolated information platforms aren't capable of integrate the information together from brokers, or forming a complete, unified and regulated underlying database, resulting in severe data missing. Worse still, the vicious competition among brokers and platforms could lead to high repetitiveness and low accuracy of the information released by separate platforms.

The third factor is the uniformity in the internal and external information dissemination, more specifically, the principle of a brokerage company to disseminate uniform information inside the company and to the public, so as to form a closed-loop of feedback and guarantee the consistent quality of the information. Under such a principle, the listings, distributed directly from the internal database to the external network, are consistent and controllable, because every adding, modification or deletion conducted on the internal database would be immediately caught up with and reflected on the external network. This could assure the customers of the latest and most accurate information and keep them from being bothered by false or outdated listings. However, if the internal database isn't uniformed with the external network, or the database cannot be updated in time due to the employment of information of other databases, we would fail to make sure that the information acquired by the customers be authentic and timely.

2   International Experiences in the Generation, Distribution and Matching of Information

2.1   The Generation of Housing Resource Information

2.1.1   The Listing of Housing Resources shall be Legal and in Writing

In America and Japan, the listing contracts signed by the home-sellers and the brokerage companies are clearly stipulated: the form of most American housing resource listing contracts is unified by regional broker associations, while Japan has made the Real Estate Business Law as the legal basis of what content should the contract basically include, (as is shown in Fig. 3), and more specified templates are provided by industrial associations. Only by fully implementing a system of housing resource listing in writing, can we set the stage for the authentic listings, and the regulated disclosure of information.

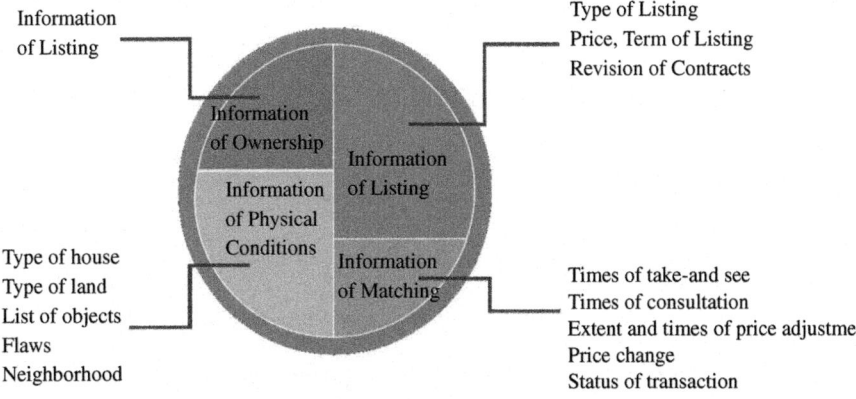

Information
of Listing

Type of Listing
Price, Term of Listing
Revision of Contracts

Information
of Ownership

Information
of Listing

Information
of Physical
Conditions

Type of house
Type of land
List of objects
Flaws
Neighborhood

Information
of Matching

Times of take-and see
Times of consultation
Extent and times of price adjustmei
Price change
Status of transaction

Fig. 3 The contents and information included in listing contracts (in japan and America) *Source* Market Research Centre, Homelink

2.1.2   The Exclusive Right-to-Sell Listing is Dominating the Market

The Exclusive right-to-sell listing is employed in almost all housing resource listings in America. In the 1880s, the brokerage industry sprouted in the form of open listing; after 1950s, the MLS (multiple listing services), designed to promote the cooperation of brokers, has gradually evolved as the core of American brokerage industry. And the regulations developed in MLS have also been adhered to as the industrial norm. Generally, MLS requires contracts of exclusive right-to-sell listing for all home resource information uploaded by brokers. After 1970, the exclusive right-to-sell listing edged out open listing, and took off as the dominant type of listing. So far, almost all members of American regional and urban broker associations have joined the MLS, which means that exclusive right-to-sell listing is the most widely used listing contract.

Japan's brokerage market adopts all three types of listing contracts, namely, exclusive right-to-sell listing, exclusive brokerage listing and open listing, and the last type is further categorized into: explicit open listing and inexplicit open listing. The explicit open listing requires the seller's exposure of a list of all the real estate agents he has entrusted, and if a deal is cut with a brokerage company beyond the list, the agents on the list are entitled to a certain amount of commission; while inexplicit open listing doesn't have requirement on such exposure. Both types of open listing contracts require the seller's immediate notice to the entrusted agents of the very agent with whom the deal was finally closed (See Table 1).

In recent years, the proportion of open listing contracts in Japan's real estate brokerage industry has dropped, while exclusive right-to-sell listing, with its close rate drastically higher than that of open listing, has been playing a larger role. According to the statistics of Japan's home resource entrusted in 2014, exclusive right-to-sell listing took a proportion of 26% ~ 29%, close to that of open listing and

Table 1 The comparison of Japan's different types of listings

Type of listing	Exclusive right-to sell listing	Exclusive brokerage listing	Open listing
Entrust other brokerage companies	Not allowed	Not allowed	Allowed
Self-dealing	Not allowed	Allowed	Allowed
Time limit of register at REINS	In 5 days	In 7 days	No requirement
Report to REINS the result	Required	Required	No requirement
Regularly report to the seller	Once a week	Once every two weeks	No requirement
Regularly report to REINS	Once a week	Once every two weeks	No requirement

lower than that of exclusive brokerage listing. In the aspect of close rate, though, the exclusive right-to-sell listing performed much better than the other two counterparts. (As is shown in Table 2).

In respect of future development, during 2002–2014, the home resource entrusted in exclusive right-to-sell listing contracts increased by 131%, in exclusive brokerage listing contracts by 25%, and in open listing contracts by 40%, which shows that exclusive right-to-sell listing is growing much faster, and gaining a much larger market share. (As is shown in Fig. 4).

British brokerage industry adopts three types of listing contracts, including sole agents (i.e. exclusive brokerage listing), multiple agency agreements (i.e. open listing), and joint-sole agreement, in which two designated agents corporate in providing services and share the commission. The joint-sole agreement, in nature, is a special form of exclusive right-to-sell listing.

Evidence from developed countries, such as America and Japan, has shown that as the size of transactions being larger and the change of themes from sellers' market to buyers' market, the trend of transforming the type of listings, from open listing to exclusive right-to-sell listing, is irreversible, and is essential for expanding the exposure of housing resource information. (As is shown in Fig. 5) Due to the low industry threshold and the scattered housing resources, a brokerage company with little information would fail to attract enough costumers, while the agents' solo fight will not meet an expected large-scale exposure of the resource. In open listing contracts, both sellers and buyers should consult with several brokers simultaneously, resulting in less efficient information transmission and problems like "hitchhiking" which discourages the wide exposure of housing resources. However, a legally protected information mechanism—the premise of the wide disclosure of housing resources as well as the basis for deals to be cut, is indispensible and essential to attract more prospective customers. Comparatively, in an expanding market, the exclusive right-to-sell listing features higher efficiency.

Table 2 The number of houses registered and traded on REINS for eastern Japan in 2004

	Registered (set)		Proportion (%)		Traded (set)		Transaction rate (%)	
	Detached house	Apartment	Detached house	Apartment	Detached house	Apartment	Detached house	Apartment
Exclusive right-to-sell listing	25028	42354	26	29	6704	16155	26.8	38.1
Exclusive brokerage listing	46111	63696	48	44	8365	16534	18.1	26.0
Open listing	25516	38846	26	27	2679	3688	10.5	9.5

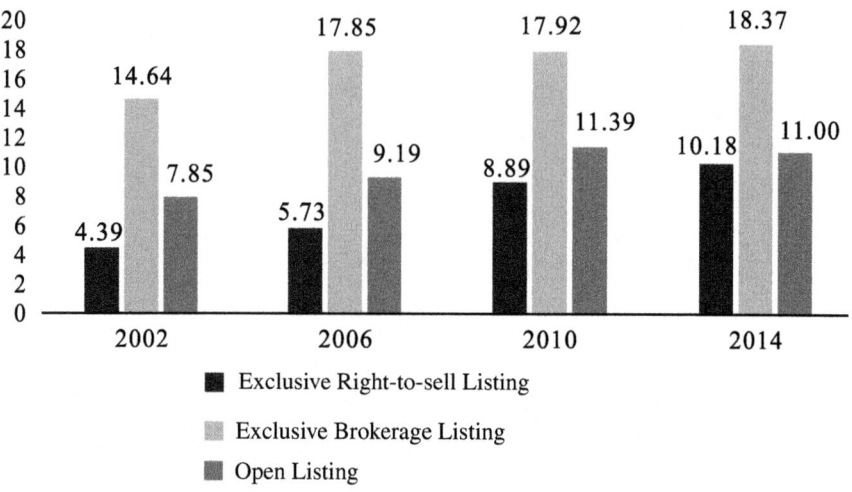

Fig. 4 Quantity changes in the number of listings on REINS (%) *Source* Market Research Centre, Homelink

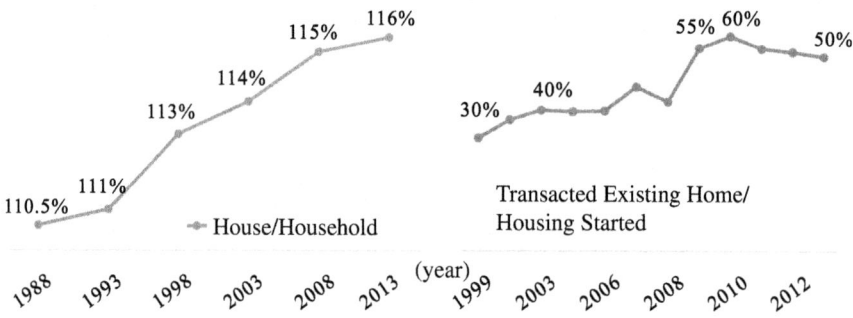

Fig. 5 The trend in Japan's existing home market (%) *Source* Market Research Centre, Homelink

2.2   The Distribution of Housing Resource Information

The history of brokerage industry could be interpreted as a record of the development of information medium: from dispersed to concentrated, and from divided to united. Sellers and buyers highly dispersed, a market maker is demanded to set rules for the industry, gather information of supplied and demanded housing resources, and make sure that the sellers and buyers at both ends could get what they needed through a highly concentrated information-sharing platform. The market maker, once played by MLS, REINS and some other traditional information-sharing platforms in the pre-Internet age, now belongs to the Web, in this era of Internet.

2.2.1   Traditional Information-Sharing Platforms

As different types of listing contracts having been clearly studied, researched and compared, large housing resource information-sharing platforms started to show in American and Japanese existing home industries, where the once concealed and monopolized information were disclosed and shared, representing a maturing brokerage industry.

The MLS is a platform created by American local association of real estate agents for housing resource sharing. The scale of existing home transactions were not large until 1880, with the brokerage industry yet been formed and most of the deals featuring randomness; with the increase in such transactions, agents started communicating and sharing housing resources in hand through small meetings or collecting-and-printing. The first MLS was set up in New York, 1907. And since 1970, America's existing home transaction volume has been rocketing, the transaction scales were much larger and the need for sharing and cooperation among agents were strongly intensified. Consequently, numerous MLSs were set up by local associations of agents, with the members of the associations growing significantly. By 1973, nearly all members of regional and urban associations of agents have joint MLSs. Now there are nearly 900 local MLSsin America.

It is generally required that all sellers' agents in an MLS shall, save as clearly rejected by the seller, upload the copy of the entrustment contract, housing resource information sheets and other information in respect of the entrustment to the MLS within 24 h after an exclusive right-to-sell contract is concluded. Included in the information are, generally, the location and type of the house, the selling price proposed by the seller, the term of the entrustment, commission rate, commission splits, etc. Having matched the information and helped cut a deal, the buyer's and the seller's agent would respectively acquire 3% of the commission. The MLS weaves all of the resources owned by agents together, where only a single agent is needed for a buyer or seller to announce his supply or demand to the whole market. The complete exposure of housing resource information is thus realized, and the efficiency of information-matching and deal-cutting has been increased and improved. (As is shown in Fig. 6).

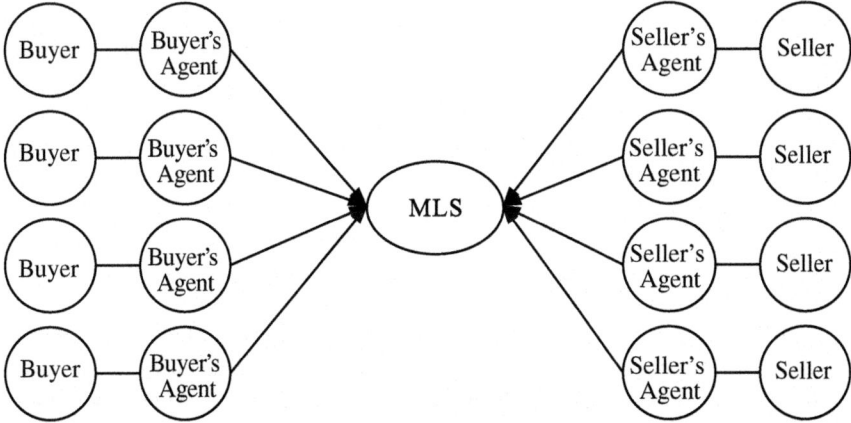

Fig. 6 The information co-sharing among exclusive right-to-sell listings under MLS system. *Source* Market Research Centre, Homelink

The REINS (Real Estate Information Network System) in Japan is a housing resource information sharing platform run by transaction institutions designated in the Real Estate Transaction Business Act. Different with the MLS which was spontaneously formed in the market, the emergence and development of REINS is partly attributed to the continuous effort of the government.

Japan's existing home market was once confronted with a messy system of housing resource information as well until the 1970s. In 1978, the Ministry of Construction (now known as Ministry of Land), together with the brokerage enterprises, discussed and issued the Report on the Promotion of the Modernization of Real Estate Transaction, advocating the sharing and verification of housing resource information, the establishment housing resource entrusting systems, the assurance of fair-value price and the improvement of the quality of brokers. In 1984, the Joint Real Estate Transaction Promotion Consortium was founded by five major Japan's brokerage companies, namely, Mitsui Fudosan, Nomura Real Estate Development, Odakyu Real Estate and Touwa Real Estate, and later joined by Mitsubishi Estate and Seibu Real Estate in 1985. Altogether, the seven major companies established an information sharing system. And at the same time, small and medium-sized companies found their solution by establishing "the Real Estate Transaction Centre" and other information exchange organizations. More than 100 confirmed transaction institutions were set up in that period of time, which is a small progress in the sharing of information, for the communication and sharing of information among the institutions were still limited. And for larger progress, the "Real Estate Transaction Modernization Centre", a guidance organization set up by Japanese government, and the transaction institutions jointly developed the REINS, for brokers from 37 regions all over the country to register and retrieve online. And the rule of employing REINS was legally included in the Real Estate Transaction Business Act. From 1985 to 1997, the transaction institutions were ultimately incorporated and merged into four covering the whole country: the Eastern, the Mid-Region, the Kinki Region and the Western. After 2000, the development of REINS reached a peak, and by 2010, the amount of the registered housing resources was doubled. (See Figs. 7 and 8).

Compared with the development and rules of MLS, REINS is different in organizational forms and ways of operation, and is somewhat similar to an early MLS (See Table 3).

MLS features spontaneity, while REINS, run by designed transaction institutions, funded by major nationwide brokerage industrial associations and clearly specified in law, is characterized by administration. Before joining the REINS, Japan's brokerage companies are required to join the local affiliate of the industrial association in the first place. The biggest real estate transaction association consortium in Japan was founded in 1968, with as many as 97,529 member companies, accounting for over 95% Japan's brokerage companies.

The REINS, less opened than MLS, features less information transparency. The housing resource information available on an MLS is no different with that available on public information websites, such as Realtor.com, Redfin or Zillow. Conversely, the housing resource information on REINS is available only to

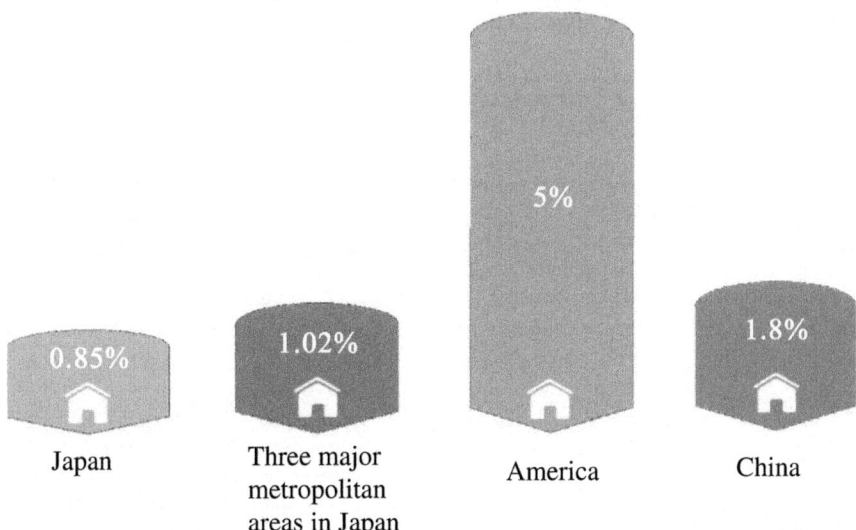

Fig. 7 Circulation rates in America's, Japan's and China's existing home markets. *Source* Market Research Centre, Homelink

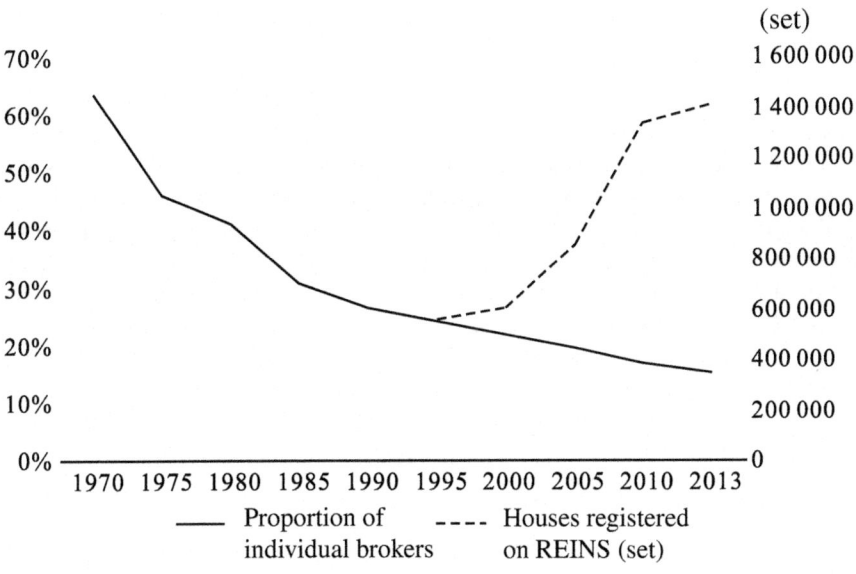

Fig. 8 The proportion of individual brokers drops while the number of houses registered on REINS increases. *Source* Market Research Centre, Homelink

Table 3 The comparison of America's MLS and Japan's REINS

	MLS	REINS
Initiator	American local association of real estate agents	The Real Estate Transaction Modernization Center and transaction institutes of Japan
Forming	Spontaneously formed in the market	Formed by the government
Major managers	State association sets up regulators; regional associations perform management	The founders set up regulations; specified transaction institutions enforce management
Scale	More than 900 regional platforms	4 regional institutions
Duty of brokers	Upload the housing resource information in 24 h	Upload the information in 5 to 7 days
Type of listings	Exclusive Right-to-sell Listing	Compulsory upload: Exclusive right-to-sell listing and exclusive brokerage listing Voluntary upload: Open Listing
Members	Brokers	Brokerage companies
Requirement of joining in	The broker should join in agent associations of all three levels	The brokerage company should join in agent associations
Users	The public	Brokers

brokers, thus it's the brokers that decide to what extent the information is exposed, making the concealed information one of the chips for bargains and profits.

The details and terms of the REINS need further improving and completing. In terms of time limit, for example, an exclusively contracted housing resource is required to be uploaded on the MLS by brokers within 72 h, while five or seven days are permitted for the REINS. Usually, 72 h is hardly enough for a broker to find a buyer, yet 7 days greatly increases the chances. Tending to act as the broker for both sides for a doubled commission (usually, the home seller and the home buyer are respectively accountable for 3% commission), Japan's brokers are motivated to bargain for a lower price with the home seller and stall for time before registering the housing resource on the REINS, or even falsely claim the resource as "reserved" upon registration to keep it from being taken up or transacted by other firms. The REINS, inevitably, has employed several measures in preventing brokers from concealing housing resources, including demanding brokers to provide the certificate of the registration of the housing resource to the seller, holding debates on the sellers' accessibility to the REINS to verify registration, and adding the selling status of a home as part of required registration information, etc. The proportion of bilateral brokering and the total rate of commission thereof in Japan's major brokerage companies are shown in Fig. 9.

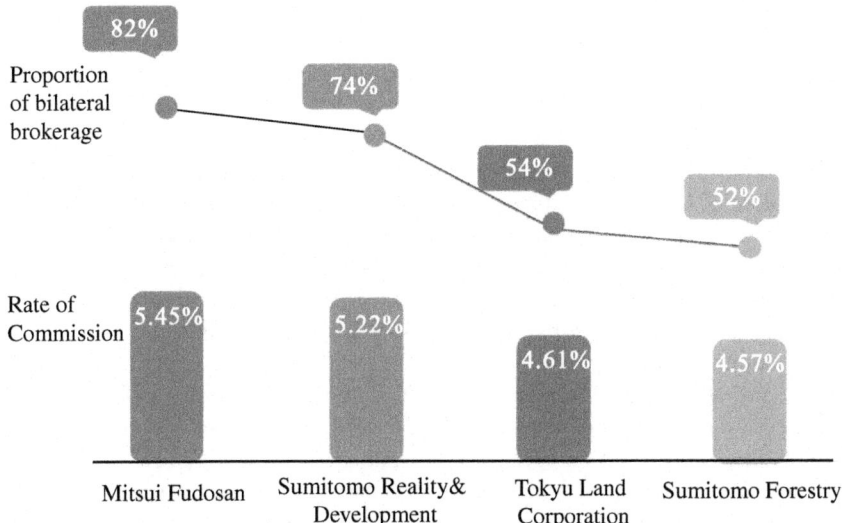

Proportion of bilateral brokerage

Rate of Commission

Mitsui Fudosan   Sumitomo Reality& Development   Tokyu Land Corporation   Sumitomo Forestry

Fig. 9 The proportion of bilateral brokerage and the rate of total commission thereof (%) *Source* Market Research Centre, Homelink

2.2.2   The Distribution System of Housing Resource Information in an Era of Internet

The Internet has changed the system of information distribution. In the era of the traditional mass media, the brokers, as the only owners of housing resource information, are information resources and information channels. Only by ads on newspapers, recommendation of friends or word of mouth can customers contact with local brokers and get access to housing information. In that era of "offline" marketing, the MLS, open only to brokers, was a closed information system with no direct access for either sellers or buyers. Consequently, the dissemination of information was comparatively small in scope, poor in timeliness and low in efficiency (See Fig. 10).

In the 1990s, the popularization of the Internet and the offline-to-online transmission of the customers' focus gave rise to contracts between Internet enterprises

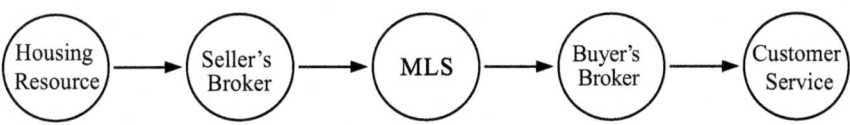

Fig. 10 The dissemination of information in America before the internet Era. *Source* Market Research Centre, Homelink

and information sharing platforms to publish the traditional, once closed housing resource information on websites available to the public.

MLS distributes information automatically on the Internet. In the era of the Internet, the information disclosed in the MLS is available to customers on online platforms in three ways: first, to directly disclose the information on MLS.com; second, to distribute the information to Realtor.com, the official site of the National Association of Realtors, and then for the official site to distribute the information to third-party websites like Zillow and Trulia; third, to distribute the information to searching engines like Google, Yahoo and Being, and to share it on brokers' or brokerage companies' websites via Internet Data Exchange (IDX) provided by Tigerlead and other platforms. These made a breakthrough in terms of space and time, maximized the exposure of housing resources to home buyers and provided the buyers with an online access to listed homes and brokers. Automatically operated, the MLS market is characterized by higher spontaneity, and no-different-information on each website. (As is shown in Fig. 11).

The information exposed on the REINS is partial and selected (see Fig. 12), thus lags behind in transparency when compared with the mature information distribution system in America. For one thing, REINS don't automatically distribute information to external websites. Any distribution would require the permission of the broker that registered the home; what's more, the housing resource information usually flows among brokers, which means that the only access to the information of the customers is to consult a brokerage company. For another, as the automaticity of Japan's information distribution system remains low and the information channels are fragmented, small and large companies respectively start creating distribution channels, distributing information to the public via websites or media partners of their own—on no website could all housing resource information be available, which lowered the efficiency of the dissemination of information. In general, Japan's existing home market initiated late, and still needs adjusting and optimizing.

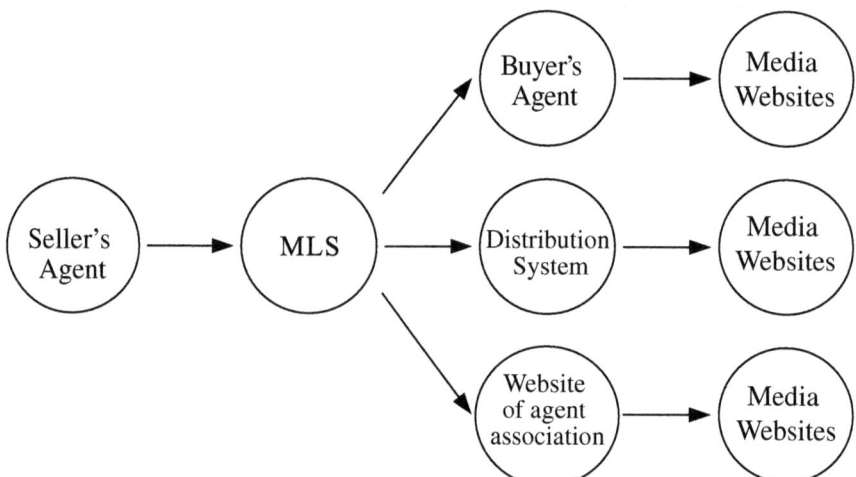

Fig. 11 The online information dissemination on MLS in America. *Source* Market Research Centre, Homelink

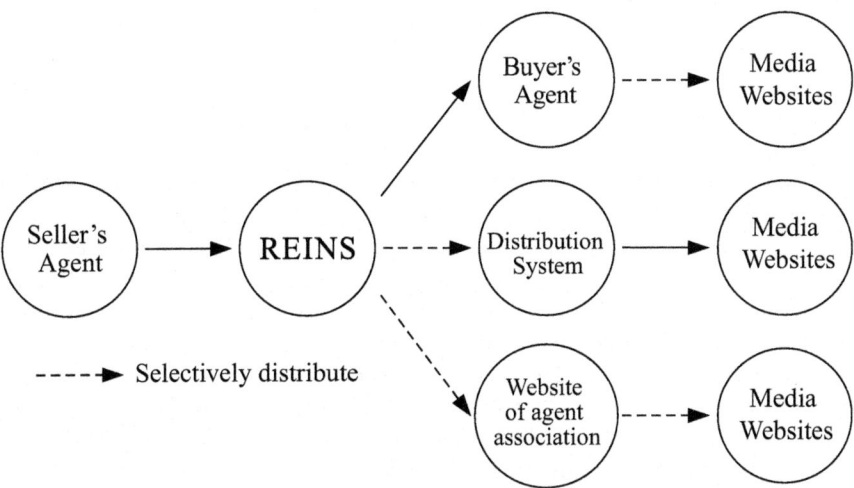

Fig. 12 The online information dissemination on REINS in Japan. *Source* Market Research Centre, Homelink

In countries without such platforms for information-sharing, the exposure of housing resource information is realized by the connection between the internal systems of brokerage companies and the Internet. Australia is one of these countries without information sharing platforms like MLS or REINS. In the mid to late 1990s, REA Group Limited, an Australian real estate media group, integrated and internet-enabled housing resources by connecting with ERP, the internal system of Australia's largest brokerage company. With swelled housing resources and users, the platform starts to show signs of monopoly—nowadays, 90% of Australian agents are paying users of REA.

In Web 2.0 era, the development and application of housing valuations, neighborhood information, searching engines and UGC (User Generated Content) business models helped established a user-centered Internet-based housing resource information distribution system. Internet enterprises, for example, can attach detailed housing resources on maps, and home buyers are directly shown the municipal facilities around the home, and even records of earthquakes, fires or hurricanes, so that they could make faster choices by filtering out homes without desirable conditions. Under the UGC model, users are able to add or update home or community information on the website by themselves, and to choose or comment on an agent online. As mobile Internet has been developing rapidly in the whole world, more and more housing researches are initiated on mobile terminals, and more and more choices are provided to costumers.

In this era, the popularity of the Internet has reshaped the system of our distribution of housing resource information. First, it has diminished the agents' role as information matchers, while a great proportion of the information were matched on the Internet by users themselves. In 2015, more than 45% American customers found their desired home on the Internet, yet only as low as 30% of them found homes through brokers. Second, the monopoly of housing resource platforms such as MLS, was reduced by the mobile terminals basing on the Internet; home sellers could directly post their home information on media platforms without turning to agents, and a new closed loop: home sellers—media platforms—home buyers, came into being. And echoing with MLS, systems like Pre-MLS and Off-MLS appeared in American real estate market. Pre-MLS means for brokers to post housing resource information on the Internet before uploading them on the MLS system, while Off-MLS means that some brokers post the information only on the Internet—in this user-centered Internet Era, the MLS is, to a certain extent, being substituted by online platforms as the core media of information dissemination.

In the future, the distribution of housing resource information might be taking on three characteristics. First, the involved information, including the local information and evaluation of a home, and the evaluation of an agent, would be counted as an increasingly essential part of housing information. Second, the method of generating information would then be transformed from PGC (Professional Generated Content) to UGC. With the Internet, agents would be less prioritized in the generation of information, and the disadvantages of their being the only channel of information dissemination would be eliminated, because the presale and brokerage executed by house owners and other methods could be direct ways to generate information. Third, the interaction will be more flattened, with direct exchange of information between buyers and sellers, and agents would then be sent acting as "offline" servers.

2.3   The Matching of Housing Resource Information

It's true that the match of information is extremely important for a successful transaction, and that the exposure of matched information would indubitably boost the efficiency of the whole market. But in practice, the complete exposure of matched information is hardly within the realm of possibility. For now, the exposure of matched information is realized in two ways: the in-time feedback requested by traditional information sharing platforms, and the recording of brokerage companies' internal ERP systems.

For MLS, transaction information should be timely updated by entrusted agents after a deal has been cut, and the genuine transaction price should as well be filled in the system. If a home seller withdraws his house before the contract expires, the agent shall provide MLS with the copy of the written contract between him and the home seller, and then MLS would label the home as "withdrawn". If the price on a listing contract is to be changed, the agent should, within 24 h (weekends and holidays excluded) after the change has been issued, provide the written authority of the seller, according to which MLS will update the listed information. And if a member broker declines or fails to report the change of the information timely, MLS are entitled to delete that information.

According to REINS, exclusive right-to-sell listing demand brokerage companies registered on REINS report their transactions as least once a week; for exclusive brokerage contracts, the companies shall report their transactions every two weeks, while for cut deals and conducted transactions, immediate reports are requested.

2.4   The Verification and Assurance of Housing Resource Information

For a smooth and successful transaction, the authenticity of housing resource information, especially the physical and title information of a home is an essential factor. To ensure the authenticity, developed markets have established full and mature assurance and verification systems.

Verification systems have been instituted to check the information of physical condition. Mainstream markets have already been equipped with comprehensive information assurance systems, which clearly outline the home sellers' duty of exposing genuine home information and the brokerage companies' and independent institutions' duties of conducting home inspections and disseminating information; also, appropriate authorities have established transparent databases of housing information accessible to the public (See Fig. 13).

In American real estate market, it's stipulated by the Residential Property Condition Disclosure Act that the home seller is responsible to disclose the actual condition of his home; when the identity of the buyer has been confirmed, a property condition disclosure statement from the seller is requested and should be signed by both parties; the seller is responsible to update the statement with new information at any time until the transaction is closed, and if he fails to state or update, he could be required to pay the buyer an extra price for credit

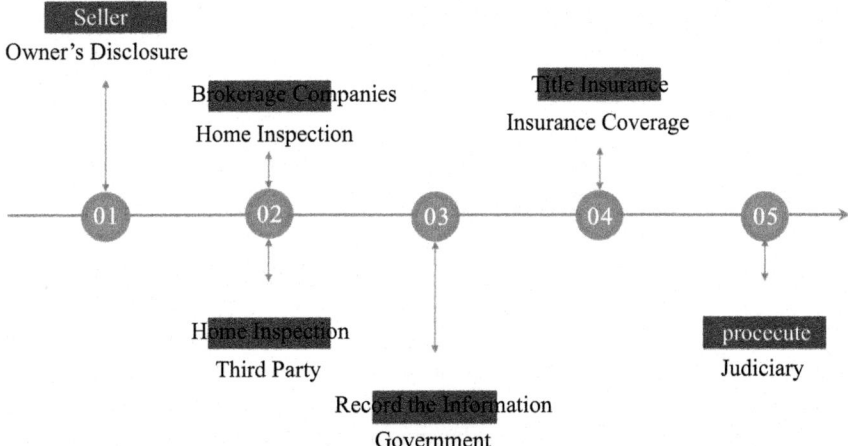

Fig. 13 The inspection of the information of physical conditions of a house. *Source* Market Research Centre, Homelink

compensation; and if the buyer discovers that the home seller have stated falsely or misleadingly, the seller is to blame. Similar responsibilities concerning disclosure are prescribed in the Real Estate Transaction Business Act of Japan. For the part of home inspection, in America, usually an independent institution is entrusted by the home seller to conduct home inspection and issue reports. But in Japan, it's often conducted by a brokerage company or an institution entrusted by the brokerage company, and the information of physical condition and material facts, i.e. results of such inspections, will be included in "Important Notices" in statuary form by certified real estate notaries.

Additionally, both American and Japanese public sectors have reserved part of the private information from public inquiry, such as records of transactions and of specific information. What's more, the insurance is an important issue. American title insurance covers all physical issues concerning gas pipes, drain lines, etc. In Japan, agents' insurance covers the loss resulting from false information filled in the "Important Notice". And one last point, an integrated legal system and the written record of information communication during transactions is the last line of defence for consumer protection. Japan has also legally stipulated a term of one year, during which full responsibility shall be held by the seller.

Secondly, verification systems have been established to check the information of ownership. In developed markets, mature systems consisting of pre-transaction interagency information sharing and post-transaction risk sharing and transferring. In American real estate market, all property information is open to the public, and most is electronic and internet-enabled. But the huge variety of the information makes it difficult for non-specialized customers to cover all of them, so often they'll rely on property inspection services provided by property insurance companies. The services are usually included in long-term property insurance contracts, and the companies can provide their customers with a detailed inspection report within 24 to 48 h, by connecting to the public database as well as private databases established during transactions. In Japan's real estate market, housing property information is open to everyone, while customers often entrust professional judicial scriveners with home inspections, which are secured by the scriveners' professional qualifications and professional liability insurances.

3 The Present Situation and Its Causes of the Generation, Distribution and Matching of Information in China

China's existing home transaction is still in its initial stage, with institutional defects in the generation, distribution and matching of information, featuring poor customer experience. The housing resource information is incomplete, high-repetitive, less immediate and mixed with false information—far from the expected completeness, authenticity and timeliness. False information gravely wastes the time and energy of both brokers and customers, and has become a huge barrier to the whole industry.

By drawing international experiences of America, Japan and other developed countries, we can conclude five reasons that the present chaos of Chinese housing resource information should attribute to:

The first is the lack of written listing contracts. At present, written housing resource listing contracts are not demanded in China, while the commonly employed telephone entrustment and office offers, are verbal, random, and hardly binding. Verbal listings have several drawbacks: there is no verification of whether the actual home is as depicted, and the low-cost of disclosing false information might lead to the brokers' frequently breaking rules; it's hard to verify whether the home is "genuinely entrusted" and the price is "genuinely offered by the home seller"; to rapidly conclude the transaction with a higher price, the home seller might conceal some information essential to the trade, which not only violates the buyer's right to know, but makes it harder to sue should a dispute arise; what's worse, the weak legal binding of the sellers' information disclosure in such entrustment results in no record of necessary written evidence, thus making it rather difficult to hold accountable the seller or to indict after the deal's been cut.

The second is the lack of exclusive right-to-sell listing. The American MLS became an open platform for genuine information sharing among its members, with private property of housing resource generators secured by 50% of the commission on the basis of exclusive right-to-sell listing. In China, the widely employed open listing could hardly protect the property title of brokers, and in order to avoid being "hitchhiked" by other agents, most brokerage companies and brokers would not disclose or disseminate accurate and authentic information, thus making the internal ERP unreliable, reducing online medias' corporation with ERP and the exposure of genuine housing resources. Competition vicious, the brokers would more often than not make up false information to attract customers.

The third is the inconsistency of internal and external databases. China has neither a sharing platform like the MLS nor a media like the REA. Instead, there are two ways of disseminating housing resource information in China: traditional brokerage companies' online dissemination of housing resources; and non trade-supported internet companies that acquires information from brokers and brokerage companies and functions as the media. After brokers or brokerage companies have acquired the housing resources, they distribute the information on their websites, while the lack of quality control over the information hinder internet companies from verifying or timely updating the information, and further result in the repetition, stagnation and inaccuracy of housing resource information, with false information widely disseminated and spread through the network.

The forth is a gap in information supervision. The NAR (National Association of Realtors) in America has strict rules over agents, and MLS has got a system to guarantee the authenticity of its information, while Chinese supervision over housing resource information is comparatively imperfect. China lacks a penalty and accountability mechanism against false information, and the blurred definition of false information, inconsistent standards and the lack of written contract system makes it hard to collect evidence and low-cost for agents to breach the rules. Chinese supervision over housing resource information is effective only over traditional brokerage industries, yet not over online dissemination of information, and the false information online is not monitored by either housing or Internet supervision department, so to establish an interagency and united supervisory system in China is necessary, essential and urgent.

The fifth is the lack of an information verification and guarantee system. The information of physical condition of Chinese real estate is highly dependent on inspections conducted by brokerage companies or the buyers themselves, while the sellers are rarely held accountable for the accuracy and authenticity of the information. Public sectors, as well, fail to disclose property information of homes completely, and fail to provide the public with comprehensive, timely and effective information services. In practice, appropriate authorities in most cities have limitations on time, location and identity of the applicant of the inspection they provide, and in some highlighted areas where transactions are prosperous and popular, a property inspection may even take as long as ten days. The regular procedures demanded in existing home transactions are complex, and a delayed update of a change in property information might also lead to the buyer's financial loss. To prevent such losses resulting from inaccurate or incomplete information, we must establish an information management system, with pre-transaction information sharing, in-time feedback during transactions and post-transaction risk sharing.

4 Summary and Suggestions

Generally far from the required completeness, authenticity and timeliness, the generation, dissemination and acquisition of Chinese housing resource information are in a chaotic status, due to the immature existing home market and incomplete supervision systems. The housing resource information in China doesn't have basic institutional framework or supervision systems, the problems of which, catalyzed by the rocketing development of the Internet, are rapidly confronting us: the disorder and troubles of the generation, dissemination and acquisition of housing resource information are gravely impeding the healthy and standard development of Chinese real estate industry. To make the information as complete, authentic and timely as expected, and to help the customers with making wiser and clearer decisions in transactions, we are required to make fundamental changes to the generation and dissemination of housing resource information.

4.1 Regulate Home Entrusting Systems, Provide Property Information Inquiry Services

4.1.1 Compulsively and Comprehensively Implement a System of Written Housing Resource Entrustment

Comprehensively implementing of a system of written home entrustment is the primal factor to tally with the standards and regulate the exposure of housing resources. To entrust one's home with a brokerage company, the seller should issue a written listing contract with the brokerage institution, and make records of basic conditions of the house, terms and price of entrusted sale, forms of listing and other information. The seller shall also produce relative certificates and sign on the entrustment contract. And if the seller rejects providing relevant documents, provides documents that don't conform to reality, or rejects signing on the written contract, the brokerage institution is supposed to decline his entrustment, and should never expose the information of an entrusted home without a written contract of entrustment. Brokerage companies should also establish a numbering system for contract management, and the housing resources exposed to external platforms shall be attached with their numbers in internal networks, which are one-to-one correspondent to the numbers on listing contracts.

4.1.2 Comprehensively Implement the Property Condition Disclosure Statement

On the basis of executing Article 22 of Measures of the Management of Real Estate Brokerage, we should further require a Property Condition Disclosure Statement issued by brokerage companies and brokers as the written disclosure of important trade information. Upon entrustment of a home, brokerage companies and brokers shall immediately issue the Property Condition Disclosure Statement of that house; when disclosing housing resources to the public or introducing homes to customers, brokerage companies and brokers shall provide customers with the Statement of that home (paper or electronic); and while signing the contract, the Statement should be provided as an appendix to the contract, with the same legal force of the contract. Sellers should disclose the actual information of the home in the Property Condition Disclosure Statement and confirm with signature; brokerage companies shall faithfully perform their duties of home inspection and be responsible for the authenticity of the result of the inspection. The administrative department for real estate and industrial associations could work on a standardized model of Property Condition Disclosure Statement for brokerage companies for unified supervision.

4.1.3 Establish Online Platforms for Property Title Inquiry Services, Provide Housing Information Inquiry Services to Registered Real Estate Institutions and Certificated Brokers

Administrative departments of real estate at all levels should speed up the establishment of online service platforms; for those lacking the required conditions of such establishment temporarily, public windows providing inquiry services should be opened, and the online platforms shall be set up within a time limit. All registered and qualified real estate institutions and certificate property brokers shall be entitled to query property information on online service platforms or at public windows. After such inquiries, brokerage institutions should provide customers with written investigation reports on property title verifications.

4.2   Integrate the Housing Resource Information Supervision System and Standardize the Information Release Mechanism

4.2.1   Establish a Information Supervision System that Covers Multiple Participants

Multiple-participant will continue to be a feature and tendency of the brokerage industry at present and in the future, with Internet enterprises engaging in the dissemination of information, and traditional brokerage companies regarding the Internet as the direction of future development. However, the gaps in oversight of the overlapping sections have been affecting the authenticity of housing resource information, thus an interagency supervision system, jointly established by ministries of housing and rural-urban development, industry and information technology, industry and commerce and other fields, is necessary and urgent. The information providers shall be set as the object, and "whoever releases is responsible" as the rule, to establish an information release standard covering multiple market participants.

4.2.2   Implement a Real-Name Housing Resource Information Release System

The release of housing resource information shall require the broker's real name; fake names should be prohibited. Online information platforms shall not provide information services with brokerage institutions that haven't registered on the administrative department of real estate, or brokers who haven't been certificated. Personal release of housing resource, as well, shall be registered with real names.

4.2.3   Establish a Deposit Mechanism for Authentic Housing Information

Real estate brokerage institutions and online platforms that provide housing information release services shall pay cash deposits to industrial associations, and the associations shall be open to public report and complaint. For any institution that has been proved releasing made-up or false information, the association should be entitled to withdraw a penalty on money from the deposit it has paid, and to award the informants. Also, housing information service institutions shall not provide any information release service with brokerage companies before they've paid the cash deposit.

4.2.4 Set up a Blacklist System for the Release of False Housing Information

If a broker has repeatedly released false housing resource information, he shall be blacklisted. And apart from publicizing such blacklist, it's demanded that, in a certain period of time, information release platforms shan't provide any information release services with those brokers on the list. The associations should enforce their verification and inspection of the registered information, and establish complaint channels for the public. And customers can resort to China Internet Illegal Information Reporting Centre and other information management departments for rights protection.

4.3 Optimize the Information Disclosure System and Establish a Generic Information Assessment System of Housing Resource Information

To improve the customers' efficiency and experience in decision making, we need to establish a generic information assessment system of neighborhood information and home appraisal.

4.3.1 Add Basic Information to the Disclosed Housing Resource Information

The government should cooperate with enterprises in adding into the disclosed list basic information of the cities, such as educational, medical and shopping facilities, traffic conditions, natural disasters and criminal records.

4.3.2 Set up and Standardize a Market Information Disclosure System

Except for the entrustment contract and the Property Condition Disclosure Statement, the market dynamics of a house, for example, the number of accompanied home viewing trips, records of the sellers' price adjustments, transaction prices of the houses in the same community, a comparison of the prices of the houses on sale at the same time, should as well be published for the buyers' reference. Also, a unified database should be set up to further establish a home appraisal system.

Chapter 3
Transaction Systems

- The nature of existing home transaction is an exchange of property title and funds conducted under the bind of contracts. And the complex procedures, numerous participants and frequent information exchanges in transactions render the mismatches of title and funds much riskier.
- Transaction system refers to a system of all procedures that are required in transactions, from the buyer and seller's reaching a consensus on transaction terms, to the property title being transferred to the buyer and the capital being delivered to the seller. The system includes: pre-transaction preparatory works, such as home inspection and property title verification; capital distribution, paper work, tax payment, registration and other procedures required during transactions, and long-term post-transaction services and supports.
- Security, efficiency and customer experience are the three cores of transaction systems. Given that China has not yet established a standard existing home transaction system, a start could be getting to grips with information disclosure and custody of funds. At the same time, the government should encourage the involvement of payment enterprises and strike a balance among security, efficiency and customer experience in the market-oriented existing home transaction.

The nature of existing home transaction is a dynamic exchange of property titles and capital conducted under the bind of contracts. In contrast to common commodity transactions, the dynamic existing home transaction could be haunted by overlapping flows of information, capital and titles as well as their mismatches in time, and the intricate, complex procedures, various participants, entries and exits of creditors and the long cycles have only added to the risk and uncertainty of the transactions. What's more, as a non-standard product, existing home features complex property title information, and the changing market lengthened the odds on the seller and buyer's cutting deals on their own and rendered it much more riskier—a rare event could end up with the buyer's disastrous loss.

Mainly, the participants have got three essential requirements: the security of capital and property title, the high efficiency of capital and time, and an enjoyable

© Xiamen University Press and Springer Nature Singapore Pte Ltd. 2018   43
S. Ba and X. Yang, *The Rise of New Brokerages and the Restructuring of Real Estate Value Chain*, https://doi.org/10.1007/978-981-10-7715-9_3

transaction experience. In practical, most of the gravest problems of our brokerage industry stem from the complicated and complex transaction procedures. And as the transaction volume is rocketing and the complexity in trading is increasing, to improve the transaction system is now the top priority. An integrated transaction system requires not only the security of the transaction, but also the improvement of efficiency and experience, which reduces the resistance in existing home circulation, smoothes and speeds up trade processes, and increases the efficiency of the industry as a whole.

1 The Connotation, Determinants and Present Situation of Existing Home Transaction Systems

1.1 One Connotation: Six Key Procedures

The connotation of existing home transaction systems mainly includes six procedures: pre-transaction home inspection and property title verification; custody of funds, paper work, tax payment required during transactions; and post-transaction services to ensure that the property title and physical conditions of the actual home are and remain consistent with the description in the disclosure statement without any dispute or defect (See Fig. 1).

Home inspection refers to the investigation and inspection of physical conditions, operational conditions, defects, and other aspects of homes. The information suppliers and conductors of home inspections usually include home sellers, home buyers, real estate brokers and independent inspection institutions.

Property title verification refers to the examination of the property title, debt, household registration, school district and other supplementary rights attached to the home, and the confirmation that the bills of utilities and property charges of the home have been paid, so that the actual price paid by house buyer shall not exceed the agreed price.

The custody of funds is the core of existing home transactions, and a basic measure to guarantee the security of fund and property right. Generally, the custody of funds is realized by entrusting the fund to an independent third party, and for the third party to deliver it to the home seller when the home transaction has moved to a certain stage. And the toughest problems in the custody of funds are to reasonably deposit the fund, to cope with the transference of debts and the mismatches of capital flows, and to deal with tax payment and other problems of capital distributaries.

Paper work is a necessary link in the circulation of funds. In many countries and regions, the work is usually done by designated professionals, given the complex procedures, multiple participants and frequent communication and confirmation of information among the parties as required.

A transaction closed doesn't mean that troubles are gone as well: problems concerning titles and the information of physical condition will continue to show,

Fig. 1 Major procedures of existing home transactions. *Source* Market Research Centre, Homelink

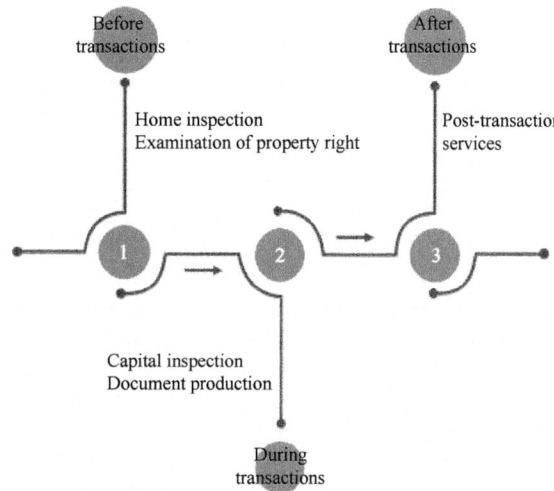

thus the core of post-transaction services is to clarify the responsible party in the use of the house and to set up a reasonable compensatory mechanism.

1.2 Three Key Words: Security, Efficiency and Customer Experience

Security, efficiency as well as customer experience are the three key words in the evaluation of an existing home transaction system. The three take different priorities in different markets.

The security shall be the principal one. As the base of trades, the security of a transaction assures the seller of the agreed price, and the buyer of the property title of the house and the housing tenure. To guarantee the security of housing transactions, we need to not only secure the transacted capital and titles, but also set up a post-transaction accountability mechanism and a compensatory mechanism.

The second comes the efficiency. High efficiency means horizontally influent and immediate communication and interaction among all parties, and vertically, efficient links between the procedures of transactions, including capital allocation, property title inspection, legal instrument writing and post-transaction services. As the communication between brokers and customers play a major part of transactions, to improve the efficiency and accuracy of such information communication could significantly shorten transaction cycles, and reduce disputes in housing trades.

The last key word is customer experience. Satisfying customer experience could be interpreted as, with security and efficiency safeguarded, customers spend less time and energy in transactions, have got more flexibility in time and space, and are kept informed of all and the latest status of the transaction.

The development of existing home transaction market is still in its initial stage, and for further progress, both participants and supervisors are required to: improve relevant laws and regulations, optimize the articulation between archives and cash flows, improve the capabilities of brokerage professionals, inspect defects carefully lest disputes occur afterwards, and work hard to guarantee the security of transactions. However, focusing on security would inevitably result in much more complicated and complex transaction procedures, and far more extensive and detailed industrial supervision; with trade volume and complexity increasing, and the risk-management of rare events upgraded, the efficiency as well as customer experience would be indubitably affected, while to completely eliminate risks is literally beyond the realm of possibility. Home transactions feature high-price and low-frequency, and accidents that seldom happen but lead to customers' severe losses, so to establish a risk-sharing and liability mechanism that safeguard all procedures in transactions is essential and necessary. The relationship and different priorities of security, efficiency and customer experience are shown in Fig. 2.

1.3   Background and the Current Situation

The reform and perfection of existing home transaction system is urgently needed.

The amount of money involved in existing home transactions is larger. As of now, nearly half of the existing home transactions were closed in first-tier cities

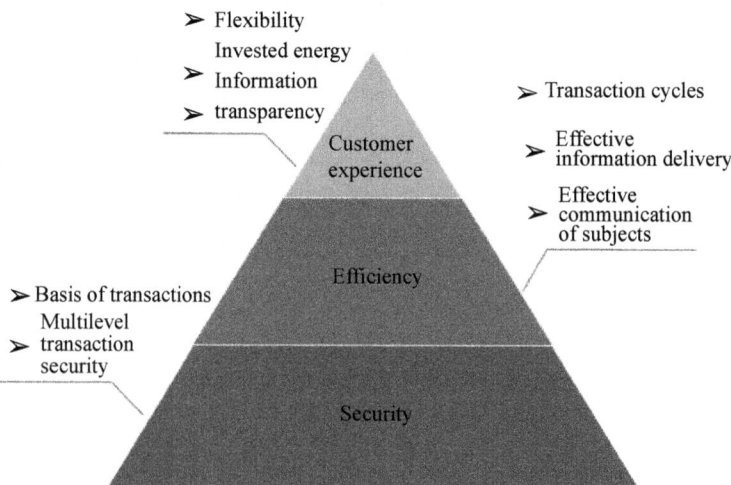

Fig. 2 The relationship and different priorities of security, efficiency and customer experience. *Source* Market Research Centre, Homelink

featuring high prices: in 2015, the average price of second-hand houses in Beijing is as high as 3.3 million Yuan per set. Among the circulating fund, smaller single payment for as small as a 5% deposit could amount to over 150 thousand Yuan. Besides, for fear that the home owner should raise prices, many buyers in first-tier cities would rather pay hundreds of thousand Yuan as a deposit and all other kinds of cash deposits, which in turn renders existing home transactions all the more risky.

The rights and titles involved in existing home transactions have become much more complex. Apart from the down-payment and the mortgage loan applied from commercial banks, the fund involved in existing home transactions usually include the earnest payment to confirm a transaction, the cash deposit to guarantee property delivery, the cash deposit to ensure the relocation of household, and the outstanding mortgage repaid to the commercial banks—each of the cash flow shall be realized on the basis of the confirmation of the title transfer hereof. For example: the earnest money is paid by the home buyer to the home owner while entering in a sales contract; the down-payment is always paid as soon as the transference of property title has been registered and a new certificate of title has been obtained; while the cash deposit to guarantee property delivery is usually paid after the property has been transferred and the home buyer has entered into the new agreement.

The improvement of efficiency and customer experience has become rather more important. The hindrance of such improvement mainly lies in the limitation of time and space, as well as the lack of communication channels among participants. In active markets, it's popular that people need to wait in lines or even cut in lines so that the title inspection, tax payment and title transfer could go on smoothly: an ordinary-in-complexity transaction could probably take longer than two months. And the extended timeline also adds uncertainty to transactions.

The most thorny and outstanding problem in the present existing home transaction system lies in the custody of funds, which directly affects the security of transactions. Firstly, the custody of funds isn't compulsory in all regions in the country—where it's not necessary or not required, active supervisions are rare. Secondly, the present approaches of fund custody—government supervision, commercial bank regulation and four-party fund custody, are mainly based on commercial bank services, which could be less satisfying due to commercial concerns, constraining procedures, capabilities of the system and other features. With regard to security, the three approaches could only guarantee safe down-payments among all cash flows; as to efficiency, the time limitation of banking hours and the timeliness of the procedures in such custody greatly hinders the actual demands from being perfectly met; and concerning customer experience, the requirement thereof varies in different cities and different banks: for example, it's not stipulated that the home owner and buyer shall both attend in person or shall apply for banking services in person, which result in that customers have to prepare different materials when applying in different banks; besides, some banks require that the customers should open accounts and apply for cards in their banks. What's more, the interactive experiences of the system, the display of such funds in custody, and the accesses on official website or mobile apps of such custody are far from

satisfying, resulting from the capabilities and features of the IT systems of commercial banks.

With regard to the inspections of home and property title, the lack of essential
information disclosing system and dynamic information feedback mechanism
renders weak protections of the buyers' interests, between which, the inspection of
property title is more decisive: the property information that has not been online
updated would lead to the parties being unable to be informed of mortgages,
attachments or other situations of the home in time. What's more, the complex
limitations in time, space and agents of property title inspections result in far too
long inspection circles in active markets.

By far, the reforms of existing home transaction systems have been centred on
improving the security of transactions, implemented through investing executive
efforts and enhancing government control over transactions. However, the present
existing home market confronted with much more pressure has made it clear to us
that merely investing administrative power no longer suffices in eliminating risks
completely or ease the stagnation generated with new transaction demands, and is a
high-cost and the least elastic solution.

2   Transaction Systems in Different Countries and Regions

The transaction system is a trade-off of security, efficiency and customer experience, and the choices and balances hereof differ from countries to countries. (See
Fig. 3) Different regimes and situations naturally breed different models of transactions systems: (1) market-driven and industrialized transaction systems—"very
active market" like American market adopts a combination of the fund custody
system and the title insurance system; (2) independent and judicial third-party
systems—in Japan where markets are less active and the U.K. where markets are
active yet has only one party involved, independent and judicial third-party systems
are adopted; (3) comprehensive transaction systems—operated in Taiwan, where
markets are active and Torrens Title[①1] with an effect of registration is working,
combined with Japan's independent judicial third-party system and American
market-driven fund custody system. International experiences of different systems
show that the market-oriented development and specialization of trading procedures
are vitally important to guarantee security, increase efficiency and improve customer experience in transactions.

---

[1]Torrens Title denotes a system of land registration, in which registration authorities substantively
review the instrument of transfer, record the new property owner in the Register and issue an
official Certificate of Title to the owner, so as to ensure the credibility of the register of land
holdings.

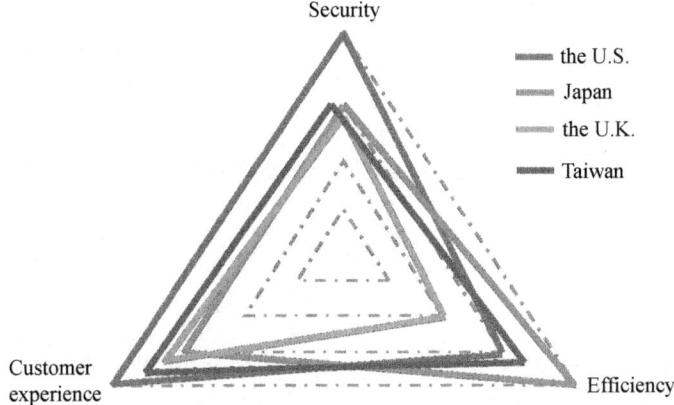

Fig. 3 The weights of security, efficiency and customer experience in different transaction markets. *Source* Market Research Centre, Homelink

2.1   The Security of Transaction Systems

The security is the core and essence of transaction systems. Therefore, to improve the security of transactions has long been the very goal of optimizing transaction systems.

Compared with common commodities, the transaction of existing homes is threatened by rather different risks—different in the sources of risk and in the impact of the losses that the risks could cause.

The risks in existing home transactions are rooted in the mismatch of funds and titles in time. First, the ownership of a property isn't fully mirrored or reflected by the use and occupation of the property, while demands a certificate issued by the authorities as well, which is the only access to title information of the public and requires re-registration for information changes. This is practically a huge investment of time. Second, large amounts of funds owned by individuals or banks are involved in real estate transactions, thus the order of payments and title deliveries are decisive in securing transactions. Third, the allocation of funds, including earnest payment, security deposit, down payment, loans, deposit for utility fees, deposit for household registration and other capital flows, is usually executed in batches, while the rights and titles thereof are not completely separated. So the transfer of title and delivery of funds are often haunted with mismatches in time.

The losses that home transactions could cause are also far more devastating than that of common commodities. The huge amount of money involved in home transactions makes it disastrous for the participant when an accident, rare though, occurs. Law makers should make a clear accountability mechanism to protect the parties involved, and the authorities should establish correspondent systems of risk sharing and risk transferring.

Coping with the mismatches of fund and title in time has been the focus of enhancing the security of existing home transactions in many countries and regions. The first method is the one adopted in Japan: unify the time and space of title and fund transferences, and directly solve the problem. The other method, the more popular one, is adopted in America, Taiwan, Britain and many other countries and regions: the funds of the buyer is escrowed to an independent third party, and are not delivered to the seller until the title has been transferred or certain requirements have been met. These major markets have got the custody of funds highly popularized.

2.1.1   Japan: The System Eliminating the Risks of Mismatches Completely

By rearranging procedures in transactions, Japan's home transaction market unifies the time and space of funds and title transfers, realizes the "cash on delivery" in transactions, and efficiently reduces the problems. What's more, they adds judicial scrivener as an independent third party in transactions, so as to enhance the security of home transactions.

The Closing Date is the most decisive part in Japan's home transactions. On that day, all participants, including the buyer, the seller, judicial scriveners and agents in brokerage companies involved, would meet in bank (usually the one the buyer applied for the loan) to complete the payment of the balance and loans, and meanwhile, the transference of property title (See Fig. 4).

(1) Procedures in Japan's Classic Existing Home Transactions

First, after the home buyer and seller have confirmed their intent for transaction, the brokerage company should inspect the property title of the home, including the examination of the information of physical condition, payment of taxes and property management fee and the utilities of the home. By title inspection is guaranteed the clarity and tradability of the title thereof.

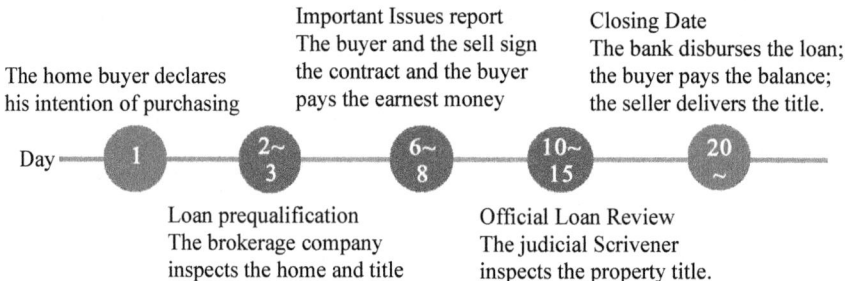

Fig. 4 Time and order of the procedures in japan's existing home transactions. *Source* Market Research Centre, Homelink

Second, the broker age company informs the buyer and the seller of the closing of the inspection, and both parties could then hire judicial scriveners. The seller's judicial scrivener, mainly functioning in assisting the seller in dealing with mortgage issues, is sometimes not required and necessary as the buyer's judicial scrivener is. So both two scriveners for both parties and one scrivener for only the buyer will do. Before entering into contract, real estate companies would send real estate notaries to report important issues to the home buyer in face, which usually lasts two to three hours. The home buyer's confirmation of the transaction is followed by his signing on the contract and the payment of the earnest money.

Third, the home buyer, by himself or with the assistance of his judicial scrivener, applies for a loan from banks; the judicial scrivener(s) conduct the title inspection, and inform the buyer and seller of final delivery after the loan has been approved.

Forth, on the closing day, the judicial scriveners will review the agreement. Generally, the buyer, the seller, the judicial scrivener(s), and the agents will all attend the Closing in the bank which the buyer applied the loan from. And the bank usually offers meeting rooms for existing home transactions, and has its employees participating in the meeting. After the brokers have read and explained in detail every provision of the contract, which often lasts for more than an hour, and both parties have shown acceptance and approval to such contract, they will sign on the contract; then the bank will disburse the money to the buyer's account, and the buyer will finish the transference of the down payment (minus the earnest money) —all completed in person during the Closing.

Fifth, in case of an unpaid existing mortgage, the buyer, the seller, the brokers, as well as the judicial scrivener will meet at the bank that the existing mortgage was applied from upon all funds of the transaction in question having been transferred to accounts, complete the pay-off of the old mortgage on-site and the copy of the certification of such pay-off issued by the bank will be respectively kept by the judicial scrivener and the home seller. After the pay-off has been completed, the buyer, the seller, the broker and the judicial scrivener will return to the bank of the Closing and continue the transaction.

Sixth, the brokerage company usually provides a detailed plan for fund allocation, listing out fixed assets tax advanced by the seller, property charges and other payments that the buyer needs to complete, for the buyer's and the seller's agreements before their signing the contract. The bank will then transfer the balance to the seller according to the plan, after which the judicial scrivener would require both the buyer and the seller to sign on the agreement of the title delivery. For now, all procedures that demand the presence of both parties have been finished.

Seventh, on the same day, usually, the judicial scrivener will apply to and register in Legal Affairs Bureau with all documents of the transaction, on behalf of the buyer and the seller, for the change of the homeowner. The modified Certificate of Title will be delivered to the buyer after a week or so. Japan's Certificate of Title, different with that of China, records the information of all previous transactions, loans and pay-offs of the home, including the time of the transactions, the identities of the two parties, the amount and the interest rate of the loans, as well as the date and amount of the pay-offs.

(2) Guardians of Japan's Transaction System—Independent Judicial Scriveners

The judicial scrivener in Japan's transaction systems, as the independent third party, safeguards the security of property titles in transactions. The "Cash on Delivery" code on the Closing Date in Japan's market has resolved the mismatches of fund and title flows in time, the problems of sedimentary funds, and the sellers' misappropriation of the loans, yet the inspection of title conducted by judicial scriveners is still vitally important to protect the right of the buyer's and to avoid post-transaction disputes over property titles. The judicial scriveners, a legal profession originating in the Judicial Scrivener Law, are specialized in preparing documents and filings of real estate registration, litigation, private debts and other legal affairs, and are authorized to represent clients in civil litigations, while their main job is to assist clients in real estate transaction procedures. The overall past rate of the certificate examination is lower than 3%. Different with barristers, whose duty lies in defending for cases, judicial scriveners are assistants in private procedures, especially those of private economic activities'.

The profession of judicial scrivener was established more than 100 year ago. Now, judicial scriveners may be qualified by passing an examination—an annual exam with a pass rate of lower that 3%, or by working for ten years as a court secretary or a prosecutor's secretary, before undergoing background checks and being filed as a member in the judicial scrivener association. Nowadays, Japan has over twenty thousand judicial scriveners, operating more than eight thousand judicial scrivener offices, with annual industrial income as high as ten billion yen; their services are provided in cities, towns and villages with a coverage rate of 78%, much higher than the 33% coverage rate of barristers'. (See Fig. 5) Obviously, the high thresholds and the high coverage rate of the industry play a prominent role in safeguarding the security of Japan's real estate transactions.

In the real estate market, judicial scriveners participate in all activities involving titles, including gift, inheritance, financing as well as purchase and sale of real estate. Generally, the judicial scrivener's duties in common home transactions are: assisting the client in transfer procedures, drawing up and applying for documents required for the buyer's loan, applying for the lift of the original mortgage and so on. Judicial scriveners only assist their clients in procedures and documents, yet stay clear of the clients' fund managements. What's more, the judicial scriveners are only responsible for legal issues of the security and transfer of titles, whereas physical conditions thereof are in the charge of real estate notaries.

It's not compulsory to hire judicial scriveners in home transactions—civilians can conduct all procedures on their own. The judicial scrivener, however, can effectively reduce the workload of both parties and the risks in transactions. Fully authorized by the law to represent his client in title inspection, transfer procedures in Legal Affairs Bureau, tax payment and many other procedures in transactions, the judicial scrivener could save the client a lot of trouble, which is also why judicial scriveners can be seen running and participating in almost every transaction.

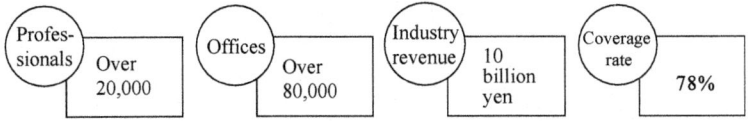

Fig. 5 The status of judicial scriveners in Japan (2012) *Source* Market Research Centre, Homelink

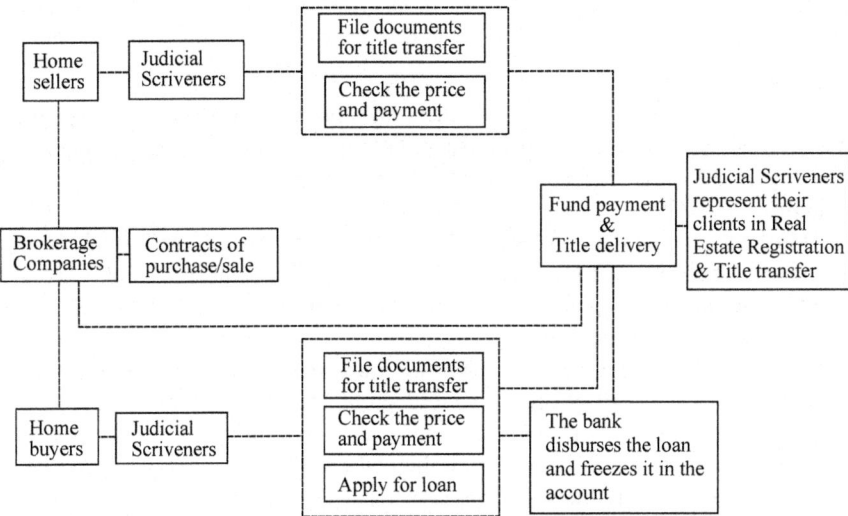

Fig. 6 Major duties of judicial scriveners. *Source* Market Research Centre, Homelink

Generally speaking, one judicial scrivener is able and adequate to handle a transaction. Brokerage companies are allowed to recommend judicial scrivener offices to their clients, yet are not allowed to charge them for commission or referral fee. As the independent third party, judicial scriveners don't involve in any negotiation or consultation, and function only as title inspectors and assistants in document processing and title transfer. The major duties of the judicial scrivener are shown in Fig. 6.

(3) Preconditions of Japan's Transaction System

Japan's "Cash on Delivery" code stems from certain institutional and social conditions.

First, it takes a time-conscious and honest society. The Closing, for example, requires the five parties' participation and usually last for as long as three hours. Japanese people are customarily punctual and time-conscious, which guarantees the transaction could proceed as scheduled, and allows room for less elastic or negotiable procedures.

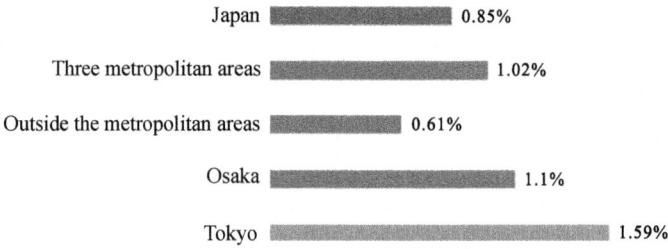

Fig. 7 Circulation rates in Japan's real estate market. *Source* Market Research Centre, Homelink

Second, the brokers, judicial scriveners and the bank staff should be qualified and professional, so as to adhere to the strict transaction rules, have all documents ready by the Closing Date, complete all required procedures, and guarantee as well as improve the efficiency of the transactions.

Third, the cooperation of the banks in providing venues and staffs is also important. The personal financial products provided in Japan's banks are still simple, and the resulting fierce competition among banks actually works as an incentive to provide better services.

Last, the plenty of time and space for transactions due to the lower home circulation in Japan can effectively avoid problems like market congestions. In Japan's most active market, Tokyo has only 120 thousand set of homes circulated each year. Comparatively, those with higher circulation rates and less evenly developed markets would face harsher situations. The circulation rates in Japan are shown in Fig. 7.

2.1.2   America: The System Double Protected by Fund Custody and Title Insurance

Every year, there are averagely five million homes traded in American's existing home market, accounting for 90% of all homes transacted in its real estate market. As one of the most active existing home markets, America's existing home market began to flourish after the Second World War, and has developed a transaction system centring on fund custodians and a market-oriented model connecting title insurance, brokerage companies, home inspection and several other industries.

The custody of funds means that the funds of the buyer is escrowed to an independent third party, and are not delivered to the seller until the title has been transferred or certain requirements have been met. The funds and title is the core of home transaction, thus the custody of funds is the core of a successful transaction. Vertically, it links procedures including title inspection, home inspection, paper works and post-transaction supports; horizontally, it's a vital part connecting the buyer, the seller and other participants involved.

Fig. 8 Flows of documents and funds bound by fund custodians. *Source* Market Research Centre, Homelink

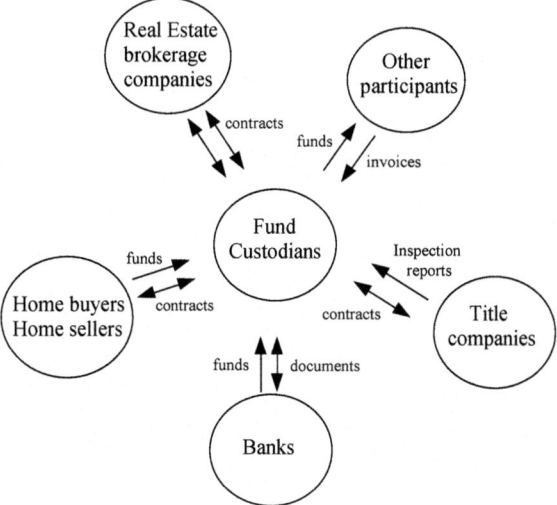

The participation of custodians weaves the flows of time and capital into a uniform system, provides a cushion for the mismatches, and safeguards the security of funds and title. Different with Japan's Cash on Delivery, America's system doesn't require the presence of all parties involved in a transaction, and this kind of flexibility also catalyzes and cultivates the prosperity of American existing home market. In America, fund custodians are participants of almost 98% of the transactions involving brokers, and 90% of the private transactions involving no brokers (See Fig. 8).

(1) Procedures in America's Classic Existing Home Transactions

In America's existing home transaction system, the fund custodians, as the independent third party, functions together with title companies in safeguarding the clients' transaction security. The transaction procedures in this system are comparatively more complex, yet most of the procedures are finished by the custodians and the insurance companies (See Fig. 9).

The Procedures and their Time and Order in America's Classic Existing Home Transactions are shown in Fig. 10.

Firstly, the home seller and the buyer confirm their intention to trade, and agree on a fund custodian that takes custody of funds in their transaction.

Secondly, a custodial account should be opened. The account could be established by the buyer, the seller, or the buyer's brokerage company together with the lender. If neither party has employed a broker, then it's usually the seller's duty to open such account. Then the buyer should deposit the earnest money, usually 1% ~ 2% the amount of the price of the house, as well as the dawn payment to the account. It's required, in some cities, that the seller should also deposit home insurance and taxes in the custodial account.

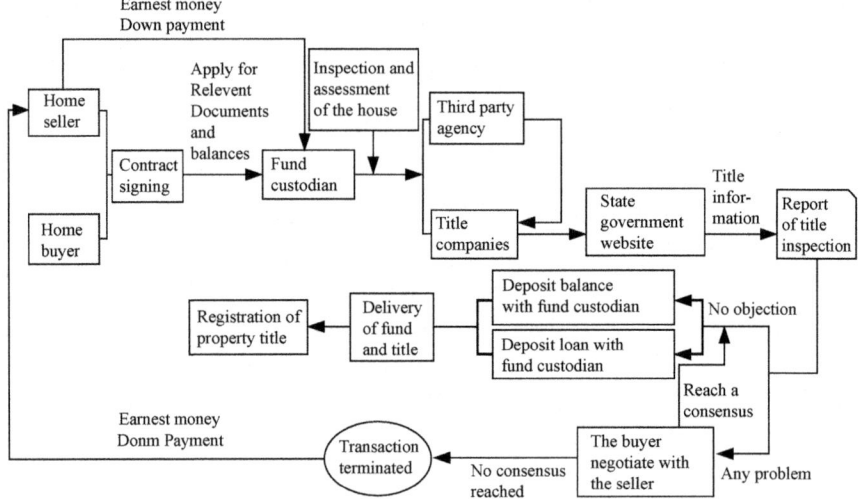

Fig. 9 Procedures of America's existing home transaction with the participation of fund custodians and title companies. *Source* Market Research Centre, Homelink

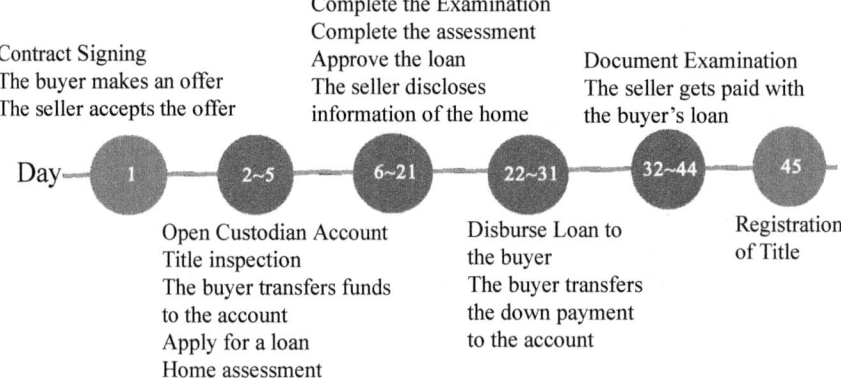

Fig. 10 Time and order of the procedures in America's existing home transactions *Source* Market Research Centre, Homelink

Thirdly, the buyer would inspect and assess the house. Usually, the buyer would employ professional and certificated third-party institutions to inspect and issue inspection reports. It's also possible that the seller would employ licensed termite inspectors and roof inspectors to conduct inspections and issue reports before the house is sold. The report could then be provided for the buyer in transactions as part of the inspection. The buyer can demand necessary repairs according to the reports. And in case that such repair is indicated in the contract while isn't approved by the seller, the buyer is entitled to withdraw from the contract.

The buyer would apply for a loan from the lender if it needed be. The lender would assess and evaluate the house to ensure that the amount of the loan worth the evaluation of the home.

Fourthly, the property title will be inspected, aiming at safeguarding the right of the buyer and of the creditor. The title company and the fund custodian, except in South California, are usually combined. The title company would issue a report including title transfer, mortgage, will, decree of divorce, tax payment, lien and other information of the house according to the information disclosed to the public, and would present the report to the buyer, so as to confirm whether the title of the house is clean. If the answer is yes, then the buyer would deposit the down payment to the custodial account. And both parties would deposit their respective custody fees and title insurances into the account at the same time. In the event of any problem concerning the title arises and cannot be solved by negotiation, the contract might be terminated.

Fifthly, fund custodians will complete all procedures of the transaction within 24 h after the loan's been deposited to the custodial account, which include: paying off the seller's bank loan (if any) and other mortgages and transfer the rest money to the buyer; allocating the funding of title insurance, custody fee and brokers' commissions; and applying for a new certificate of title.

Sixthly, on the next day of the delivery of title and funds, the fund custodian will send its employee registering with appropriate authorities for title changes with the new certificate of title. Usually, the new certificate is issued one month after the registration.

(2) The Guardian of America's Transaction System—the Custody of Funds

The market-oriented development and industrialization of America's existing home transactions are majorly attributed to the employment of fund custodians. By gathering the matches of time flow and capital flow into the same system, fund custodians realize the Cash on Money on the Closing Day, and guarantee the security of title and funds. The custody of funds is not a business, but rather a service which can be conducted by various participants. Companies that provide only custody services, usually with less than 100 employees and rarely large in scale, can work for local existing home transactions after they've acquired custodian licenses and paid deposits. Often they are under strict surveillance. Almost half of the custody services, though, are provided by title companies, brokerage companies or lawyers. It's estimated that the industry could worth at least 12.2 billion dollar. The percentages of different types of fund custodians in America are shown in Fig. 11.

(3) Preconditions of America's Transaction System

The market-oriented custody mode dominated by the industry of fund custody in America, as well, is closely related to its present situations: ① the service of fund

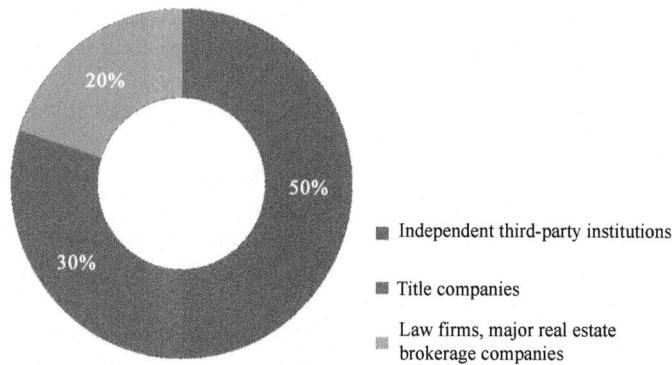

Independent third-party institutions

Title companies

Law firms, major real estate
brokerage companies

Fig. 11 Percentages of Different Types of Fund Custodians in America *Source* Market Research Centre, Homelink

custody in America originated from its middleman system, and became prosperous in major transactions like real estate trades. To prevent frauds and disputes in transactions, and to guarantee the security of title and fund deliveries, the services were gradually professionalized with the pace of American economy, and have also given birth to a fund custody system, an approach to cope with the mismatches of fund and time in existing home transactions. ② America boasts a huge existing home market. In America, the annual circulation rate is averagely about 5%, and the annual total volume over five million sets, with expenses on transaction procedures thousands of dollars per set, and revenues from fund custody and title insurance both exceeding hundreds of billions—enough to prop up the development of the whole industry. The industry of title insurance, especially, has started to show signs of economies of scale, with the four biggest title companies taking over 70% market share. Among them, FNF, the biggest one, takes a market share of 30% with a market value of nine billion dollar. ③ The government allows the market with ample room in three ways. First, the government rarely involves in existing home transactions except when issuing the official certificate of title transfer. Second, the authorities have passed fund custody laws covering all details in the operation of the custody in exiting home transactions, which provides a legal base for the industry regulation. Third, the custody of funds is barely limited to some specified companies, which means that third-party companies are granted with ample space to innovate and develop their services, as long as they are legal. ④ The housing information in America's market features higher accessibility and easy availability. Title information is absolutely transparent and mostly available online. FNF's offshore teams in India, for example, can conduct most of their inspection works in America.

2.1.3   Taiwan: The System Combining Independent Third-Party Judiciary and the Custody of Funds

Existing home transactions in the Province of Taiwan are influenced by those in Japan: Taiwan's land administration agent is the equal of Japan's judicial scrivener. The agents, as the judicial third-party, safeguard the security of the transactions by verifying rights and entitlements of the home, re-inspecting the title thereof, assisting in title transfer, and so on. However, Japan's cash on delivery on the Closing Date isn't realized in Taiwan—the funds are paid after the transference of title, so mismatches of title and fund still occur. By borrowing the mode of fund custody in America, Taiwan introduces third-party fund custodians to its existing home transactions, usually realized through performance securities and conducted by real estate management companies. The Payment System among banks runs over debt transference, which means that the banks that the parties applied loans from are entitled to conduct payments of the loans, and that both parties are separated with the fund flow, which could reduce the risk of the misappropriation of loans (See Figs. 12 and 13).

The existing home transaction in Taiwan consists of five major procedures: deposit payment, contract signing, stamping (paper work of title transfer), tax payment and title transfer and home delivery. And the money paid by the buyer often includes the earnest money, down-payment, balances and so on, among which the earnest money is always part of the down payment. And it is usually structured as: earnest money (for contract signing, 10%) + mid-term payment (for stamping, 10%) + mid-term payment (for taxes, 10%) + balances (the loan, 70%). See Fig. 14.

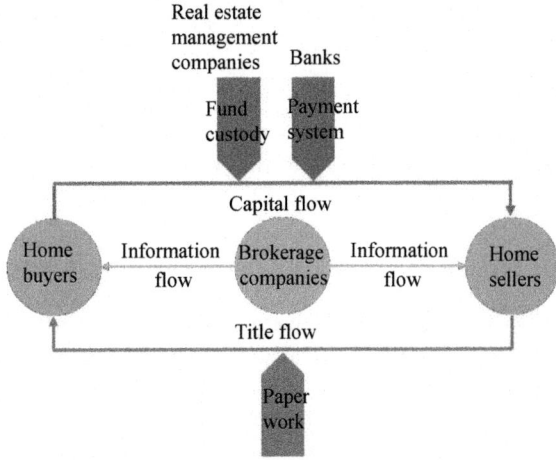

Fig. 12 Japan's transaction system that embodies land administration agents and the custody of funds. *Source* Market Research Centre, Homelink

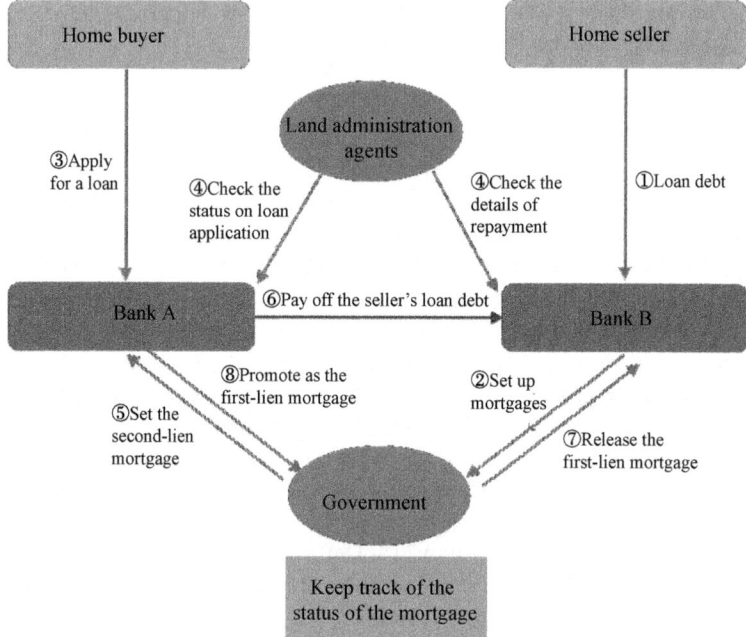

Fig. 13 The payment system of banks in Taiwan's existing home transactions. *Source* Market Research Centre, Homelink

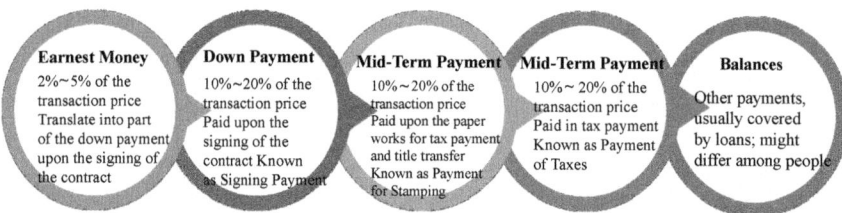

Fig. 14 Structure of the funds in Taiwan's existing home transaction. *Source* Market Research Centre, Homelink

(1) Procedures in Taiwan's Classic Existing Home Transactions

First, the buyer pays the earnest money when the intention of both parties to trade has been confirmed. Then the employed land administration agent, the building management company that in charge of fund custody, as well as the brokerage company would conduct a preliminary inspection of the title of the house, so as to make sure that the seller is the rightful owner of the home. And both parties could then prepare for the signing of the contract.

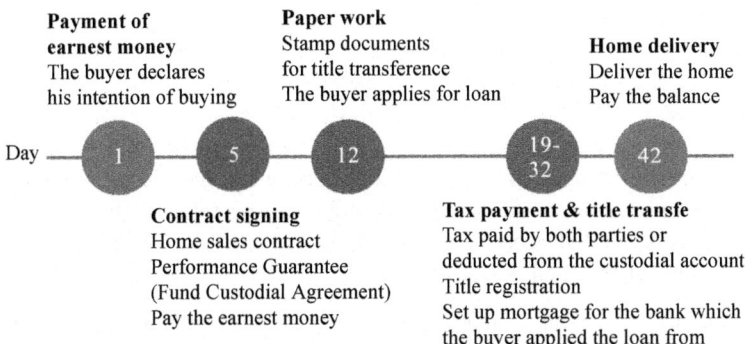

Fig. 15 Time and order of the procedures in Taiwan's existing home transactions. *Source* Market Research Centre, Homelink

Secondly, the two parties sign contracts. The buyer and the seller, with the assistance of the land administration agent, will sign the home sales contract, and an application together with a contract for their performance of the transaction, both of which are provided by the building management company. The land administration agent will issue a Performance Guarantee and the buyer will deposit the down payment into the custodial account opened by the building management company. The land administration agent would then provide the company with relevant documents and files, and start a second title inspection, which will be more detailed and careful than the preliminary one (Fig. 15).

Thirdly, documents and filings are prepared for the title transfer. The buyer as well as the seller will submit the stamped documents required in tax payment and title transfer to the land administration agent. During this time, the buyer can apply a loan from the bank, settle the amount of the loan, and complete the loan application, by himself or with the land administration agent's assistance. Then the buyer would deposit a mid-term payment (10% ∼ 20% of the transaction price) in the custodial account.

Fourthly, the tax will be paid and the title will be transferred. The land administration agent is entrusted to declare taxes, both parties shall pay the taxes or for the management company to pay by deducting from the custodial account. Then, the land administration agent will provide the land administration office with the sales contract attached with the confirmation of payment to register the title transfer. And if the buyer have applied for a mortgage loan, a new mortgage should be set up for the bank that the buyer applied loan from, and the buyer shall issue a promissory note securing a sum of money equating to the balance (apart from the down payment and the mid-term payments), identifying the seller as the payee, and deliver the note to the agent. If there is no mortgage loan on the home to pay off, the buyer shall deposit the loan in the custodial account.

Fifthly, the custodian account will be cleared and the home will be delivered. Between the tax payment as well as title transfer and the home delivery, the custodial account will be cleared: the income and expenditure of the account, the commission of the brokerage company, the payment for performance security and the payment deposited by the buyer will be checked and examined. If there was a mortgage loan on the home, the land administration agent will organize the buyer's loan to pay off the loan and release the seller's mortgage. The buyer and the seller will complete the home delivery with the broker or the land administration agent. After the home delivery, the promissory note will be returned to the buyer; the money in the custodial account will be deposited in the seller's account, which marks the end of the fund custody.

(2) Guardians of Taiwan's Transaction Security—the Comprehensive System

Taiwan not only brought in Japan's judicial scrivener as its land administration agent to safeguard transaction security by taking charge of right inspection, re-inspecting the property title, and offering assistance in title delivery, but learned from America's transaction system and introduced the fund custodian as its real estate management company to secure transactions. For now, more than 90% transactions in major cities are under the fund custody conducted by real estate management companies, far higher than the coverage rate in smaller cities or rural areas. Meanwhile, major brokerage companies are much more frequently covered by fund custody than small brokerage companies. By introducing land administration agents and real estate companies in its transaction system, and maintaining their high levels of coverage, the security in Taiwan's existing home transactions is safeguarded and guaranteed.

Real estate management companies took its shape in new home markets, and mainly function ① as the custodian of pre-sale payment; ② in assisting development financing works and as the custodian of loan, so as to safeguard the security of funds. To enhance the security in existing home transactions, in 1996, Sinyi Real Estate and Taishin Bank established the first real estate management company, An-Sin Real Estate Management as a joint venture to provide real estate management services. As the range of existing home transaction market is swelling, major brokerage companies start establishing their own real estate management companies, providing services for and not only for transactions conducted by their brokers. Anshin Escrow, a 2009 spin-out of An-Sin Real Estate Company, provides services for home transactions not completed by Sinyi Real Estate. At the same time, some long-established real estate management companies start taking on fund custodies, as well. The development of Taiwan's real estate management companies is shown in Fig. 16.

Due to the important role that real estate management companies plays in the security of transactions, they are strictly regulated in from establishment through requirements in custody to the company's articles and businesses. In Taiwan, most of the management companies providing fund custody services are joint ventures set up by brokerage companies and banks. Part of the reason is that the Real Estate Management Practices Act outlines to jointly establish a real estate management company, the bank shall hold more than 30% of the shares. It may also attribute to

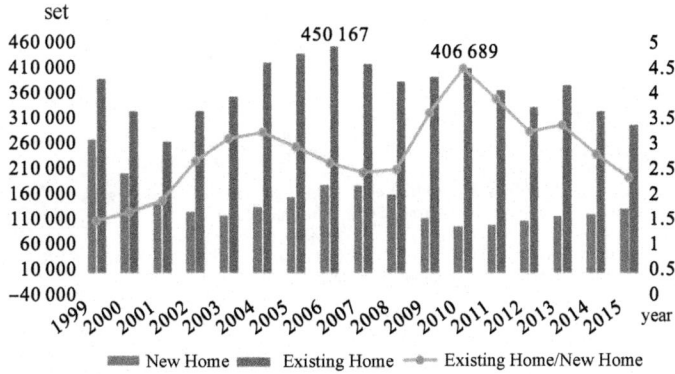

Fig. 16 Development of Taiwan's real estate management companies. *Source* Market Research Centre, Homelink

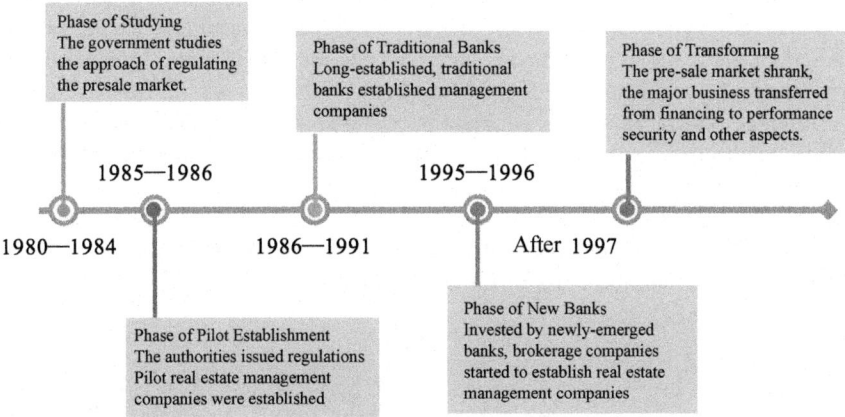

Fig. 17 Trading activity in Taiwan's real estate market. *Source* Market Research Centre, Homelink

the fact that the bank's taking shares could render the fund custody more reliable and trustworthy.

2015 records a transaction volume of 290 thousand set of houses in Taiwan (See Fig. 17), with a GMV (Gross Merchandise Volume) of nearly 600 billion yuan. And if taking the management companies' penetration rate as 70%, and the charging standard as 5 yuan per 10000 of the GMV, we can estimate that the total revenue from the industry could be as high as 210 million yuan. Moreover, the interest generated during the custody also belongs to the management company: with an annual interest rate offered by the checking account of 0.3%, and a 40% custody fee (the ratio of the custody fee to the price of the home), the revenue from interest of the industry could amount to 50 million yuan.

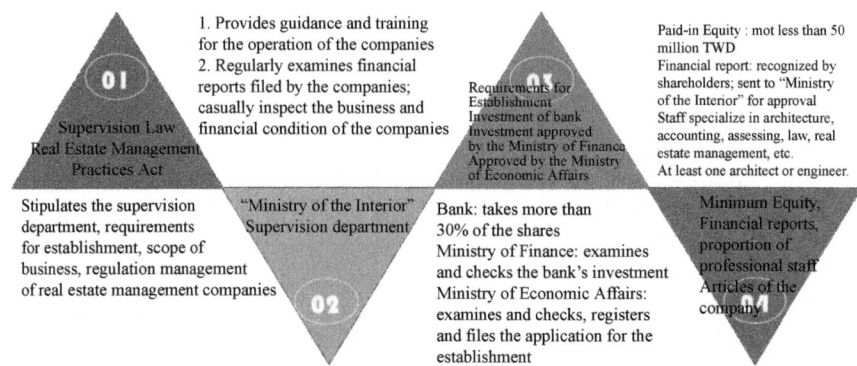

Fig. 18 The supervision system and requirements for the establishment of Taiwan's real estate management companies. *Source* Market Research Centre, Homelink

Another major participant in Taiwan's existing home transactions is the land administration agent (See Fig. 18). They are employed in over 90% existing home transactions to assist in title transfer, and represent the clients in the application and processing of documents (See Figs. 19 and 20).

Different with Japan's rules, land administration agents in Taiwan are allowed to acquire the broker's license, and most of the management companies, consignment companies and brokerage companies have fixed land administration agents. This weakens the agents' effectiveness in supervising as the independent third party, and consequently, the once independent industry of land administration is now being reduced to an affiliate business of the companies.

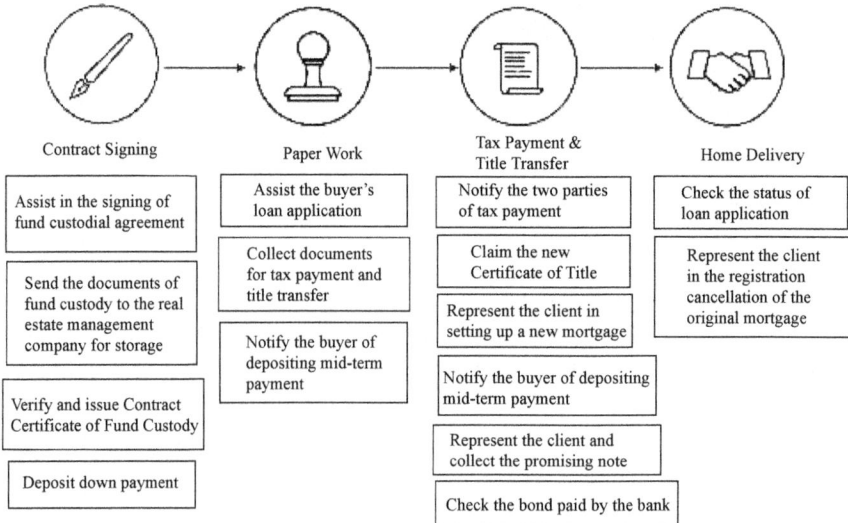

Fig. 19 The land administration agent's duties in existing home transactions. *Source* Market Research Centre, Homelink

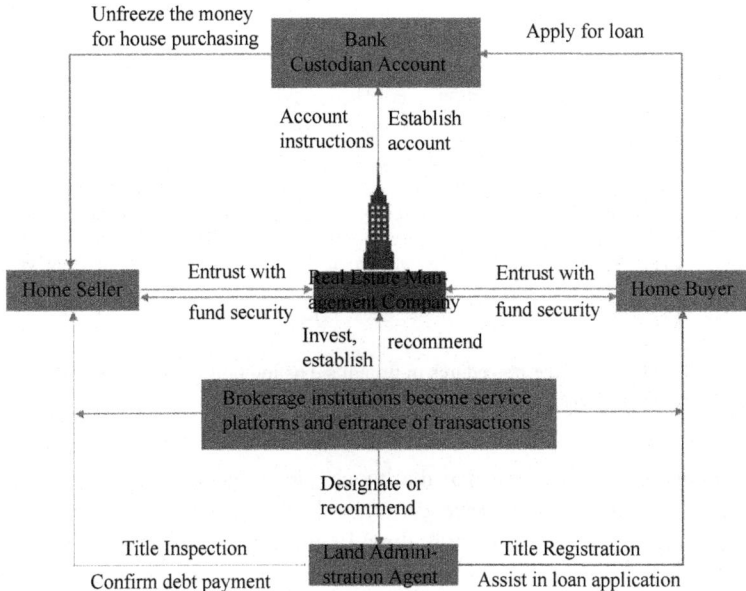

Fig. 20 The roles of real estate management company and land administration agent in Taiwan' home transactions. *Source* Market Research Centre, Homelink

(3) The Development Tendency of Taiwan's Transaction System

The custody of funds conducted by real estate management companies in Taiwan differs from that in America's transaction system in three ways: ① the fund custody in Taiwan does not cover all money circulated in transactions—the fund for releasing the house's mortgage is handled by and among banks; ② real estate management companies cannot finish the custody work alone, for they need to cooperate with land administration agents and brokerage companies to complete the paper work; ③ the custody of funds in Taiwan doesn't develop into an independent industry, and instead, functioning as a supporting player, it is more often than not provided as a transaction service by brokerage companies. With swelling amount of money invested and increasing transaction activity, the core of Taiwan's existing home transaction system will transfer from land administration agents' paper work to the custody of funds in the long run. By then, customers will be promised with more security and efficiency.

2.1.4   Britain: The System Highly Dependent on Solicitors

The procedures in Britain's existing home transaction resemble those in Japan's, while one of its major participants, solicitors, shoulders more duties than Japan's judicial scriveners. The judicial scriveners' main mission is to file legal documents,

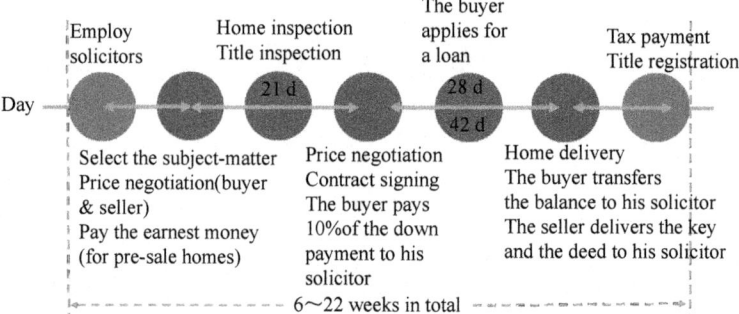

Fig. 21 Time and order of the procedures in britain's existing home transactions. *Source* Market Research Centre, Homelink

provide assistance, and assure that the buyer's loan and the seller's unpaid mortgage are handled by banks. However, other than processing documents and providing assistance, Britain's solicitors directly engage in the custody of funds. The time and order of the procedures in Britain's existing home transactions are shown in Fig. 21.

The mismatches of funds and title in time in Britain's transactions are solved by solicitors, and thus is the security of funds safeguarded. The money for the purchase, rather than directly transferred from the buyer's account to the seller's, is handled via solicitors, and the buyer's loan, as well, will firstly be transferred to his solicitor's account after approval. The buyer will directly transfer the fund for home purchase after the transaction has been confirmed, and the fund will not be disbursed to the seller's solicitor until all legal documents are filed and completed, where cash transactions are not permitted. For fund security, the solicitors must acquire certificates of real estate professionals and buy occupational insurances, so misappropriation of funds rarely occurs—if it occurs, the lawyer association (comprised by all lawyers and solicitors of the country) will then be held accountable to compensate for the buyer's loss. And for title security, all homes in the U.K. are online registered at UK Land Registry, kept available to the public, and the buyer's solicitor will assist his client in registering at the Land Registry upon the closing of the transaction, after which the buyer, as the rightful owner of the house, will be secured with his title to the home, even if he loses his title deed by accident.

2.2   The Efficiency of Transaction Systems

The efficiency of transaction systems is measured by the effectiveness of the connection between procedures and the smoothness of matching the title flow and the fund flow with effective communication among participants. Practically, we can measure the efficiency of a system by its transaction cost (the transaction cycle plus the transaction fees). The transaction cycle could stand for the time invested, and the transaction fee represents the payment apart from commission and taxes.

The different efficiencies of different transaction systems result from diverse arrangements of transaction procedures and various engaged parties. America' system, with fund custodians as the core that connects title insurance, home inspection and paper work, features an average transaction cycle of 30 ∼ 50 days, and transaction fees of 17 to 20 thousand yuan, mainly comprised by custody fee and title insurance, features high transaction costs and medium efficiency. The centre of Japan's system is brokerage companies, which links home inspection, the custody of funds and the paper work conducted by judicial scriveners. Due to a transaction cycle of about 20 days, and that the only payment required from the customer is a judicial scrivener's commission of about 6,000 yuan, Japan's transaction system features low transaction costs and high efficiency. Similar to Japan's system, Taiwan's transaction system is, as well, propped up by brokerage companies. Taiwan's system boasts a transaction cycle of 28 ∼ 35 days and transaction costs less than 5,000 yuan, and is thus characterized by low transaction costs and high efficiency. In Britain, all procedures in existing home transactions, from home inspection through the delivery and custody of funds to paper work, are handled and dealt with by solicitors. Consequently, the Britain's transaction system, with an average transaction cycle of as long as 42 ∼ 82 days and transaction costs as much as 4720 ∼ 14,000 yuan, features ultra-long transaction cycle, ultra-high transaction costs and very low efficiency.

Measured by cycles and costs of transaction, generally, the systems with brokerage companies at the core in Japan and Taiwan is highly efficient; America's custodian-centred system ranks the third; and Britain's transaction system led by solicitors features the lowest transaction efficiency (See Fig. 22).

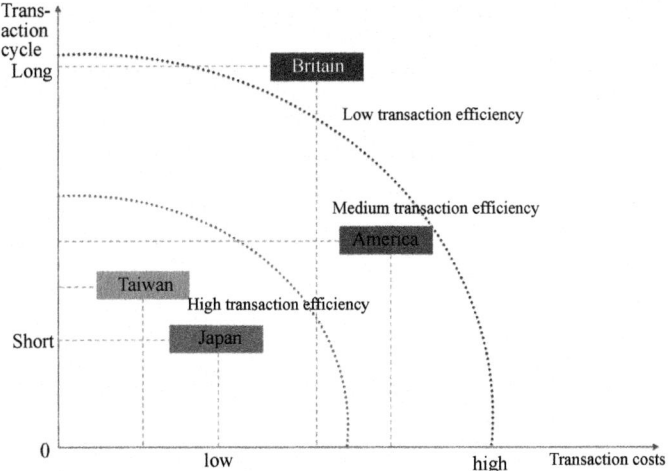

Fig. 22 The comparison of transaction efficiencies in different transaction systems. *Source* Market Research Centre, Homelink

2.2.1   America: The Transaction Efficiency in a System Led by Fund Custodians

America's existing home transaction features many participants, among which fund custodians are the tie that connects the seller and the buyer, brokerage companies, title companies, banks and other parties, and are responsible for successful and secured deliveries of funds, titles and contracts. Not only do they take charge of the security of funds, but they also dominate the transactions—they also need to file documents, communicate with the two parties as well as their brokers and attorneys, and accelerate the transactions.

The leading position of fund custodians is reflected in three aspects:

(1) Fund custodians are responsible to select title companies for title inspection and insurance underwriting. Most title companies in America, save for those in South California, provide both title insurance service and fund custody service, so that the costs of external communications could be reduced and the efficiency could be increased. Major title companies, usually, establish their own databanks by updating and recompiling the information publicized by the government, which notably improved the efficiency of title inspection.

(2) To learn the status of the buyer's loan application, fund custodians need to communicate with banks, during which flows of documents and funds take place. (See Fig. 23) The reason lies in that American banks, highly localized

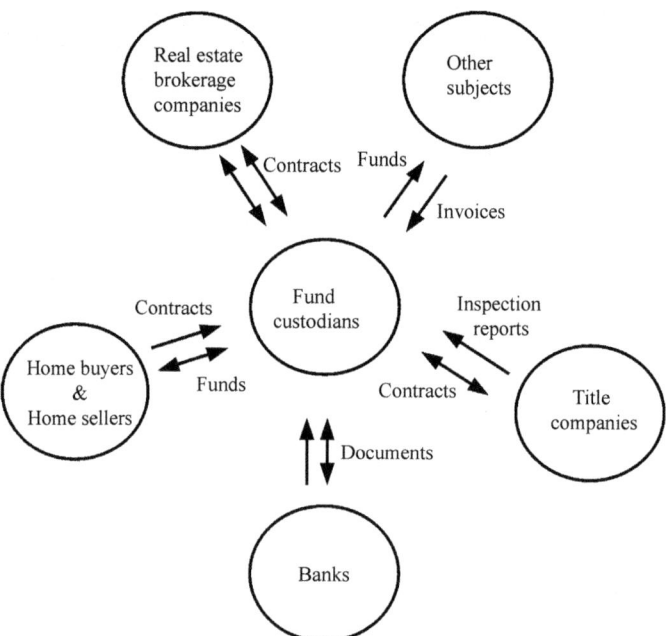

Fig. 23 The flows of funds and documents led by fund custodians. *Source* Market Research Centre, Homelink

and hardly equipped with branches in other states, often fail to conduct title inspections on houses beyond a certain territory, whereas insurance companies are not bothered by such problems.

(3) Fund custodians also need to communicate and cooperate with title attorneys. In New York State, America, the buyers usually hire title attorneys, who draft statements of custody, file legal documents, deliver the required documents to fund custodians and register the title transfer at the government. Moreover, for pre-existing title flaws, such as unpaid taxes, or unpaid property costs, fund custodians cannot conduct any repayment unless authorized by title attorneys.

In terms of transaction cycles, transactions in America usually last for $30 \sim 45$ days, while in Japan, 20 days. The main external reason why America's transaction cycle is longer lies in the different time invested in applying loans from banks. In America, it takes $17 \sim 30$ days from applying a loan to the loan being disbursed, while in Japan, the time is reduced to $10 \sim 15$ days. Fund custodians have to negotiate with several participants for transferences of funds and title, and these repetitive communications inevitably reduce the efficiency in transactions.

In terms of transaction costs, in America, the custody fee is usually 2‰ the transaction price plus a flat fee of about 250 dollar, while the money charged for title insurance differs a lot and depends on the appraisal value of the house and the specific coverage of the insurance, amounting to 5‰ $\sim$ 6‰ the transaction price plus a $200 \sim 300$ dollar flat fee. If taking the transaction price as 350,000 dollar (commission not included), the American customer need to pay an extra 600 dollar for fund custody and $1950 \sim 2400$ dollar for title insurance (about $17,000 \sim 20,000$ yuan) for an existing home.

So, when judged by transaction cycles and transaction costs, America's existing home transaction system, with fund custodians at its core, is not the most efficient one.

2.2.2 Japan: The High Transaction Efficiency in a System with Brokerage Companies at Its Core

The efficiency of a transaction system could be measured by the efficiency of the connections between its procedures. In Japan, all procedures of a transaction are gathered together on one day—the Closing, when the five parties, namely, the home buyer, the home seller, brokers, the banks that the buyer and the seller loaned from, and the judicial scriveners, will all participate in the meeting and complete the title transfer and fund delivery at the same time. This arrangement can avoid the mismatches of title and funds, and has significantly promoted the efficiency in transactions and created a unique trading environment of "Title on Funds". Consequently, Japan's existing home transactions boast the shortest cycles. The comparison of the procedures in America's and Japan's existing home transactions is shown in Fig. 24.

Procedures and Participants in Americals Existing Home Transactions

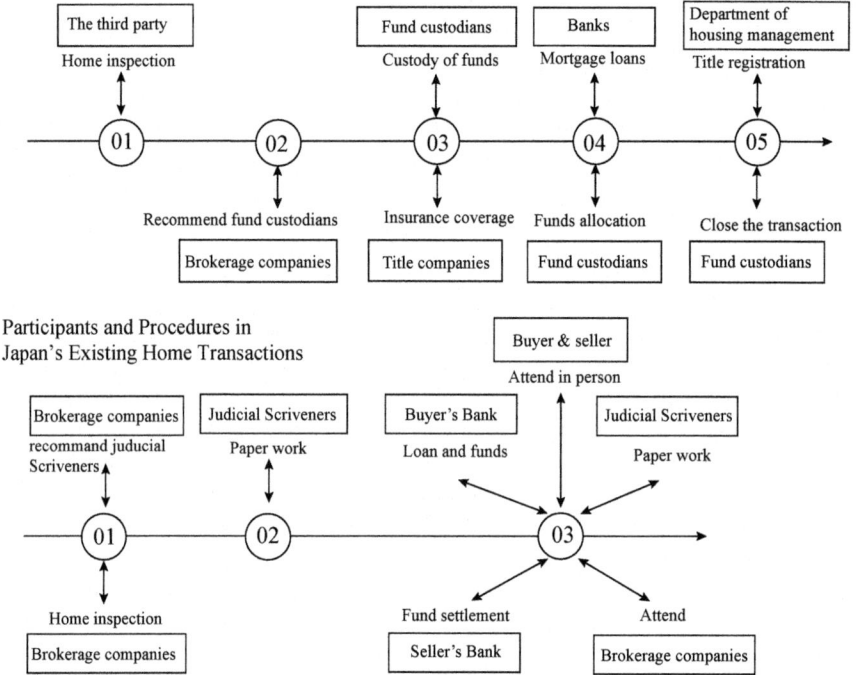

Fig. 24 The comparison of the procedures in America's and Japan's existing home transactions. *Source* Market Research Centre, Homelink

In America, the procedures and links in transactions are constructed and connected by fund custodians, which holds the key to funds allocation, title inspection and paper work. Japan's transaction system, allowing no sedimentary fund and involving no title insurance, makes brokerage companies its core, and the professional services provided by judicial scriveners the efficiency-booster.

When taking the procedures in transaction as a whole, brokerage companies are practically in charge of the collection and communication of information. (See Fig. 25) Brokerage companies hire real estate notaries to examine the house, conduct preliminary title inspection, sign on relevant documents and bear legal responsibilities thereof, recommend banks as well as judicial scriveners, and communicate with the bank and both parties so as to make sure every procedure is going on well. Judicial scriveners' duties lie in providing professional services, including title inspection and paper work, which could reduce the time invested in complex filings or title registration and further improve the efficiency of transactions. As a consequence, the average transaction cycle under Japan's transaction system with brokerage companies and legal professionals at its core is reduced to as short as 20 days.

Fig. 25 The leading position of Japan's brokerage companies in information flows. *Source* Market Research Centre, Homelink

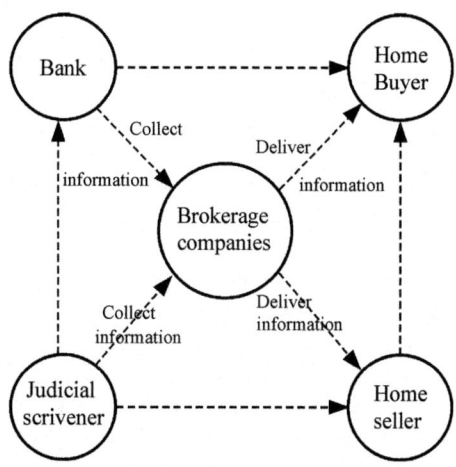

Table 1 The fees for judicial scriveners' services

Item	Average fee (RMB)
Registration of title transfer (Gift)	
Registration of title transfer (sale & purchase)	
Mortgage registration (bank loans)	
Erase mortgage registration	
Incidental expenses (certificate of tax deductions, travel expenses, survey fee, registration of change of address, etc.)	1000 ~ 5000 (according to actual expenses)

In terms of transaction costs, Japanese customers only need to pay for the judicial scriveners' charge for service, because the real estate notaries' charge has already been included in the commission. Usually, judicial scriveners charge only for title registrations, so the transaction costs, as well as his income in one transaction depends on whether he's employed by only one party, or both parties. Practically, a judicial scrivener can get an average income of 120,000 yen (about 7000 yuan) per transaction (See Table 1).

To conclude, without involving fund custodians or title insurances, Japan's transaction system, with brokerage companies at the core of its transaction procedures, is characterized by very high transaction efficiency thanks to its short transaction cycles and low transaction costs.

2.2.3 Taiwan: The High Transaction Efficiency Under a System Featuring Multi-party Communication with Brokerage Companies at the Core

Taiwan's transaction system, as well, is propped up by brokerage companies, (see Fig. 26), which, responsible for home examination, preliminary title inspection and recommending land administration agents and fund custodians—real estate management companies, functions at the centre of information exchanges. Land administration agents also play an important role in efficiency improving by providing professional services including title inspection, document processing, assisting the buyer's loan application and the banks' loan repayment, and so on. And the custody and allocation of funds are completed by real estate management companies. By weaving separate participants and various procedures effectively into a uniform system, brokerage companies significantly improves the efficiency of transactions as a medium of information.

Taiwan's transaction system has not only borrowed Japan's independent judicial third-party—land administration agents, but introduced America's fund custodians as its major participant, and the multi participants inevitably resulted in increased communication costs. Besides, different with America's fund custodians that take charge of all and any fund issues, Taiwan's loan repayment is completed through the banks' Payment System, yet the allocation of funds is conducted by real estate management companies with performance securities. The doubled fund managers inevitably reduced the efficiency of funds allocation and the efficiency of transactions.

With the steady and long-term cooperation between brokerage companies and land administration agents, however, Taiwan's transaction system still features a shorter transaction cycle, averagely 28 ~ 35 days, when compared with those in America, Britain and Mainland China.

In terms of transaction costs, Taiwan's land administration agents, as well, charge by services and items. Averagely, a land administration agent charges 10,000 to 20,000 TWD (2000 ~ 4000 CNY) for each existing home transaction. Real estate management companies charge 0.05% the transaction price as fund custody fee, and if we take the transaction price as seven million TWD, then the custody fee is approximately 3500 TWD (about 720 CNY). So customers need to pay a fee ranging from 2720 ~ 4720 yuan for a transaction.

To conclude, with brokerage companies at its core and land administration agents providing professional services, Taiwan's transaction system is characterized by short transaction cycle, low transaction costs and high transaction efficiency.

2.2.4 Britain: The Low Efficiency Under a Transaction System with All Burdens Taken on by Solicitors

The solicitors are the absolute core of Britain's transaction system, taking on almost all duties in transactions: there are no fund custodians or title companies, and

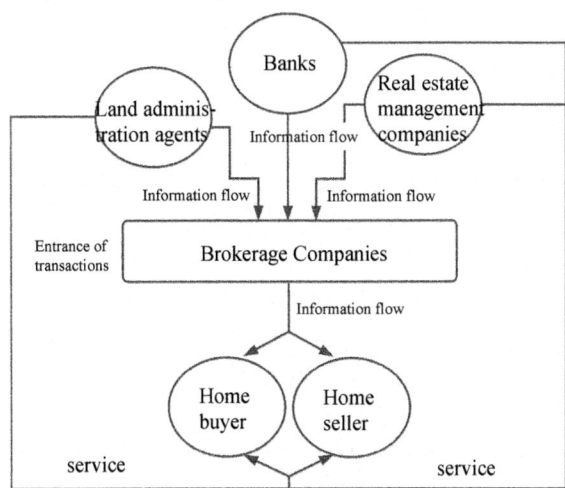

Fig. 26 The information flows connected by brokerage companies under Taiwan's transaction system. *Source* Market Research Centre, Homelink

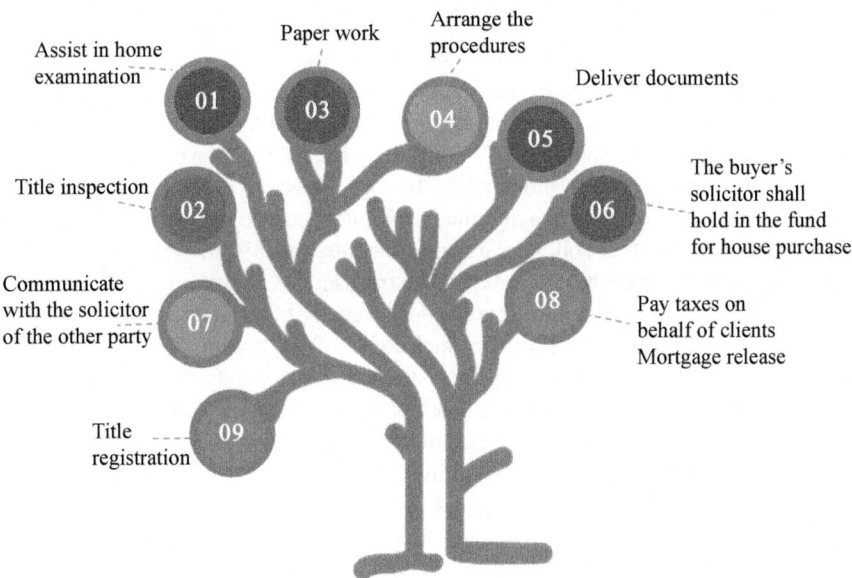

Fig. 27 The duties of solicitors in Britain. *Source* Market Research Centre, Homelink

brokerage companies merely functions in matching home resources. The solicitors need to contact with third parties for home examination, take custody of and deliver the funds, and take on all paper work (See Fig. 27).

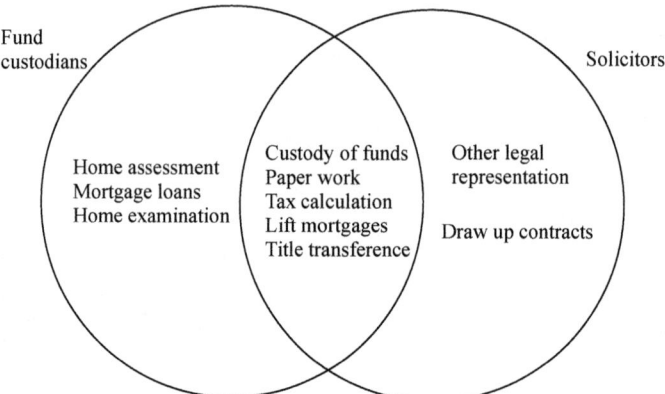

Fig. 28 The comparison of the duties of fund custodians in America and solicitors in transactions. *Source* Market Research Centre, Homelink

As the absolute leading party in home transactions, the solicitors need to take on so many duties that the transaction cycles are incredibly longer. In every transaction, the solicitor needs to communicate for several times with the solicitor of the other party to confirm the contract and collect the information of both parties, applies for relevant information and documents from the appropriate authorities, and cooperates with professional companies to complete the inspection report of the physical conditions of the home in question. Consequently, the transaction cycles are extremely long: the solicitors of both parties need three to six weeks to prepare for contract exchange, and another two to four weeks to conduct the exchange. What's more, the cycles are usually uncontrollable, because the buyer and the seller are assisted only by their solicitors as professionals, and it's possible that accidents occur, yet will not be dealt with in time. The transactions in Britain could take six to twelve weeks, nearly twice the time needed in many other countries.

Guaranteed by the mature professional codes of the country and personal reputation, the solicitors in Britain are entrusted with the custody of funds—the most important part in home transactions. And as legal professionals, they also provide customers with paper work services. In transactions, they not only take on the custody of funds, but take the responsibilities for document drafting and processing as well. (See Fig. 28) When compared with America, where brokers' roles are relatively minor as well, the transaction efficiency in Britain is decided by solicitors; and when compared with Japan and Taiwan, where independent judicial third parties are also involved, the solicitors' duties are heavier due to the absence of brokerage companies in Britain. So for all these reasons, the transaction efficiency under Britain's transaction system is comparatively low.

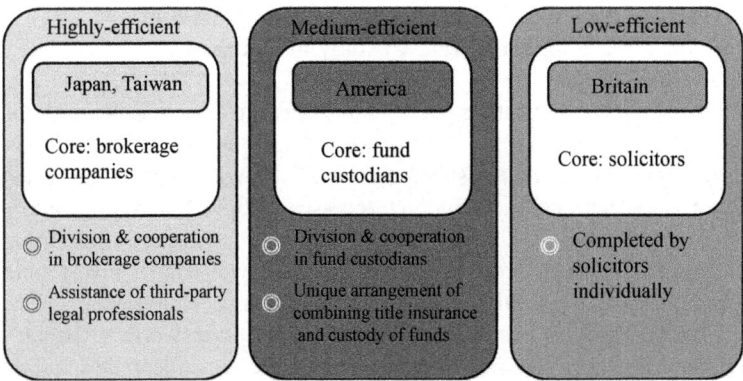

Fig. 29 The cores of different transaction systems. *Source* Market Research Centre, Homelink

The solicitors have got much more work to do, so naturally they charge for more in transactions when compared with other countries or regions: averagely 500 ~ 1500 lb (about 4650 ~ 14000 yuan) per transaction.

In general, the absolute leading position of solicitors in transactions results in ultra-long transaction cycles and high transaction costs. The transaction system is characterized by extremely low transaction efficiency.

According only to transaction efficiency, transaction systems can be divided into: highly-efficient systems with brokerage companies at core, medium-efficient systems with fund custodians at core, and low-efficient systems with solicitors at core. The first two kinds improve their efficiency by the cooperation and team work in companies, while the third one, propped up by individuals, is comparatively less efficient. Among them, Japan and Taiwan further increased their transaction efficiency by adding legal professionals as the independent third party (See Fig. 29). In a nutshell, the improvement of transaction efficiency depends on the scientific specialization of service providers and effective arrangements of the procedures in transactions.

2.3 Customer Experience

The customer experience of a transaction system is an indicator of the time and energy customers have invested, the flexibility of the time or place where the transaction is completed and the transparency of the information of the transaction. Great customer experience always has several features: the work are completed by third parties, lower time and energy investment, higher flexibility of the time and places to complete transactions and timely report of the latest status of the transaction.

2.3.1 America: New Customer Experience Brought About by the Emerging Electronic Custody of Funds

Title information of real estate is highly transparent in America. Records of titles, mortgages, liens, taxes and other information of the house are available to everyone through official websites of the state, county or city with zero or low charges. In counties or cities without such Internet accesses, people can acquire information through telephone hotlines. With title companies emerging, the information acquisition became much easier, and the buyer now needs to invest much less energy and time to acquire title information of the house. After having selected title companies (usually fund custodians will do the selection work on behalf of the clients), the customers can resort to the companies to collect title information, which will surely be faster done and loaded with more details. During transactions, fund custodies would also inform the customers of the progresses of the transaction by e-mails at all times, so as to protect their right to know.

Fund custodians plays a significant leading role in America's existing home transactions, while the buyers and the sellers are saved the trouble of investing much energy or time in it, endowing the system with good customer experience. American fund custodians are also improving their efficiency and services to survive competition in the industry. It's estimated that a single employee in an American fund custodian is capable of handling 40 transactions per month, and if dividing transactions into certain procedures and allocating work by specific procedures, an employee working at one procedure might then need to deal with about 200 transactions per month. With the development of science and technology, the efficiency of transactions are further improved: on one hand, customers are provided with a brand new approach to pay the fund custodians: telegraphed transfer—apart from traditional cash payment, or check and cash mailing—a much time-saving and energy-saving choice. On the other hand, electronic custody of funds frees fund custodians from complex and intricate document processing work, and significantly increases their working efficiency.

The electronic custody of funds gathers banks, brokers, notaries, title companies, registration staff in appropriate authorities and other participants of transactions into a uniform system, where standardized samples of documents are provided and every single person has got an electronic (digital) signature of his own. In this system, a series of documents and agreements are drawn up (usually) by fund custodians and banks (of mortgages and loans), delivered to relevant participants online for signatures, and confirmed with electronic signatures. The electronic way of document delivery notably reduces the time once invested in on-site communications, saves the trouble of several parties' adjusting time for certain meetings, avoids the concern of waiting in queue for registration and renders the deliveries much faster and safer. After training and learning, a fund custodian can finish a closing in $15 \sim 30$ min, which, compared with the days or even weeks needed for the same procedure before, is a significant progress in efficiency and in customer experience.

Table 2 The comparison of traditional and electronic custody of funds

	Traditional custody of funds	Electronic custody of funds
Time needed to close a transaction	From several days to several weeks	15 ~ 30 min
Deliver of documents	Express	Internet
Type of documents	Paper	Data stream
Type and features of signatures	Hand written; can be imitated or changed	Digital; encrypted, difficult to imitate
Storage of documents	File boxes, offices, warehouses	Computers, CDs, flash disks

After a transaction has been closed, the electronic fund custodian will collect all files with digital signatures into a CD or a flash disk and send copies to each participant for storage and filing. Those fund custodians who introduced the new electronic technology earlier have attracted customers with higher efficiency and better customer experience, and significantly had their market share expanded; in the future, the development of technology as well as people's recognition of electronic signatures will help popularizing the electronic custody of funds, through which the transaction cycles will be further shortened, and the customer experience further improved (See Table 2).

2.3.2   Japan: The Customer Experience Affected by Fixed Time and Place of Transactions

Japan's title information is open to the public as well, yet not easily acquirable. Individuals or institutions need to apply for a copy of the certificate of title at the Ministry of Justice, who will deliver a copy of the certificate several days upon the supplication. The inquiry fee is usually about 1000 yen, and online application will be cheaper. On Japan's certificate of title are recorded location and property area, ownership, buying and selling, mortgages, and other information of the house. It's worth noting that Japan's apply-before-acquire information, not publicized online or open for inquiry as the information in America, is severely reduced in flexibility, convenience and timeliness. However, the development of the society and the popularization of the Internet breed some title information companies, which can provide the consumers with an electronic certificate of title immediately after they have applied and paid a fee—the acquisition of real estate information nowadays is becoming easier and easier.

The existing home transactions in Japan, mainly completed and done by real estate notaries and judicial scriveners, don't require much time or energy of buyers and sellers. Besides, they are informed by the real estate notaries and judicial scriveners of the latest progress of the transactions at all time. However, the Closing day demands the attendance of the buyer, the seller, brokerage companies, judicial scriveners and banks, which guarantees the security of funds and title, yet reduces the customer experience due to the specified and fixed time and place of the meeting.

2.3.3   Taiwan: The Customer Experience Improved
with the Development of the Internet

The title information in Taiwan is also highly transparent to the public. Individuals
and institutions can acquire information including property titles, registration of the
house on government websites. Land administration agents are also exclusively
provided with special access to verified information of the identity and right of the
home seller, detailed information of property title, property area, ceiling of mortgage, attachment, and other information of the house. In transactions, real estate
management companies start to employ the Internet technology in their services,
and now customers can set up online accounts, deposit money through online
banks, and keep up with the latest status of transactions through mobile APPs,
through which the transparency of transaction information is further improved.

The existing home transaction in Taiwan, mainly completed by brokerage
companies and land administration agents with the assistance of real estate management companies, reduces the time and energy needed from home buyers and
home sellers, yet the capital structure featuring multi-payment increases the home
buyer's time and energy burden. Besides, the home delivery that shall be accom-
plished by both the seller and the buyer together with their land administration
agents lacks the flexibility in time and space, and affects the customer experience as
well.

2.3.4   Britain: Good Customer Experience at the Cost of the Solicitors'
Heavy Burden

Property title information is highly publicized in Britain. Before transactions, home
buyers are always willing to learn the price of a satisfying home, so as to decide
whether it is under budget. In Britain, customers have got two property websites,
namely, RIGHTMOVE and ZOOPLA, on which they can learn the transaction
prices of all properties in Britain in the last more than ten years. Meanwhile,
without a "certificate of title" like China has, Britain's property information is open
to the world on the Internet, and when the buyer or home owner need to prove their
ownership, they just need to log in the website, search for relevant information, and
download a statement of ownership after paying a certain fee—the whole process
could be very easy and short. However, the statement only shows the name and
address of the owner, yet not displays other information such as title transfer,
mortgages, tax payments or liens of the house. So, when compared with America,
the housing information in Britain is opener to the public, yet the publicized part is
not so comprehensive, and procedures like title inspections have to be conducted by
solicitors. Besides, there are no insurance institutions like title companies held

accountable for the existing title flaws, and customers can only resort to legal processes once disputes occur. Although highly publicized, Britain's tile information is comparatively less comprehensive, and the procedures and processes in transactions are less transparent or clear to the consumers.

The solicitor in Britain plays a dominant position in existing home transaction, while the buyer and the seller need to invest little energy and time in it, thus enjoying flexibility and freedom in transactions. The transactions begin with both parties' hiring solicitors, who will then safeguard the security of funds as fund custodians, protect the security of titles as title inspectors, communicate and negotiate with all participants, complete paper work, and conduct title transfers in transactions. While the seller and the buyer can enjoy much more freedom—they can have their house sold or buy a new home without even meeting the other party. Moreover, the solicitor would communicate with their customers a lot during transactions, so the buyer and the seller can separately hire the solicitor that they cooperate or communicate well with. When compared with Japan's transaction system, Britain's is more flexible and thus boasts better customer experience. While putting almost all duties on the shoulder of solicitor's makes the progress of transactions dependent on and limited by the time and energy arrangements of the solicitors', therefore the long transactions cycles, to a certain extent, affect customers' transaction experience.

3 The Present Situation and Problems of Chinese Transaction Systems

The home-ownership rate increasing, China's existing home transactions, once rare and small, are now playing an important role. However, the procedures of existing home transactions differ a lot as the result of unbalanced economic development and population migration. In general, China's existing home market, an emerging one, lacks a comprehensive regulation mechanism, featuring relatively separate settlement systems among banks, immature transaction service businesses, and not satisfying security, efficiency and customer experience. Nowadays, the swelling transaction volume in existing home market together with the more and more complex trading environment and the diversifying participants makes it significant to notice and focus on the risks in transactions and people's demand for transaction security. Obviously, the present transaction system needs modifying and adjusting to suit a market where existing home transactions are going to take a leading position.

Hence, we need to develop market-oriented transaction services, understand the connotation of transaction service industry, lead a healthy and standardized future of the industry, prepare suitable soil for the emerging and flourish of service companies on the basis of title and personal credit information co-sharing as well as the acknowledgement of the third parties' authorization and credit, and make

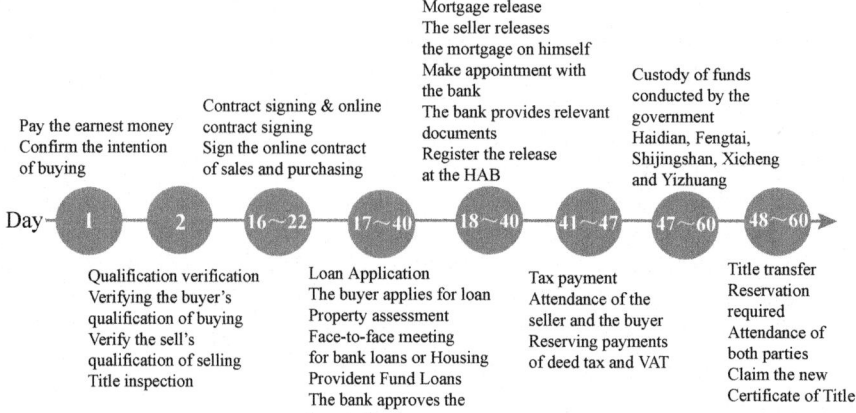

Fig. 30 The procedures of the existing home transactions in Beijing. *Source* Market Research Centre, Homelink

third-party fund custodians and supporting participants the most important guardians of customers' right and bearers of duties and responsibilities.

3.1   Transaction Security: The Present Situation and Problems

China's existing home market features regional characteristics. Not only transaction volume, government regulation and consumers' demand, but procedures in transactions differ a lot from region to region. Generally, China's existing home transactions could be divided into five major procedures: earnest money payment, contract signing, loan application, tax payment and title transfer. Firstly Beijing's existing home market will be taken as an example to introduce the procedures in China's existing home transactions (See Fig. 30).

3.1.1   Procedures in Beijing's Classic Existing Home Transactions

Firstly, the buyer will pay the earnest money and confirm his intention to buy the house. Brokerage companies will start verifying the buyer's qualification of buying and conducting title investigation.

Secondly, the seller's qualification of selling will be verified, and the property title will be inspected. With the development of existing home market is gaining pace in China, the government has issued strict limitations on the buyers' qualification of purchase, the verification of which will cost 10 ~ 15 working days.

What's more, the home inspection conducted at the same period of time, once completed on the inspection day, now takes 10 workdays. The prolonged transaction cycles would inevitably add to the uncertainty in transactions.

Thirdly, the sales contract and an online contract will be signed. The buyer's qualification of buying and the title of the property having been verified, the buyer and the seller will sign the sales contract, an agreement with brokerage companies, and an online sales contract at the online contract system of Beijing Municipal Commission of Housing and Urban-Rural Development.

Fourthly, the buyer will apply a loan from the bank upon the signing of the contract and start home assessment. Usually, it takes $10 \sim 20$ work days for the commercial bank to issue an approval letter of the loan from the face-to-face meeting application. However, for Housing Provident Fund Loans, the face-to-face meeting will not happen until the home assessment has been finished, and the approval will take another $15 \sim 20$ work days. Therefore, the transaction cycles tend to vary according to the buyer's income, debt-paying ability and other credit records and information.

Fifthly, the existing mortgage of the house will be released. While the buyer's applying for a loan, the seller with mortgage on his house shall, by raising money on himself or employing the buyer's payment for the house, repay the bank or other debtors and release the mortgage. It might take $10 \sim 15$ work days from setting up appointment for repayment to the mortgage being released by the House Administration Bureau: the accurate time is decided by the time that banks need to issue the documents of the mortgage release.

Sixthly, taxes will be paid. After the buyer has received the approval of letter of the loan and the seller's mortgage has been released, they will make appointment and pay taxes according to the home in question and the seller's qualification of home selling.

Seventhly, the government will conduct the custody of funds. In five districts, namely, Haidian, Fengtai, Shijingshan, Xicheng and Yizhuang, the custody of funds are fully implemented by the government, which means that in all existing home transactions, the money involved minus the down payment as well as the loan will be deposited in the sub-accounts set up jointly by the House Administration Bureau and its bank partners for the custody of funds before the transference of titles.

Eighthly, the title will be transferred and the transference will be registered. Given that the existing home markets of some regions in Beijing show high activity, the Home Administration Bureau implements a title registration system where meeting reservations are demanded. And it usually takes $5 \sim 10$ days for a reservation to be set and scheduled. Upon the meeting, the buyer as well as the seller shall present and provide the HAB officials with the documents for title transfer and tax payment for verification. And for the five custody-covered districts, the allocation of funds will as well be verified and supervised. The title transfer will then be completed and registered, and the home buyer can acquire the new certificate of title on the very day.

Due to the rocketing transaction volume as well as the changes in trading environment, the appropriate authorities in Beijing, to guarantee the security of

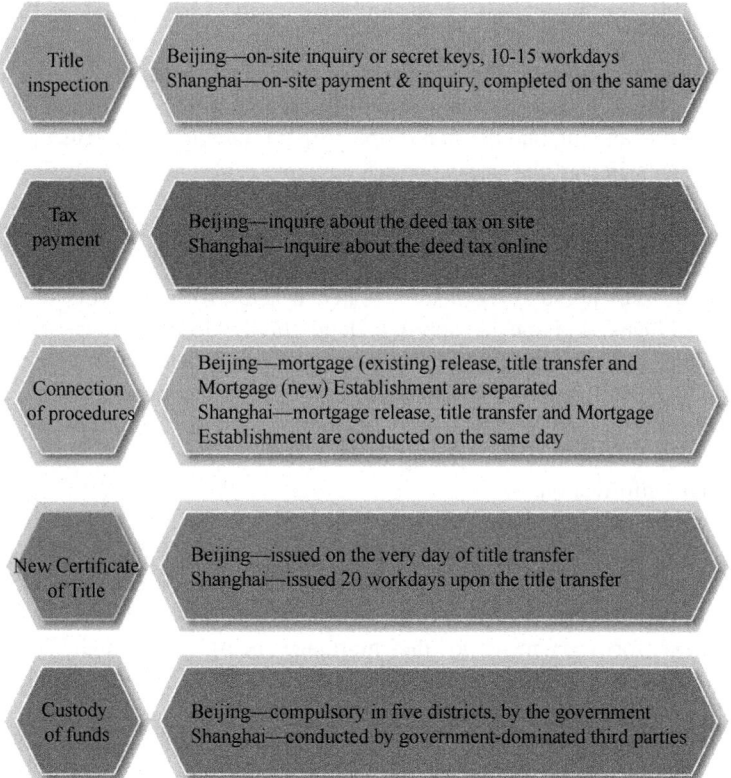

Fig. 31 The comparison of the procedures in Beijing's and shanghai's existing home transactions. *Source* Market Research Centre, Homelink

transactions, have set strict limitations on the buyers' qualification of purchasing, title inspection and title registration. As a consequence, customers' waiting in queues and making reservations and appointments became a routine, and the efficiency of transactions is indubitably reduced.

Existing home market playing a dominant role as well, the procedures in Shanghai's existing home transactions, however, differ a lot with those in Beijing (See Fig. 31).

3.1.2 The Risks in the Procedures of China's Existing Home Transactions

Also, China's existing home transaction system is not immune to the mismatches of funds and titles in time: several payments are conducted before the transfer of title, and the collection of outstanding balance is not yet regulated. Meanwhile, the rocketing house prices in first-tier cities are rendering the unexpected losses more and more severe and devastating. Worse still, China's home transactions are haunted by special risks, such as the risk exclusively attached on the school district housings.

We can categorize the risks in China's existing home transactions into three groups.

(1) The risks may result from the absence of or delayed title inspections. In some cities, the title inspection conducted by the authorities could take as long as $10 \sim 15$ days, resulting in an even later information update. A successful transaction stems from the timeliness, completeness and authenticity of title information, which, rather implicit when compared with physical conditions of the house and possibly involving debtor of another transactions, requires in-time feedback and features more difficult and challenging inspections. Naturally, disputes might occur.

(2) The risks may result from the absence of custody of funds, the staggered fund delivery and title transfer, and the limited scope of present custody of funds that doesn't include down payment or loans, which is true to most areas. (See Fig. 32) China's existing home market is a typical seller's market, where the sellers may demand the payment of earnest money and down payment without fund custody, so as to get the money as soon as possible. As a consequence, great risks of fraud and default have been posed to the security of funds and transactions.

(3) China's fund custodians are not entitled to allocate the funds, so the existing mortgage shall be released by the sellers on themselves—during which extra fund flows and new debtors are introduced to transactions. This is another cause of risks. As a prominent point of entries and exits of new and old debtors, the release of mortgage is one of the most risky procedures in existing home transactions. America's regulation of fund custody has forged a mature system for the debtors' entering and exiting without bringing risks to the very trans-action, and the Payment System of banks employed in Japan, Britain and Taiwan works well in allocating the buyer's loan for the repayment of the seller's mortgage without involving the two parties or requiring the seller to raise money by himself. In China, however, the seller has to raise funds himself or apply for another loan to repay his existing mortgage, which will introduce new debtors (apart from the buyer's bank) and extra loan funds into the transaction.

4   The Inadequacy of the Custody of Funds

Unlike Japan, who eliminates the mismatches of funds and titles by dealing with them on the same day at the same place, or America, who employs fund custodians to keep and allocate the funds according to transaction processes, China's strategy of dealing with the mismatches of funds and titles, still in its initial stage, has

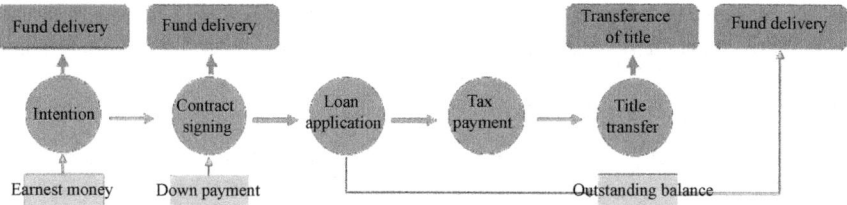

Fig. 32 The staggered fund delivery and title transfer in the absence of the custody of funds. *Source* Market Research Centre, Homelink

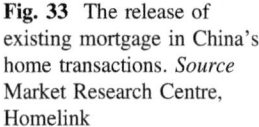

Fig. 33 The release of existing mortgage in China's home transactions. *Source* Market Research Centre, Homelink

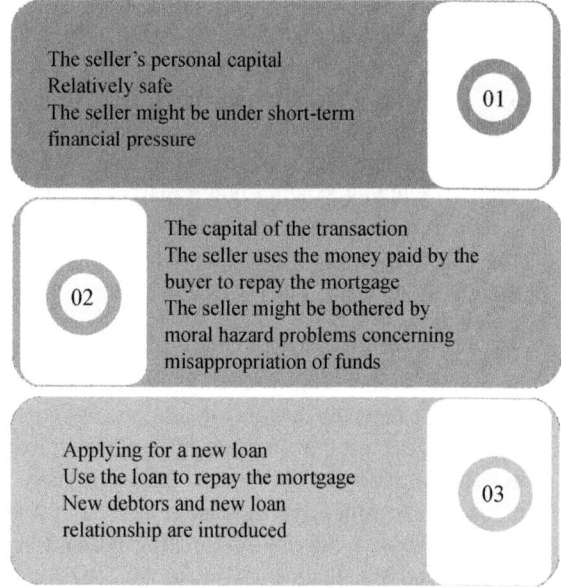

formed into a unique pattern: a combination of market-oriented self-custody, four-party custody, professional third-party custody, as well as the government supervision and third-party platforms for fund custody dominated by the government—a multi-layered kind of fund custody practiced by multi-layered participants (See Fig. 33).

Under the current pattern, the coverage rate of the custody of funds in Chinese existing home market is far from satisfying, with rather low rate and volume of fund custody. The rate of fund custody is the ratio of the number of existing home transactions completed with custody on fund to the number of all completed transactions; the volume of fund custody is the ratio of the amount of funds under custody to the total amount of money circulated in transactions. In Beijing, for example, the custody of funds is compulsorily implemented in the five districts (Haidian, Fengtai, Shijingshan, Xicheng and Yizhuang), where the rate of fund custody is high, but the volume of fund custody remains low, and the funds under custody doesn't include the down payment or the earnest money; in other areas where fund custody is not demanded, the rate of fund custody is as low as less than 40%. In Shanghai, given the overall voluntary policy of fund custody and the seller-dominant trading environment, the rate of fund custody in existing home transactions is even less than 10%.

4.1 Transaction Efficiency: The Present Situation and Problems

The efficiency in existing home transactions is decided by the connection between its procedures and communication among its participants, and is directly indicated by the cycle and costs of transactions. The procedures in China's existing home transactions have not yet been specialized and allocated; as a result, the brokerage companies not only function in the matching of houses and customers, but are responsible for home examination, paper work, tax calculation, providing loan and brokering services, assisting in tax payment, title transfer and many other duties. What's more, due to the varying levels of market activities and government supervisions in different regions, the transaction cycle in China could vary from 30 to 65 days. In general, China's existing home transactions are not highly efficient.

4.1.1 Transaction Procedures that Feature Low Efficiency

Without America's custody of funds practiced by fund custodians and title inspection as well as title insurance provided by title companies or Japan's and Taiwan's assistance from independent third parties, the procedures in China's existing transactions are absolutely dependent on brokerage companies and brokers, between which the companies takes the leading position. It's true that most of the major brokerage companies have started allocating jobs with their employees of particular spectrums: there are title-transfer specialists, title inspectors and mortgage brokers, but the reduction of transaction cycles is still hindered by the general trading environment and arrangements of trading procedures.

In Beijing's market, for example, all procedures are propped up by brokerage companies, and the transaction cycles are handled and controlled by the government. The brokerage companies prepare documents for the verifications of the buyer's and the seller's qualifications of purchasing and selling, the precondition of a successful transaction, then it'll take 10 ~ 15 work days for the government to verify the buyer's qualification and the seller's property title. The buyer's loan application are complex and take much longer time: for loans from commercial banks, it'll be 15 ~ 25 work days between applying a loan to the approval of the loan is issued; and for Housing Provident Fund Loans, however, the time might be as long as 20 ~ 30 work days. What's more, if the seller needs to raise money and repay his mortgage, his broker will assist him in making reservation with the bank for repayment, and it'll take 3 ~ 10 work days for the bank to issue relevant certificates, after which can the broker register the release at the Housing Administration Bureau on behalf of the seller. Reservations are always demanded for tax payment and title transfer, which are usually done by brokers, and each often takes 5 ~ 7 work days to be settled. Averagely, the transaction cycle in Beijing could be 40 ~ 60 days.

4.1.2 The Root of the Low Transaction Efficiency and the Inadequacy of the Custody of Funds

The low efficiency in transactions mainly has two reasons. The one is the long time spent queuing and waiting for the government's responses, and the other is the not-yet-specialized procedures in transaction, which are now over-reliant on brokers. In practice, however, no broker is professional at all industries and fields involved in transactions.

What's more, the unique arrangement of procedures in Chinese existing home transactions intensifies the impact of the above two reasons: the bank's not participating leads to the seller's introducing an extra loan and debtor to release his mortgage, through which the time invested is prolonged; the multi-party of fund custody, as well, results in low-efficient allocation of the funds under market-driven custody. More specifically, we divide the fund custody in China into five types according to the specific fund custodian, namely, government supervision, three-party (the buyer, the seller and the commercial banks) fund custody, four-party (the buyer, the seller, the bank, and the brokerage company) fund custody and third-party fund custody. Among them, government supervision, three-party and four-party fund custody belong to the market-driven type of fund custody.

Under the custody of funds practiced by the government, fund custody is valued as a precondition of title transfer. In some cities, represented by Beijing, the governments directly take custody of the funds, and the buyer shall deposit his personal capital (dawn payment) apart from the earnest money and the loan, into a custodial account automatically designated by the custody system jointly established by the government and its bank partners. And by title transfer, government officials will verify the deposit of the money, make sure that all conditions required are met, unfreeze the funds under custody, and transfer it to the seller's account.

In some cities, for example, Nanjing and Tianjin, the governments indirectly take custody of the funds; instead, they establish or cooperate with third-party custodians. In transactions, the buyer will deposit his money into the custodial account set up by third-party at banks, and the bank will disburse the loan in advance into the custodial account, promised with the financial guarantee of third-party custodians, and after the title has been transferred, the loan will be unfrozen.

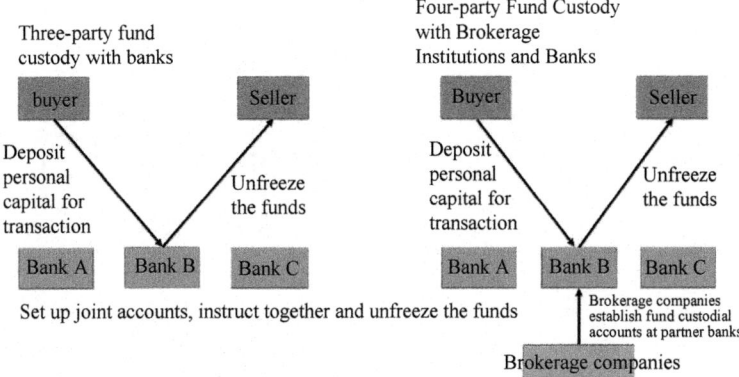

Fig. 34 Two types of fund custody with commercial banks. *Source* Market Research Centre, Homelink

The fund custody conducted by commercial banks could be categorized into three-party fund custody that agreed upon by the seller and the buyer, and four-party fund custody where brokerage companies take the leading position; in nature, however, both of them could be translated into: the commercial banks establishing joint accounts where the buyer's personal capital will not be transferred to the buyer's account until certain conditions are met (See Fig. 34).

Generally, the custody of funds in China suffers from the following problems:

Under the fund custody mainly conducted by banks, including four-party fund custody and three-party fund custody, the banks need to communicate with customers and examine the provided documents, which means that not fully engaged in transactions, however, the banks should bear the heavy burden of fund custody and deal with trivial paper work, knowing neither the customers' actual thoughts toward the transaction nor the way to tell the authenticity of the documents. The custody of funds in real estate transactions is, as well, not a major service daily provided in banks, thus it's hard to guarantee their being professional and highly-efficient.

The problems are so much worse in the fund custody conducted by governments. Being far from actual transactions, the government lacks flexibility in the custody, and specializes only in setting up key conditions to unfreeze funds. The custody of funds needs and only needs to meet the regulations set by the government before being recognized as compliant. Worse still, the limitations on working time and places makes crowds and long queues of people waiting a routine. In a nutshell, the custody of funds conducted by the government is characterized by low efficiency.

It's out of question that the custody of funds could improve the security of transaction, but all of them could severely reduce the efficiency and customer experience of the transactions. Nowadays, the mounting demand in market and the growing complexity of transactions are inevitably prolonging the transactions and adding uncertainties to the procedures.

Fig. 35 The custody of funds
with third-party payment
firms. *Source* Market
Research Centre, Homelink

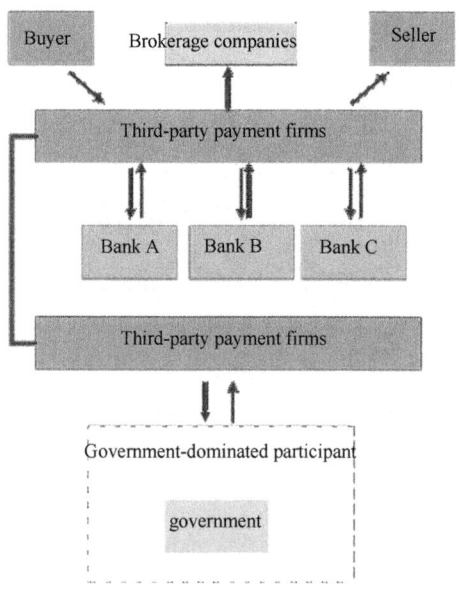

International experiences, however, show that the custody of funds conducted by third parties can well cushion such deduction of transaction efficiency. In China, the third parties are usually played by third-party payment firms, which complement the fund custody of banks by entering into cooperation agreement with banks, establishing provision accounts, and transforming the bank's personal services targeting private business into public services targeting payment firms. As a consequence, the banks are no longer the major conductor of fund custody, but a keeper of capital. Meanwhile, the payment firms, by employing online payment technology and fully engaging in transactions, can now provide energy-and-time saving services of account establishment and fund deposit, and are highly flexible in unfreezing capital at the customer's well (See Fig. 35).

Specifically, there are five advantages in entrusting third-party payment firms with the job of fund custody. (1) The payment firms, with its ability to catch up with every single dynamic change in transactions, to timely response to the customer's demands, and to tell the authenticity of documents with its professional knowledge, is more familiar with transactions than banks and the government, and can well fit in the procedures of existing home transactions; (2) under a market-oriented pattern of fund custody, the firms take the initiative to bear the responsibilities and risks in transactions, and set up provision accounts in case of the buyer's loss; (3) the profit-driven payment firms, in order to thrive in the industry, are motivated to actively improve the security, efficiency as well as customer experience in transactions, and to upgrade its efficiency by keeping up with the time and the demand; (4) the payment firms are strongly adaptive and widely applicable in different businesses, which ensures a higher coverage of the custody of funds; (5) payment firms can, to a certain extent, lower the pressure on governments and reduce unnecessary costs.

As third-party custodians, the payment firms' function of fund allocation remains approvable. The capital flow between payment firms and banks are one-way due to the accounts in payment firms are not acknowledged as be of equal status as those set up in banks—the capital can be transferred from payment firms to the banks, yet not the other way around, so the payment firms don't have accounts to keep and reallocate the loans and other payments. They can only contact with down payment and other non-debt capital (such us the deposit for household registration and the deposit for utility fees), yet cannot provide customers with one-stop services to deal with all debts on the house. To be a qualified and genuine third-party payment participant in existing home transactions, the firms should be empowered, entitled and entrusted to allocate all funds.

In a nutshell, the root of the low efficiency of Chinese existing home transactions lies in the less market-oriented procedures, the ineffective connections between the procedures, and the uniqueness of the procedures in China's home market, which ensures the deduction caused by the first two issues.

4.2 Customer Experience: The Present Situation and Problems

Good customer experience takes less time or energy of the customers, features transparent information and flexible time as well as space of transactions. China's transaction system is not able to guarantee the security and efficiency yet, thus satisfying customer experience is not yet a pressing need of customers. The rocketing transaction volume of existing homes in China is actually backed up with limited level of public services—long queues of people waiting in front of offices becomes a routine. In Beijing, for example, tax payment and title transfer must be completed at the trading centre of the Housing Administration Bureau with a reservation made five-to-seven workdays in advance. Bothered by disclosed title information, long time spent in title inspection and delayed report on the status of transactions, the customer experience under the present transaction system remains infant and undeveloped.

5 Some Policy Suggestions

International experience suggests that transaction systems are the product of markets, with the participants' and custodians' consideration of security, efficiency and customer experience—the three major elements of existing home transactions. And through comparison, we can come to three conclusions: firstly, professional third-parties are more suitable to handle the procedures than brokers, given the complexity and risks in existing home transactions; secondly, the jobs of the third party should not be performed by administrative departments, but rather, transaction participants that could fully engage in the trades, provide better services responsive to the demand, and effectively improve the security, efficiency and customer experience with a clearer role to play; thirdly, to forge a system that could prop up the genuine third-party payment, China's government should further improve the transparency of information and grant third-party firms with more accesses to the market.

Accordingly, several policy suggestions are put forward on the basis of the present situation in China's existing home market:

5.1   Conditionally Disclose Title Information to the Public

With the status of property title becoming more and more complex and diversified, the latest information of such as title inspection, title registry, mortgages or attachment of a house are necessary and demanded to be accurately and immediately delivered and communicated, so as to avoid huge losses in transactions that are usually attributed to delayed or false information.

Firstly, online service platforms should be established, and land administration departments of all level, as well, are supposed to set up their online platforms for public services; for those lacking the required conditions of such establishment temporarily, public windows providing inquiry services should be opened, and online inquiry services should also be provided. Secondly, title information should be open for inquiry at online service platforms and public windows to registered real estate brokerage companies and licensed real estate brokers. And the companies are supposed to issue reports of the collected information and provide the reports to their customers. Thirdly, online information network should be forged, so that the dynamic changes of title information, such as new mortgages or attachments of the houses that have been contracted online, could be timely known by participants. The platforms are also supposed to build a dynamic notification system to inform the brokerage companies and customers involved immediately of the updated information through online reminder, SMSs or other approaches.

5.2   Forcefully Implement the Policy of Fund Custody

To push the custody of funds is the only way to cope with the security issues of funds, which is at the root of most risks and disputes in existing home transactions. More than 90% transactions in most major markets are under fund custody and have developed certain patterns of fund custody according to the market. China's custody of funds, once conducted by the government, banks, brokerage companies and third-party firms, is still in its initial stage, and at the areas where fund custody is not compulsory, few would actively employ fund custodians to keep their money, and severe risks are sweeping in. Here we've got four proposals.

5.2.1 Regulate the Procedures of Fund Custody and Establish Standard Custody Procedures

The government is supposed to establish standardized procedures of the custody of funds, and the funds include earnest money, down payment, loans and mortgages, deposit for utility fees and other types of capital. Regulations on the time and order, specific requirements and documents demanded of the custody as well the unfreezing of the funds shall be regulated, and the procedures of registering and fund delivery of releasing the existing mortgage with the buyer's payment for the house shall be standardized as well.

5.2.2 Establish Reporting and Verification Mechanism of Information

Fund custodians should report their orders under their custody and the amount of unfrozen funds to the administrative department per month with detailed records of each day and a collection and summary of information of the whole month. The government can also encourage brokerage companies to report more detailed information, such as payment of deposits, property services, residence transfers and other information of the transaction.

Automatic verification mechanism based on IT systems should be set up, to collect, compare and examine the information of fund custody reported by fund custodians, the information of title registration and title transfer reported by administrative departments and transaction information reported by brokerage companies to make sure that all fund deliveries in all transactions have been unfrozen according to the regulation, and have been delivered securely and soundly.

The regulation on and mechanism of information verification might go like this: (1) collect and compare the information of the completed businesses (e.g. title transfer and title registration) presented by brokerage companies and the information recorded at the administrative departments, so as to confirm the accuracy of the presented information; (2) the information of completed businesses and fund flows presented by fund custodians should be compared with the business information presented by brokerage companies, to make sure that the information of businesses correspond, and that every single delivery of fund is the result of a rightful operation of the transaction; (3) the examination and verification should be conducted not only by details, but by collections and summaries, as well; (4) check the records in the custodial account: the amount of money at the beginning of the custody, the balance at the end of the custody, and the delivered amount during transactions, so as to verify the continuity of the fund custody.

5.2.3   Implement the Internet + Plan to Upgrade Customer Experience

The government should forcefully encourage real estate institutions to, with the help of Internet and mobile Internet technologies, swiftly and steadily transform the industry into an "Internet + Industry" and provide convenient, highly-efficient and transparent fund custody services. With scientific adoption of the technologies, customers might be able to complete the custody of their funds at offices of brokerage companies or even at home and participate in transactions by uploading required documents for fund custody and confirming relevant information in the future. This could effectively release the pressure of administrative departments and avoid disputes. The inquiry of information might be done through online platforms, mobile APPs, phone hotlines, SMSs and so on. What's more, the business flows of institutions and companies should be integrated and connected with fund flows, so that less time will be invested and the efficiency of fund custody will be improved.

5.2.4   Recognize Third-Party Payment Firms as Qualified Fund Custodians with Permission to Allocate Funds

The emerging third-party payment firms of fund custody in China are paving the way to an existing home market with higher custody rate, greater custody volume, and transactions featuring security and efficiency. Third-party fund custodians should be granted with the power to allocate funds, which usually involves the delivery of capital among banks. However, they are now hindered from cross-bank fund allocations due to not being recognized by the law or the banks. The biggest barriers turn out to be: one, their credibility is not recognized by government or banks; two, they are not yet granted with the permission of fund allocation; and three, they are not able to cooperate with government systems online. So, third-party firms should be acknowledged by banks as fund custodians and granted with the permission to allocate funds and autonomously operate fund deliveries when required conditions are met, so as to mature into the genuine third-party fund custodians of China's existing home market.

5.3   Encourage Professional Institutions to Provide Various and Diversified Transaction Services and Products

America's custody of funds and title insurance, Japan's judicial scriveners, Britain's solicitors and Taiwan's real estate management companies—all of them are third parties specially introduced into transactions, while as the supervisor and manager, property management companies don't involve in trades or guarantee services. To balance the security, efficiency and customer experience of the market, the most efficient method will be to develop in a market-oriented way. And with the general direction led by the demand and supply, the regulation and standards worked out by the government should be the core and code of the industry.

To cope with paper work and arrange procedures, major brokerage companies in China have set up "specialist of title transfer" as a specialized position, and most minor ones might resort to third-party institutions to deal with the work in the future. To follow the trend of customization and moving online, the government should encourage its real estate institutions, such as third-party firms and brokerage companies, to develop and provide various services and patterns to meet the diversified demands in the market.

In terms of post-transaction services, the authorities should encourage insurance companies and brokerage companies to innovate and invent new products and new services, for example, Title Insurance, Transaction Insurance and Reassuring Commitment, to enhance the co-sharing of information, the regulation on certificates and licenses, the standard settings and other aspects, and to improve the security, efficiency and customer experience of the industry in a market-oriented way.

Chapter 4
Liquidity Finance

- Liquidity finance consists of short-term capital circulation finance, loan brokerage service, third-party payment and housing insurance, etc. It exists for more effective housing transactions and less uncertainties in transactions.
- Liquidity finance is not a single product or service. It is a complete financial system consists of diverse financial services provided by a wide range of participants.

Liquidity finance is a natural consequence of the combination of second-hand house transactions and financial markets. Liquidity finance is usually based on the real estate trading scene. Its starting point is to solve the safety and efficiency pain points in house transactions and reduce uncertainties and information asymmetry so as to improve the efficiency of transactions and smooth transactions. Liquidity finance services can be divided into circulation finance, loan brokerage service, third-party payment and insurance. Only circulation finance involves short-term capital loans. Loan brokerage service, third-party payment and house insurance do not generate new loan relationships (see Fig. 1).

At present, China has basically developed a specific liquidity finance system which is based on short-term circulation finance and supplemented by loan brokerage service and third-party payment. Under the existing liquidity finance system, it can to some extent solve transaction-based problems of fund demand and transaction difficulties arising from China's special trading system. However, liquidity finance services related to the security of transaction capital and property rights verification are not yet mature and cannot cover corresponding risks.

The improvement of the trading system and the maturity of the traditional financial market will inevitably lead to the shortening of the trading cycle and the improvement of the bank settlement system. A mature liquidity financial system will be gradually formed by short-term capital circulation, loan brokerage service, third-party payment and insurance. Through information matching, funding arrangements and risk-sharing mechanisms, liquidity finance secures its transactions, improves the efficiency of transactions, and promote house circulation.

© Xiamen University Press and Springer Nature Singapore Pte Ltd. 2018   95
S. Ba and X. Yang, *The Rise of New Brokerages and the Restructuring of Real Estate Value Chain*, https://doi.org/10.1007/978-981-10-7715-9_4

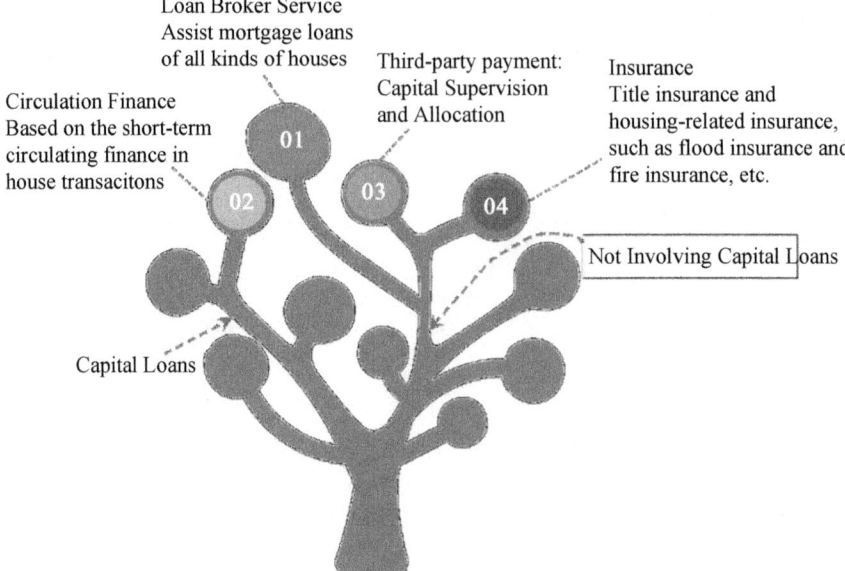

Fig. 1 Classification of circulating finance. *Source of Data* compiled by Lianjia Institute

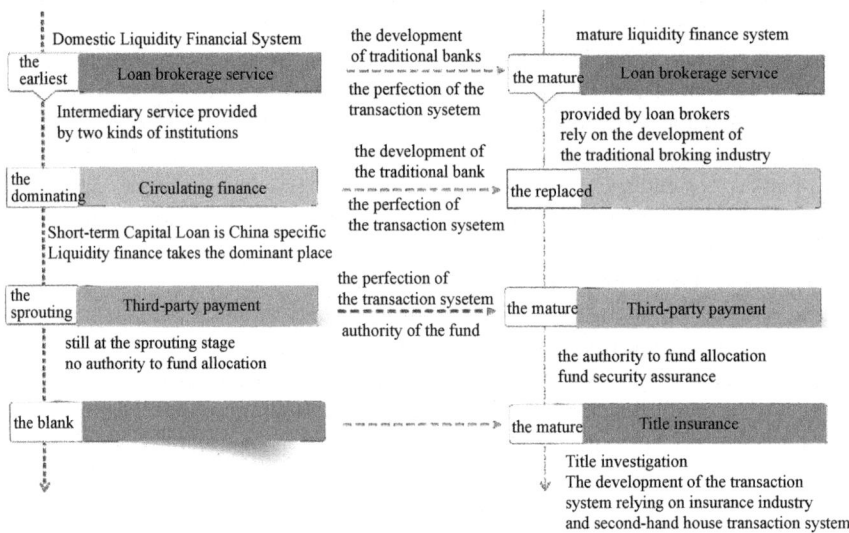

Fig. 2 The future upgrading direction of China's special liquidity financial system

Therefore, liquidity financial service is not an isolated product or service. It is a financial system consists of diverse financial services provided by diverse participants, relying on the improvements of the second-hand house transaction system and the traditional bank finance (Fig. 2).

At present, with the increase in the complexity of the domestic transaction itself and the increase in the transaction cycle, especially the increase in the demand for redemption. The demand of buyers and sellers for second-hand house transactions is increasing rapidly. From the point of the micro level, the standardization and development of liquidity finance play a more and more important role in improving transaction efficiency, ensuring transaction safety, improving users' experience and shortening trading cycle, etc. From the point of the industry's intermediate level, liquidity finance also plays a significant role in enhancing the vitality of houses in stock, expanding housing supply and stabilizing housing price, etc. Therefore, liquidity finance is an important part of promoting the standardizaiton and development of the real estate brokerage industry.

1 The Background and Function of China's Liquidity Finance

At present, the volume of second-hand house transactions accounts for more than half of the overall housing market transactions. Second-hand house transactions already play a leading role in the housing market. As the second-hand housing market is heating-up rapidly, the transaction procedure is becoming more diversified and complicated. But problems related to various capital needs and risk control are often not effectively solved.

1.1 The Background of the Generation of Liquidity Finance

China's unique liquidity financial system is based on circulation finance, supplemented by loan brokerage service and has newly begun with third-party payment. The system has its own background and the fundamental reason is that the second-hand house system is not perfect and the traditional financial market is still developing. To be Specific:

The first is the absence of bank settlement system in the transaction process. Second-hand house transactions should be based on the premise of clean property rights. However, because of the isolation of the bank settlement system, China's buyers, sellers and loan banks cannot form a capital right closed cycle. Meanwhile, the third-party payment doesn't have the capital allocation authority due to its authority insufficiency. As a result, sellers must raise their own capital to lift the mortgage, which provides a broad market basis for circulation finance.

Second, the trading environment is becoming increasingly complex, evidenced in increasing times of transactions and the associated transactional frustrations, resulting in complicated procedures of second-hand house transactions, prolonged transaction periods, and increasing demands of finances. To be specific, there are

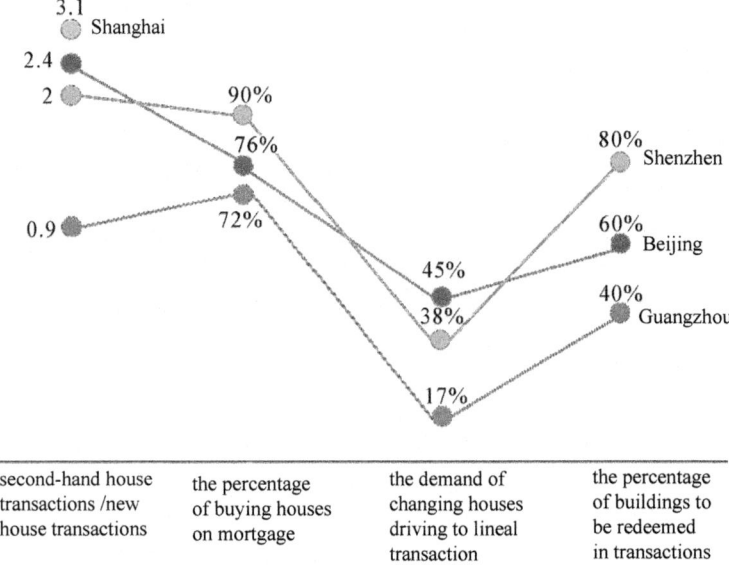

Fig. 3 The reflection of the increasingly complicated transaction environment. *Source of Data* compiled by Lianjia Institute

housing of divergent kinds joining the circulation; transaction parties increasingly demand finance security; there is a shift away from transaction of "paying deposits, signing the contract, paying the tax, and transfer of ownership" to one of "paying deposits, auditing purchase qualification, verifying property rights, signing the contract, supervising down payment, lifting mortgages, applying for housing mortgage, notarization, taxing, transfer of ownership, and delivering properties". Such a prolonged transaction period brings in uncertainties, and accordingly results in increasing demands of finance security for buyers and motivation of obtaining full payment in advance for sellers (See Fig. 3).

Third, with the continuous reform and optimization of the purchase policies, more buyers short of funds will have the opportunity to participate in the housing market. Due to the changing factors of second-hand house transactions and insufficient experience of funding budget, there are more and more difficulties in the transactions. To be specific, in the event of the temporary shortage of small amount of capital, transactions cannot continue without financial support and will face with interruption and default.

Fourth, the complexity of second-hand house transactions outlines transaction security needs. In second-hand house transactions, fund security is still the core demand. Risk can be everywhere when there is no financial supervision and protection from the third-party payment. (1) unchecked housing property will lead to a great loss of buyers if the property is sealed up. (2) When lifting the mortgage, if the seller delayed the process, misappropriate the funds of default after lifting the

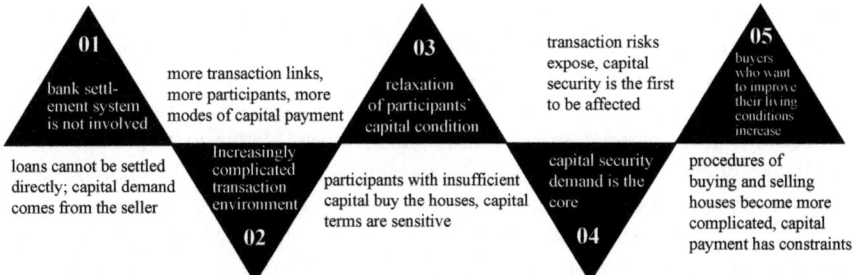

Fig. 4 The background of the formation of China's liquidity financial system. *Source of Data* compiled by Lianjia Institute

mortgage, the interests of the buyer and the seller will both be hurt. (3) If one side breaks the contract, the other side will suffer a great loss. Even if some loss can be recovered by law, it will still cost a lot of time, energy and money of the other side.

Fifth, improvement demands, such as "Changing House", are increasing continuously. House transactions need to be promoted through financial business. In China's first-tier cities, housing improvement transactions already account for more than 30%. The funds of most housing improvement transactions mainly come form the sale of the original houses. Therefore, there are strict constraints: (1) if purchases and sales of the houses alternate, any mistakes in the funds recovering process of housing selling will directly affect the next housing payment. (2) If the sale is before the purchase, the house selling period and house purchasing period will accumulate, leading to lengthy transactions. The preferred house would probably be bought by others before the buyer gets the funds from selling another house. Moreover, the procedure is very complex. It is very likely that there will be difficulties in the operation of all trading sessions, which will be great consumption of energy and time of house changers. If those who want to improve house demands pay part of the house payment through circulation financing, in other words, if they use the money from the sales of houses as the source to pay the housing mortgage, they can buy the preferred house in advance. At the same time, the transaction period will be shortened and housing circulation will be speeded up. The forming background of China's liquidity financial system is shown in Fig. 4.

2   The Function of Liquidity Finance

Despite the fact that the present liquidity finance is still undeveloped, it is very important to ensuring transaction security, saving transaction time, shortening the trading period and smoothing transactions so as to promote the sales of houses.

First, achieve the interactive verification of information, control the risk of transactions, ensure funds security. The strict control of financial services' risk management provides second-hand transactions with methods to interactively verify information, ensure transaction authenticity, which is beneficial to controlling risks. The authenticity of housing transaction is ensured through multiple measures such as interactive verification of liquidity finance service and housing transactions, information comparison, financial subject matter corresponding to the contract number on the Internet, and setting person respectful for lifting mortgages, and controlling mortgage rates, etc. Thus the authenticity of housing transactions is ensured and lots of risks are ruling out. As for funds security, the funds of second-hand houses consist of bond, deposit, down payment, loans, balance and property deposit, etc. With the payment from a third-party, both the buyer and seller will be guided to set reasonable payment node under the guidance of professional brokerages. The order to transfer funds will only be started under the agreed payment conditions, which will make housing delivery more reasonable, professional and secure.

Second, lift mortgages while secure the interests of the buyer and the seller. When the buyer help the seller lift the mortgage and the buyer's fund is paid by the third party, the third party commissioned professionals to verify the liabilities of the seller's house and go through procedures of repaying the loans and lifting mortgages, which ensure the security of the buyer's funds and also meet the needs of both sides.

Third, help people who have "Changing House" needs to solve the problem of cash flow and realize housing improvements for more clients. As for the funding needs in the "purchase and sale" process of the people who want to change houses, second-hand house transitions not only can save time of the "purchase and sale" process as well as the time cost of funds, but also help lock their favorite houses the first time and improve the houses as much as possible.

Fourth, provide safe and efficient financing options to sellers who have needs for funds and to smooth transactions. On one hand, because of the transaction period is too long, it is very common for sellers to reclaim funds in advance or to sell houses in a hurry. However, the bank loan usually can only be completed 7–20 working days after the transfer of the house ownership. On the other hand, the circulation business can provide some funds to sellers. When the ownership is transferred, the seller's need for capital is met with controllable risk. Thus, it is helpful to smooth transaction.

As the need to change houses increases, serial transactions involving several clients are also on a rise. If one of the clients has a problem with cash flow, there would be chain effects, leading to frequent disputes. However, financial intervention can smooth transactions the following process. Take Beijing as an example, the need to change houses is rising since the house purchase restrictions were implemented. At present, clients who "sell a house and buy another" account for 45% of the total. As most improvement-type clients have only one house each. They need to both sell and buy houses in a short time. However, since the procedure of second-hand house transaction is time-consuming, in order to secure purchasing new houses clients often need to get money from the one they are selling. During this period, there would be

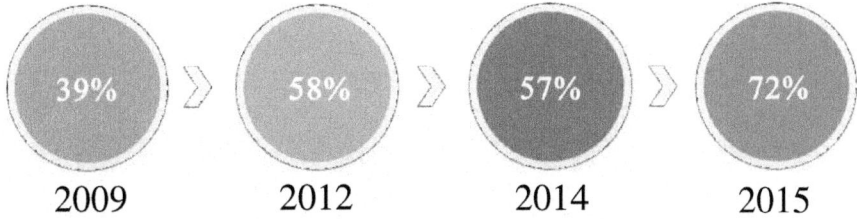

Fig. 5 The percentage of the loans of Beijing's second-hand houses sales in 2009–2015. *Source of Data* compiled by Lianjia Institute

circulation problems which will last for 1–3 months, adding great difficulties to normal housing transactions.

Fifth, it is beneficial to revitalizing stock houses and increasing supply. Take Beijing as an example again, from 2009 to 2015, the second-hand loans rose from about 40 to 70 and 80% (see Fig. 5). In the past 6 years, the average loan accounted for 53.4%, with the rising housing prices, loan amount also increased significantly. In 2016, the average commercial loan amount of the first quarter was 1.87 billion, which is 2.2 times of that of 2011 (see Fig. 6). Stock houses on mortgage also increased. In terms of the trend, the proportion of people who pay off the mortgage decreased.

At present, the scale of Beijing's stock houses is expanding continuously. On a conservative estimate, at least 40–50% stock houses are on mortgage, among which 20–30% stock houses' loans cannot be paid off by equity funds at the time of sale. In the market of more than 7 million stock houses, if there is no redeem house business, there would be hundreds of thousands of houses that cannot form a potential supply.

Early liquidity financial service generated in 2005 or so, which was mainly for the convenience of loan brokers to help buyers get loans as soon as possible. Due to the increased market demand and more flexible loan policies, more and more brokerage firms are developing financial business as their strategic services to smooth housing transactions. They launched financial mortgage products, most of which are short-term mortgages such as pledges and final payment with advance fund. They also combined with Internet technology to launch financial platforms. In 2016, more and more supervision departments introduced regulatory measures, so major brokerage companies suspend and adjust their circulation financial loan transactions (see Fig. 7).

In general, China's liquidity business has experienced cradle stage, rapid development stage and the suspension and adjustment stage. In these processes, the brokerage company is the main service provider. Liquidity finance represented by short-term loan service gradually occupies a crucial position. On the regulatory level, directors are increasingly aware of the importance of stock house transactions and related financial services. They begin to introduce relevant policies to regulate the market.

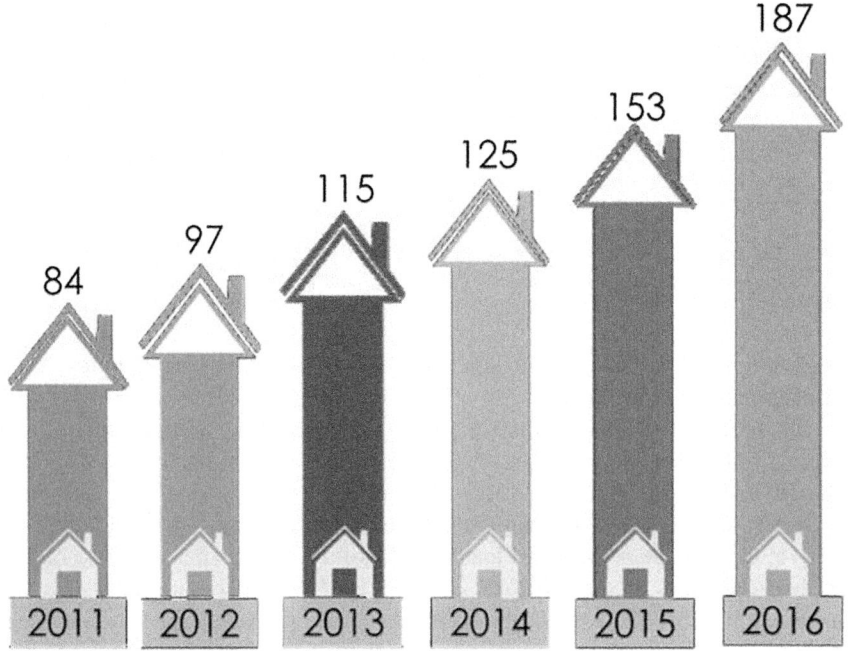

Fig. 6 The average line of credit of Beijing's second-hand houses loans (unit, RMB 10,000 yuan). *Source of Data* compiled by Lianjia Institute

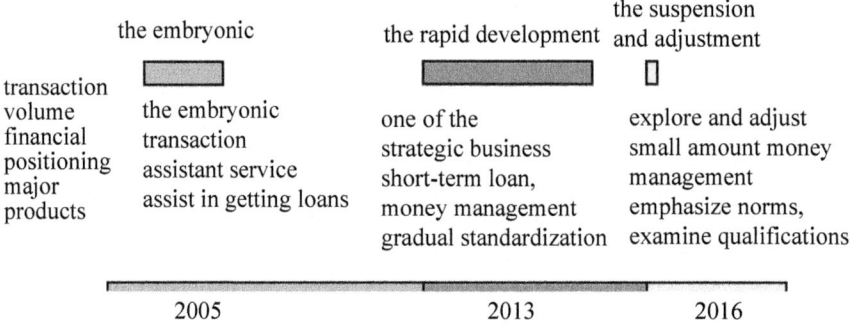

Fig. 7 Development stages of liquidity finance. *Source of Data* compiled by Lianjia Institute

3 China's Liquidity Financial Service Practice

As brokerage companies are directly involved in transaction and know customer needs better, they have become the main provider of China's liquidity financial service at present. In China's specific liquidity financial system, the brokerage agent

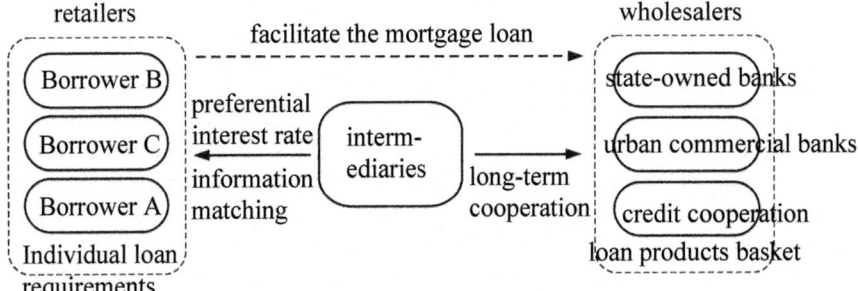

Fig. 8 China's intermediary loan brokerage service mode. *Source of Data* compiled by Lianjia Institute

function was separated from brokerage company. Later, flow cash finance was in the core position, the third party is still emerging.

(1) Loan brokerage service

As China's interest rate liberalization and bank's differentiated competition are intensified, loan products are becoming more and more diversified and transaction complexity is improved, the intermediaries will match the bank loan products with customer loan demands and help customer get loans from banks and assist them in promoting the processes of interviewing, claiming on the goods and releasing cargo, etc. Loan brokerage services' revenue comes from intermediary service commission and bank rebate income, among which intermediary agencies that have loan brokerage function can be divided into two categories: (1) part of traditional brokerage companies have customer advantage due to the in-depth transactions. They help the buyer match the loans and get prime rate. (2) The financial institutions are away from transactions, but they have capital advantage and can help financial clients find lower-cost loans. China's intermediary agency loan brokerage service model is shown in Fig. 8.

(2) Liquidity Finance Representative Short-term Loan Products

Based on the short-term financing demand of second-hand houses, broker companies and part of guarantee financing companies provide circulating capital services and generated short-term loan products, of which the most common are redeem house loans and final advance payment. Circulating capital is China-featured. It is to bring in new creditors and debts besides the buyers and sellers and the bank. In a mature liquidity financial market, circulating capital has been replaced by the bank settlement system or third-party payment.

3.1 Redeem House Loan

In China's second-hand house transaction system, second-hand house ownership can only be transferred when it is unsecured property. As a result, when the owner cannot repay the loan, financing demand is generated to repay the left mortgage loan and release the mortgage loan of the bank, and therefore help to complete transaction. That is how redeem house service came into been. Now there are mainly two kinds of the service.

The first one is limit redeem house, which is very common in the redeem house business in Shenzhen. Financing guarantee corporation use bank credit limit as short-term capital source to repay the bank mortgage loan for them. The guarantee cost is usually 0.8–1% of the loan limit.

Limit redeem house can also be applied by the owner or the buyer on the condition that the buyer must get document approval from the bank (See Fig. 4.9). If the seller applies, it needs to pay the financing fee and guarantee fee; if the buyer applies, it only needs to pay the guarantee fee.

The second one is that the internet financing platform match investors' funds for the seller as the source of loan. Compared with limit redeem house, loan rate level is lower, and its cost is lower while the time of application is shorter (See Fig. 10).

In general, in either way, redeem house loan's basic situation would be that the seller net pays off the house sold or on mortgage as the borrower and cancel the registration of the mortgage and redeem the house to transfer the ownership. Usually, the situation happens when the buyer and the seller have signed the selling contract and the price of the house is settled down. The redeem funds is offered to pay back the left original mortgage.

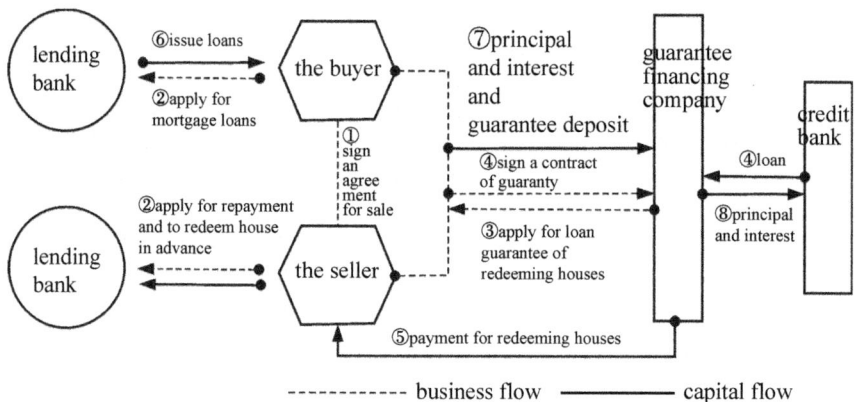

Fig. 9 Limited redeeming house business procedure. *Source of Data* compiled by Lianjia Institute

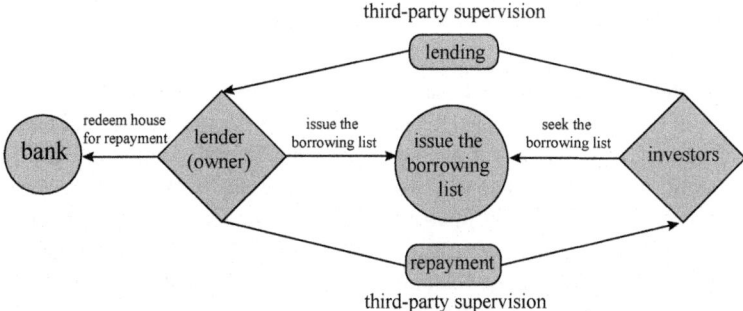

Fig. 10 Capital flow of internet financial platform redeeming house business. *Source of Data* compiled by Lianjia Institute

3.2   Final Payment on Account

According to the transaction data of 2015, despite the different procedures of different regions, the average period from bank interview to money lending is 30 days or so. In some regions, such as Haidian and Chaoyang District in Beijing, the period is over 40 days. As a result, during this period, if the seller is eager to get the final payment, the product of final payment on account is a required solution. After the bank assigns the goods, the brokerage company or other institution pays the rest payment in advance for the owner. After the bank lends the money, the seller can repay the intermediary company or other institutions.

According to the attributes of the product and the risks, the borrower usually has obtained the bank's loan approval document in the housing transaction process. Also, it is usually when the contract is signed by the buyer and seller, the price is settled down and the buyer's bank mortgage loan has been approved but the loan hasn't been given that the borrower will pay the final payment for the buyer in case that the buyer delays the payment. The limit is the total amount of the assigned goods of the bank. As a result, there is no problem of adding leverage, and the risk is comparatively controllable (see Fig. 11).

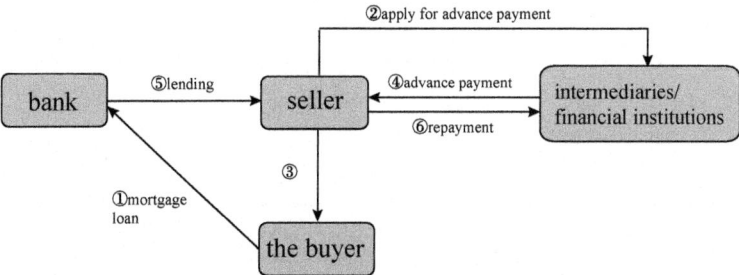

Fig. 11 Intermediary financial institution final advance payment procedure. *Source of Data* compiled by Lianjia Institute

4 The Sprouting of the Third-Party Payment

Today, insufficient trust and fund risks are still pressing problems perplexing buyers and sellers in housing transactions. To ensure the fund security of second-hand house transactions and help the buyer with risk prevention and control are the primary considerations of the government. Although the present bank-led fund supervision product covers the second-hand house transaction risk to some degree, there are still problems. For example, there is no supervision on small amount house payment like down payment, and the process of unfreezing house payment is inflexible, and the transaction can only be done on workdays, etc. Thus customers' demands cannot be satisfied. It provides innovation space for the generation of the third-party payment.

At present, the second-house payment service is still in the sprouting stage and has the similar function with Alipay. The third-party payment service also has 4 parties to participate, i.e. the buyer, the seller, the intermediary company and the third-party payment institution. The third-party payment institution solves transaction fund security issue by providing the third-party payment platform. The house payment is saved in the client excess reserve account which is under the direct supervision of Bank of China. With intermediary institutions as its offline commercial tenants, the third-party payment institutions put property transaction related funds on the platform and flexibly unfreeze the fund to the owners or repay it to clients so as to guarantee fund security and play a role of fund supervision. However, the third-party payment service does not have the right of disposing the fund and cannot fundamentally solve the problem of releasing mortgage. (See Fig. 4.12)

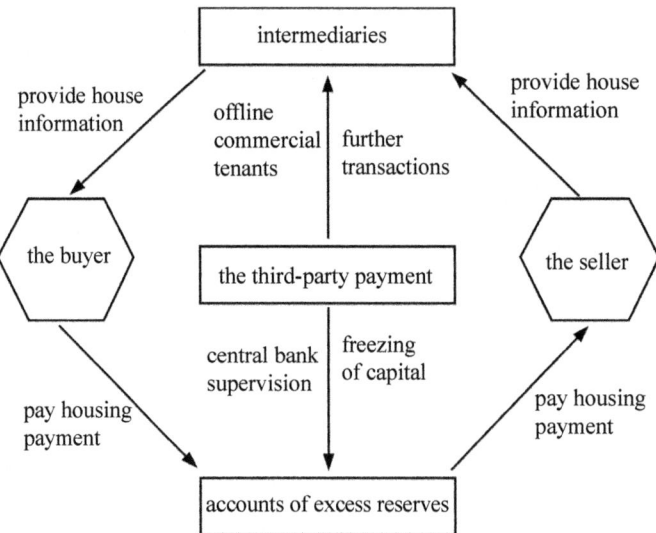

Fig. 12 The supervision process of the third-party payment. *Source of Data* compiled by Lianjia Institute

5   Mature Market Liquidity Financial System

Mature market liquidity financial system is made up of loan brokerage service, the third-party payment and insurance. The logic behind this is as follows: (1) Mortgage brokers match the buyer's demand, debt paying ability and loan products. They reduce the degree of asymmetric information and increase loan efficiency. (2) The third-party payment guarantees fund security and increases transaction efficiency by adopting the method of capital arrangement, working through the key processes of house mortgage, tax payment, etc. (3) Insurance guarantees house subject matter and property security, and promotes housing transaction circulation with risk dispersal mechanism. Its driving force lies in the maturity of traditional financial market and the development of second-hand house transition market. With plural subjects' various service, the uncertainties of transactions decreased. By smoothing transactions, the circulation of houses is promoted. The production, distribution, matching and transaction can be seen in Fig. 13.

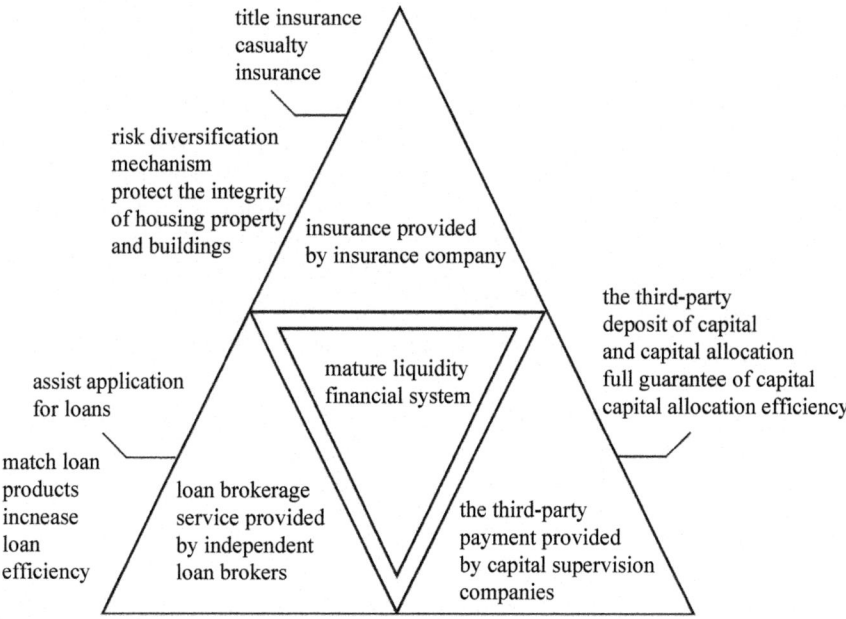

Fig. 13 The generation, allocation, matching and transaction of housing information. *Source of Data* compiled by Lianjia Institute

(1) Loan Brokerage Service

The nature of loan brokerage service is to serve the information intermediaries and the service is provided by mortgage loan brokers. Based on the professional knowledge of loan products and loan processes, loan brokers match individual loan demands, stronger debt paying ability, higher efficiency and lower cost with bank loan products, reduce the degree of asymmetric information, increase loan efficiency.

The specific mode of loan brokerage service is as follows: mortgage loan broker, as the intermediary of many sides, connect loan institutions and wholesalers, acquire an intimate knowledge of loan products and approval requirements, learn about the individual loan requirements and loan demands of retailer borrowers, connect participants of the third party, get borrowers' credit reports from credit consulting company, get assessment reports from assessment company, get property survey reports from property company, and get mortgage insurance for breach of contract from guarantee company (see Fig. 14).

Hence, mortgage loan brokers play a role of lowering transaction cost, easing information asymmetry and increasing transaction efficiency. Lowering transaction cost is embodied in reducing borrowers' search cost of loan banks and loan products, reducing the risk of no deal, helping borrowers get favorable wholesale interest rate, and lowering the operating cost of loan institutions. Easing information asymmetry and increasing transaction efficiency are embodied in connecting retailers, wholesalers and the third-party participants though individual professional credibility and specialized skills. On one hand, they replace the original information collecting and assessing functions of loan institutions with providing professional

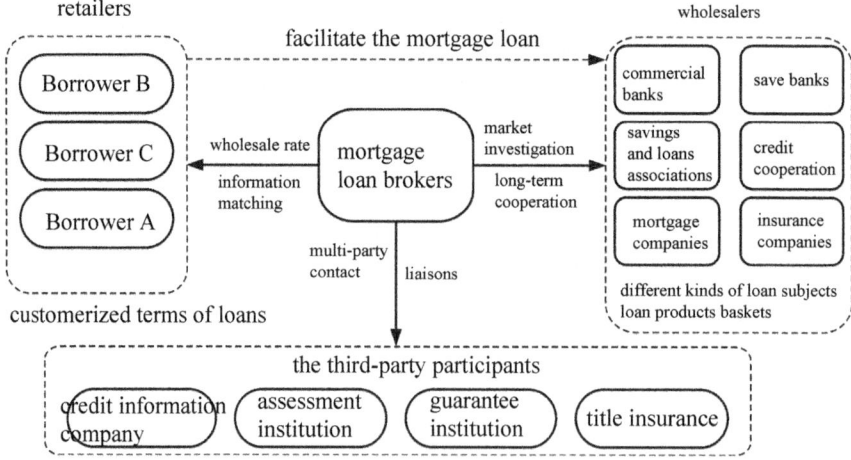

Fig. 14 The Mortgage brokerage service mode in the U.S. *Source of Data* compiled by Lianjia Institute

consulting services to borrowers. On the other hand, as the intermediary, they enable retailers, wholesalers and the third-party participants to exchange information extensively. (See Fig. 15).

1. The Function of Mortgage Loan Brokers
   The mortgage loan broker profession comes from the flexibly arranged employment of bank mortgage loan unemployed people. Before transaction, loan brokers must familiarize themselves with the mortgage loan market and develop customers. In the process of transaction, they must match information, pre-examine whether the application for loan is qualified and deal with related documents to close the loan and obtain the contract interest rate and lines of credit quota (See Fig. 16).

2. The Mortgage Loan Brokers' Development Under the Financial Innovation Background
   The rapid development of mortgage loan brokers is closely related to the interest rate liberalization of the U.S.: First, the intensifying competition of banks promotes the separation of loan origination and process services. Second, the rapid development of subprime mortgage market provides a broad market for loan brokerage service. Third, with the separation of mortgage market services, there are a group of professional loan service providers in charge of accumulating clients and creating loan business. Fourth, with the increasingly rich bank mortgage loan products, the nonstandardized difference is expanding, and borrowers' selection and matching are becoming more difficult. Fifth, the

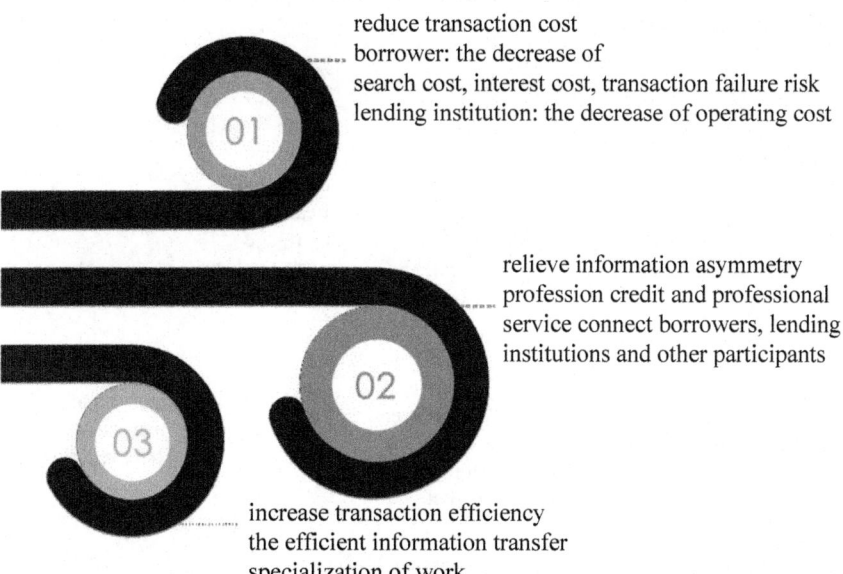

reduce transaction cost
borrower: the decrease of
search cost, interest cost, transaction failure risk
lending institution: the decrease of operating cost

relieve information asymmetry
profession credit and professional
service connect borrowers, lending
institutions and other participants

increase transaction efficiency
the efficient information transfer
specialization of work

Fig. 15 The market function of mortgage loan brokers

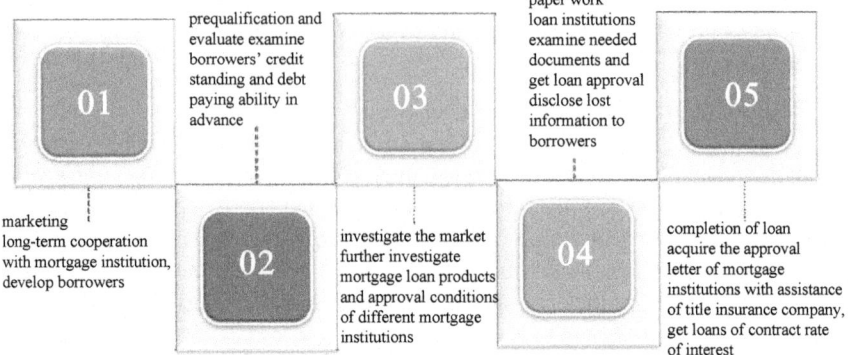

Fig. 16 The duty of mortgage brokers

megamerger of banks and asset securitization lead to a quick return of loan cash flow. The lending ability is enhanced. Non-deposit financial institutions join the mortgage loan market competition. The loan subjects increased (see Fig. 17).

3. The Revenue Model of Mortgage Loan Brokers and Industry Scale

The revenue of mortgage loan brokers mainly comes from the interest margins between the commission charges and revenues, i.e. the extra part of the actual loan interest rate over the bank's lowest interest rate, among which the commission charges account for 80%. However, with the supervision revolution after America's financial market crisis, the interest margins revenue supervision is becoming stricter in case mortgage loan brokers privately increase the interest rate's adverse selection (see Fig. 18).

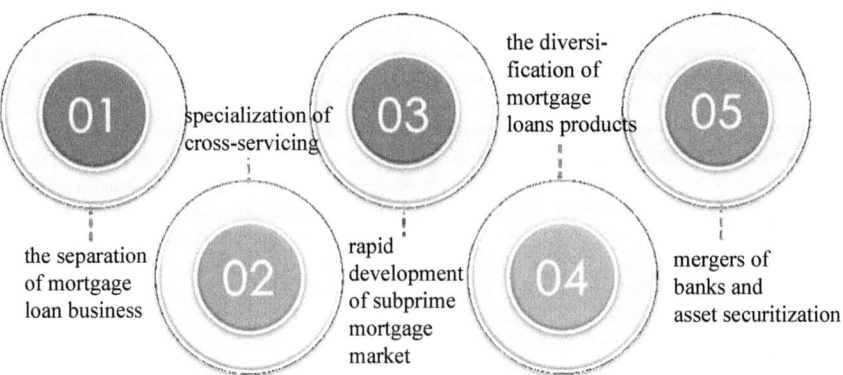

Fig. 17 The background development of mortgage brokers

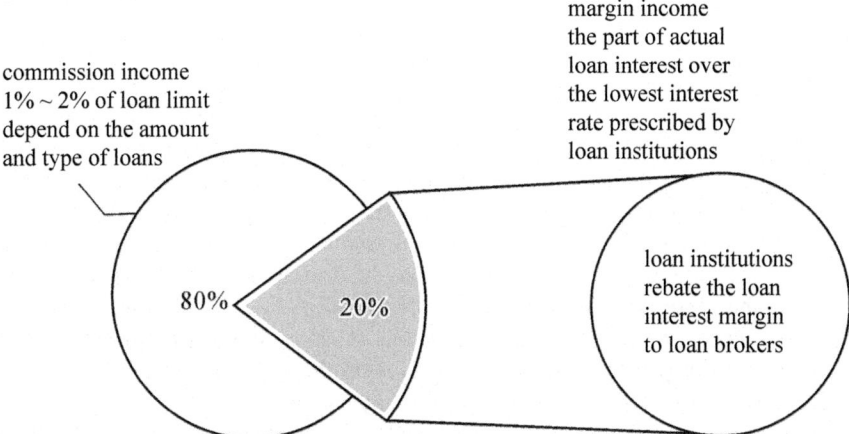

Fig. 18 The mortgage brokers' revenue model in the U.S.

Mortgage loan brokers are the crucial channel of mortgage loan in the U.S., Canada and Australia, etc. In the 1990s, the growing rate of mortgage loan brokers is over 14% per year. However, after the financial crisis, the number of mortgage loan brokers decreased to the present 5000 from 25000 in 2006. The market share decreased from 30% to less than 10% (see Fig. 19). But the percentage of Canada's mortgage loan which comes from mortgage loan brokers rises to 31% in 2015 from 22% in 2005. Among the six major banks of China, 27% mortgage loan comes from loan brokers. At present, there are 18633 mortgage loan brokers, they created 63.7% of the newly increased mortgage loan in 2014.

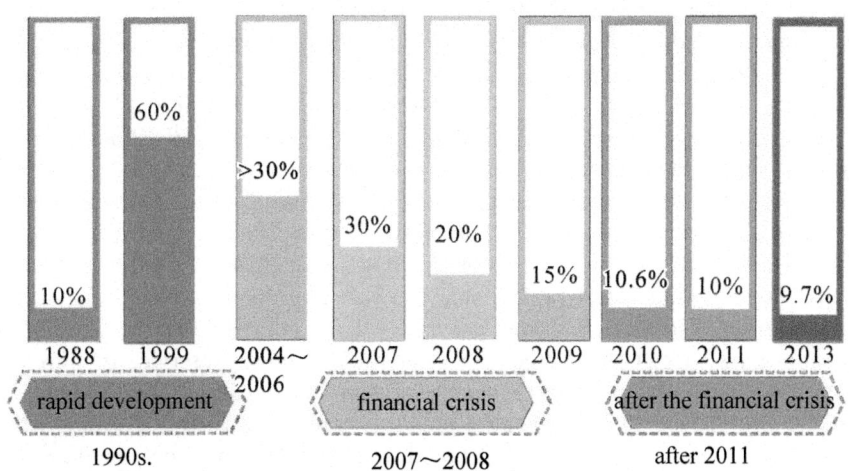

Fig. 19 The change of market share of mortgage brokers in the U.S.

6 Summary and Suggestion

In general, the key function of liquidity finance is to guarantee transaction security and to eliminate uncertainties in transactions so as to smooth the transaction process and not to leverage. The establishment of a mature liquidity financial system must be based on an impeccable transaction system and traditional financial market to achieve various service provided by plural subjects. However, with the regional, complicated and professional development, more and more financial demands generate, the same goes with some risks like the breach of contract, fraud, implicit debt and the close down, etc. Hence, professional and pointed liquidity financial service is needed to support house transactions. As a result, liquidity finance should become a crucial part to standardize and develop the property brokerage industry. Here are some suggestions in relation to policy:

First, to study sufficiently and learn about liquidity finance's lubricant function in second-hand house transaction. Ministry of Housing and Urban-Rural Development, Central Bank, China Banking Regulatory Commission, China Insurance Regulatory Commission are suggested to hold special research projects on liquidity financial service generated in second-hand house transactions. The organizational form, function and risks of liquidity finance in the market should be studied well and learned about. Related intermediary institutions can participate in the research as research members. When the projects are carried out, the participated intermediary institutions can be considered as pilot projects and experimental subjects to explore the operational details and process specification of financial business.

Second, on the basis of sufficient research, to promote trans-department cooperation, and to build a supervision system that suits China's situation. Liquidity finance is the natural product of the combination of financial service and second-hand house transaction development. Single supervision subject or method is insufficient. As a result, on the basis of adequate arguments, Central Bank, China Banking Regulatory Commission, China Insurance Regulatory Commission and Ministry of Housing and Urban-Rural Development should establish trans-department cooperation to promote related supervision legislation, be clear with the supervision subject and industry standards, build a supervision system that suits China's situation, promote liquidity financial system's mature development.

Third, it is suggested to treat liquidity financial business with different risk factors differently and to carry out different regulations. Second-hand house transaction is complicated, professional and risky. In different procedures of the transaction, risk control measures are different according to specific transaction situations. As a result, the degrees of risk of liquidity financial service are different correspondingly. The universal regulating measure cannot adapt to the development of liquidity finance. Different control policies should be carried out. Promote the healthy and orderly development of liquidity financial business on condition that the risks are under control.

Fourth, on condition that risks are under control, the liquidity financial service providers are encouraged to be diversified. One embodiment of the mature development of liquidity finance is that there are diverse participants, multiple service types, and capital demands, security demands, etc. in the transaction can be met, and the legitimate rights of the buyers and sellers are secured. Hence, when risks are under control, liquidity financial business providers are encouraged to be diversified. In promoting interest rate liberalization, banking industry is encouraged to participate in the mortgage loan settlement, loan origination and the division of labor in bank lending channels. Promote the third-party payment development based on the internet technology and the bank settlement system. Guarantee capital security. On the basis of the development of insurance industry, promote the combination of insurance and housing transactions to assist the allocation of risks. For brokerage companies that have already provided liquidity financial services, access conditions and operating standards should be cleared and the advantages of deep transaction and the good knowledge of customers' needs should be exploited.

Fifth, fully absorb internet technology to provide the two parties with better financial services. In recent years, the financial innovation and internet technology development has laid fundamental conditions for the development of China's internet financial service development. With internet technology, the demands to buy houses, to sell houses and the capital demands and investment demands can break the time limit and geographic restrictions to match with one another. Internet technology should be fully used to promote the third-party payment development and to provide better service, match the capital demands in transactions and guarantee security as soon as possible so as to achieve the purpose of increasing house circulation efficiency and promoting the development of inclusive finance.

Chapter 5
Mobile Internet

- In order to overcome information obstacles, it is necessary to extend the information dimension from the availability information to the decision-making information, and to transform the information production and interaction from PGC (professional production content)-oriented to UGC (user production content)-oriented, in particular to achieve networked commissions.
- The fundamental changes brought into the commission agency by the internet are its complete smash of the cost structure. These changes have achieved the ultimate unity of the scale effect and the network effect. The superposition of these two effects will produce a strong positive feedback effect, which brings irresistible changes to the entire industry, laying the basis foundations for fundamental changes in customer experience.

The emergence and popularization of the Internet has fundamentally changed the way people communicate, access information, and experience the services. Nowadays, the Internet has also succeeded in changing the way people shop and travel. Users can also feel the marked differences of services provided by Jingdong, Didi and traditional service providers. However, among basic necessities of life, its role in the "shelter" (house transactions) is still less obvious. Users' experience in housing transaction has been far from agreeable in relation to both online service and offline services. The influences of Internet on housing transactions have been week. In the past two years, the mobile Internet is surging, bringing profound changes in standardized areas of goods and non-standardized areas of local services. Looking ahead, it is worth exploring what changes and from which aspects the Internet will cause.

© Xiamen University Press and Springer Nature Singapore Pte Ltd. 2018   115
S. Ba and X. Yang, *The Rise of New Brokerages and the Restructuring of Real Estate Value Chain*, https://doi.org/10.1007/978-981-10-7715-9_5

1   Key Changes

So far, the Internet has changed the real estate brokerage industry for many years, and has gone through two stages:

The first stage is the so-called "O2O" (online to offline) stage. There are three typical characteristics of this stage:

(1) The buyer's Internet remains a dominating position. Compared with that of the sellers, the connection of the buyers with the Internet is much earlier, more active and much deeper. This has been reflected in real data that the commission rate of sellers is still very low, or even negligible; on the contrary, the vast majority of buyers have considered the Internet as the first channel to obtain information.
(2) Internet is becoming the prioritized media and channel for buyers to obtain information, the core driving force behind which is the shift of consumers' focus. At the same time, advertisements always follow people's attention. The business model of the Internet companies relies on online advertising, challenging and even replacing offline media.
(3) There is an embarrassing state of separation and "seemingly" integration of online and offline services. Internet media companies provide online information, and brokerage companies provide offline services. However, simple and improper online advertising model cannot fundamentally improve the efficiency of information exchange. Instead it has exacerbated the vicious competition between the brokerage firms. Especially in the real estate transaction downturn, this vicious competition will eventually evolve into intense resistance between online and offline service providers. They will move from cooperation to conflict, and eventually to breakdown. This scene has been vividly presented in the last two years. To some extent it is this internal conflict that promotes the industry to further divide (See Fig. 1).

The second stage is what we understood as the "E2E" (End to End) stage. The key changes therein are:

(1) The boundaries between online and offline begin to disappear. The Internet companies are moving from functioning as media to conducting business. Their business models change from profiting from advertisements to procuring commission fees. It can be said that the media are becoming brokerage agencies. Transaction brokerage firms are moving from offline to online, and begin to build their own online platforms, through attracting customers for brokers on the Internet, and through guiding the brokers' practices by means of rules of internal and external networks.
(2) The formation of closed-loop transactions. Representative companies of the industry at this stage are beginning to enhance their abilities to provide trading services. They begin to build their own controllable transaction ecology and

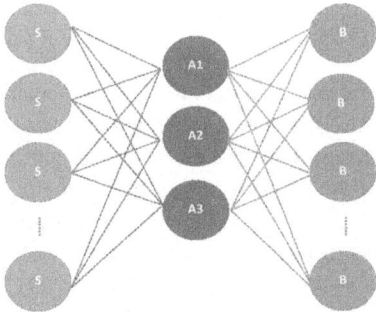

Fig. 1 The Internet and the change of the brokerage industry: "O2O" period

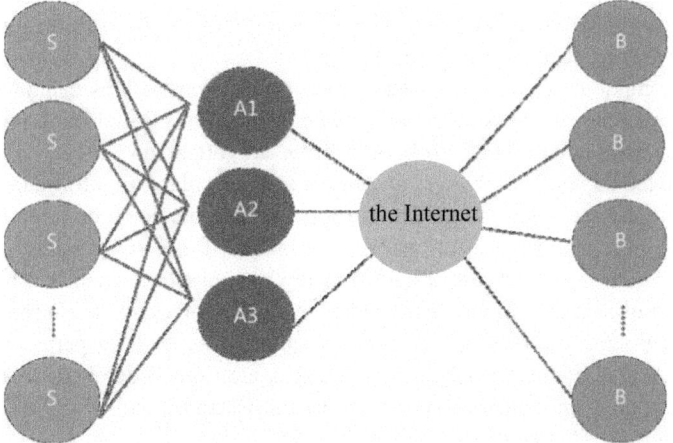

Fig. 2 The Internet and the change of the brokerage industry: "E2E"period

trading environments, in an effort to control more stages from traffic to trans-action. At this stage, central to the measurement of the company's ability and overcoming competition barriers is the transaction efficiency and transaction shares. See Fig. 2.

2   Three Dilemmas and Three Directions

In the foreseeable future, the extent to which the Internet can transform the bro-kerage industry will depend largelyon whether it can break through the "three dilemmas": information dilemma, service scale dilemma, network dilemma.

2.1   Three Dilemmas

(1) The first dilemma is information dilemma. To be specific, (1) a company with a media attributecan not guarantee the authenticity and timeliness of the information, which is determined by the intrinsic attributes of the real estate information media. If the purpose of purchasing the network port and updating available housing by the broker or brokerage firm is to accumulate more transactions, or the advertising is the only monetization model of the real estate media companies, users can hardly get real and timely information through the Internet. Even the largest and most capable media company Zilow, under the exclusive Commission system and MLS system in the United States, have not yet solved this issue. In comparison, it is hardly possible for Chinese Internet information media to provide comprehensive, timely and accurate real estate information, especially under the current situation of multi-commissions and confusing internal information. This is the dilemma of the industry and also the point that most users are dissatisfied with.

(2) The companies that are allowed rights to make transactions cannot guarantee the comprehensiveness of the real estate information. Based on the transaction and service capabilities, brokerage firms are often able to or conditionally guarantee the authenticity and timeliness of the availability information, but not comprehensive information. The transactions are bound to be large enough to obtain comprehensive information. In principle, it is only possible for a company to ensure occupying 80–90% of the market share when it achieves 40–50% or even higher in the local market share. Taking into account the efficiency of large-scale transaction services, it requires a rather long period to achieve this amount of market share, and at the same time it demands a more rigid management and supervision of information access, uploading and dynamic monitoring. This is also a challenge.

The second is the scale of service dilemma. Compared to other industries, the scale of real estate transactions is not so obvious, the reason for which is twofold: First, the offline services per se are loaded, relying on personnel, lack of scale effect, and the marginal costs for next services are less likely to decline; Second, it is not easy to reach the critical point of the scale effect, the scale of most companies are maintained under the critical point, and small companies prevail.

In most of time of the 20th century in the United States, the real estate brokerage industries are family workshops. Even the largest and nationwide brokerage firms are very small. One with 200 brokers can be considered a big company. Several start-up companies began to become nationalized and scaled through the franchise approach in 1970, *for instance, the ERA that was established in 1973…* The reason why these companies could grow bigger (such as RE/MAX has more than 100,000 brokers) is that they have adopted a light asset franchise mode. This in essence reflects the scale effects of the brank (See Fig. 3).

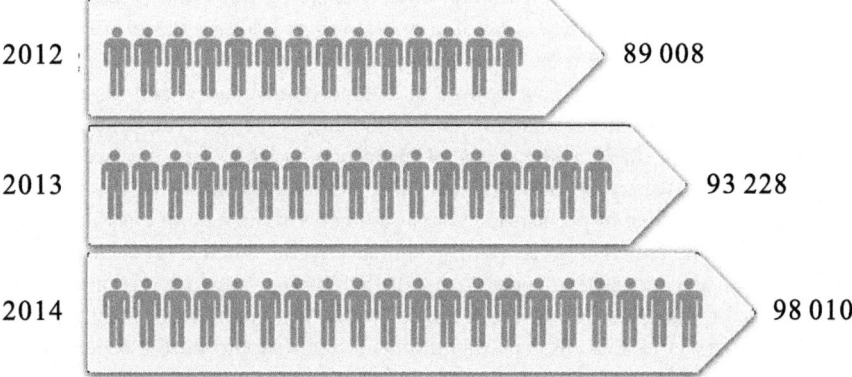

Fig. 3 The scale of brokers in RE/MAX (unit: person)

So, the possibility of achieving "heavy and efficient" can be realized from two aspects: one is the word of mouth. If the existing and previous customers can recommend new customers or continue transaction services, the marginal costs will decrease. The second possibility is service density. With the expansion of market scale, brokers service density increases and effective working hours are extended, or the value of work within unit increases, companies at this stage will have high efficiency, and thus reduces the cost of service costs, increases the scale of customers amount. Hence, the positive feedback of large-scale transactions is established.

The third is the network dilemma. The value of the network depends on the number of those who connected to the network. Connecting to larger networks can produce more customer values than connecting to small networks. In short, the bigger the network is, the better it is. The reason why network effect of this kind is more important and stronger is because it produces greater positive feedback effects. Once the positive feedback is established, it is irresistible. The final result is the winners prevail and consequently produce a monopoly. In the real estate sector, more buyers will attract more sellers, more available housing information will attract more buyers, that is, the platform between buyers and sellers has a certain degree of network effect. At the same time, if a platform can attract enough buyers and sellers at the same time, it will also attract more brokers. Eventually, "housing, buyers and sellers" establish a "tripartite interaction" in this platform.

However, in contrast, the network effect of brokerage services is generally small. First of all, the real estate trading network is not as big as what we have imagined. Although the scale of real estate transactions transcends more than 10 trillion yuan, the high price per unit means that the real estate transaction network may only involves tens of millions of people. In short, the user base is too small. Secondly, the characteristics of low-frequency transactions lead to less values of a single user's repeated transaction, and thus users' loyalty is very weak.

Based on these considerations, other ways to increase the value of the network include: (1) to increase the varieties of services and to improve the use value of a single customer' repeated uses. This can include all housing transaction services such as renting, purchasing new houses or second-hand houses, and also include associated services such as financing and furnishing; (2) to provide differentiated services to increase the transfer costs of customers so that they are given more reasons to stay loyal to the network; (3) most importantly, to move the scope of service from in-service to pre-service so that the network covers all customers who possess real estate and also includes all potential buyers. When a network does not only focus on the transaction service, it will then attend to wider customers. The annual housing transaction in China is only about 4 million units, but the number of Chinese owners is as high as tens of millions, which should be the focused customers group.

2.2   Three Directions

The first is to extend the information dimension from the availability information to the decision information and turn the information production from PGC to UGC. Although the availability, timeliness and authenticity of listings are important for trading decisions for both buyers and sellers, such information is not everything in the long period of transactions. Some "pan-decision" information is also important. To be specific, (1) the first is local information, for instance, school districts, hospitals, shops, transportation and other information are also an important part of housing decision-making. (2) The second is valuation information. When the price of the real estate ceases a unilateral rise, and shows a two-way fluctuation, the valuation of housing is of increasing importance to transactions. The significance of valuation is not about accuracy, but rather about providing customers transparent and advantageous decision-making choices. (3) The third is broker evaluation information. Consumers generally have insufficient trust in brokers, and therefore there is an urgent need to establish an objective and credible broker evaluation system. Until today, this system is still yet to be established. Those brokerage firms have the ability to do so, but they do not have the motivation. By contrast, the network companies have the motivation, but not the ability.

In addition to the information dimension, the way information is produced is equally important. The information production method nowadays is still largely dependent on "PGC", which is called by brokers. In the absence of information protection, it is against human nature to require brokers to produce and disseminate authentic information. Therefore, in order to fundamentally change this situation, a potential direction is to remove barriers for users to produce information through internet, and consequently create more UGC ways, for example, to use "owners' pre-sale" method to reduce the broker's influence in the process of information production. If the "owners' pre-sale" is further and gradually changed into "owners commissioned", it will then become the determining force of the future of the brokerage industry. If the future first contact point of sellers commissioned housing comes not from the broker or the store but from the Internet, then the entire transaction process will be fundamentally changed.

In addition, the way information interacts is also an important aspect influencing the quality of information. Nowadays, sellers and buyers to a large extent still interact through brokers to exchange information. In the future, there will be more ways for buyers and sellers to interact directly to exchange information so that brokers will appear to offline services.

The second is the reshaping of organizational relationships. Internet can be regarded a new type of organizational relationship that reshapes relationships between firms and brokers, brokers and brokers, and brokers and managers.

The practice in the United States shows that the Internet has changed the traditional "MLS + broker" organizational relationship into one of "Internet information platform + broker", which led to the decline of the old MLS platform in some cities. And brokers move to a more independent direction relying on the Internet. For example, brokers today can list available houses in the MLS on the Internet; or they can directly skip over the MLS and only display such information on the Internet, and the current proportion is rising rapidly.

Australia is another interesting case. Before the Internet Era, the country has nothing similar to the traditional platform of the United States MLS. The core organizational relationship in the brokerage industry is the 'company + broker'. In the late 90s of the 20th century, with the rise of Internet, the real estate media company REA works with the largest local brokerage firm, docks their internal ERP system, integrates the housing information and shares the information in the Internet. The adequate housing information further promotes the growth of customers. When the real housing data and user platform develops to a certain degree, REA's monopoly on brokerage firm and brokers starts to emerge: today, more than 90% of Australian brokers are REA paid customers. Hence, REA has actually become an Internet version of the MLS (See Fig. 4). Unlike the United States, the main function of the Internet in Australia is to remodel the relationship between the Internet and the brokerage firm; whereas, the relationship between the brokerage firm and brokers does not change substantially. If the Internet in the United States brings about organizational changes in 'Internet + independent brokers', then, the Australian change is 'Internet + broker Company'. The situation in the UK is very similar to Australia; the company RMW in the United Kingdom is a UK version of REA.

Compared with the United States and Australia, China has neither exclusive commission, nor MLS as well as a set of complete game rules. This means that it is difficult for any Internet company to achieve a real housing data through docking ERP information of a brokerage firm. This also means that it is not possible to have

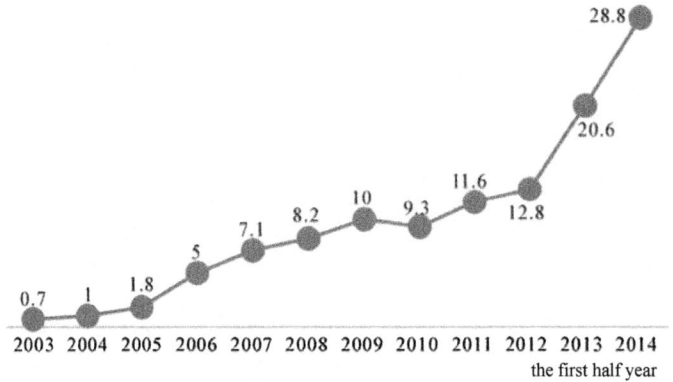

Fig. 4   The housing integration of REA in Australia led to the expansion of users

the organizational relationship of independent brokers in a short term. Under the wave of the Internet, China's future organizational structure is likely to be a complex, namely the structure of 'the company's internet platform + management + broker'. (1) The internet platform may emerge from within the company. Only those brokerage firms in a monopoly position can achieve online listing of authentic housing information, so as to attract potential users and establish a bilateral platform for housing information and customers. Therefore, it makes sense to say that if America has the MLS in its market, then China will have the MLS in its big companies. (2) The combat units on the platform are neither the companies nor independent brokers, but a mixture of the "a + M" (broker + manager). In the absence of rules in the market and low profession qualities of the brokers, the existence of M (manager) requires necessary management to replace markets without common rules, so as to enhance transaction efficiency. (3) From a long term, if the era of the professional brokers may finally arrive, this organizational relationship may eventually transit to a 'firm platform + professional broker'.

The third is the remodeling of the transaction process. The second-hand house transaction is more complicated compared with the first-hand. However, the second-hand transaction still follows the basic procedures: the agreement of house transactions, the payment of transaction money, and the related property transfer procedures. Judging from the current process, there are at least five types of agencies that may get involved in the whole house transaction procedures, among which the brokerage companies mainly participate in intermediary commission and contract terms negotiation. The follow-up transaction procedures involve the collaboration with other agencies (See Fig. 5). Due to the business needs, the majority of large brokerage companies in the market has gradually infiltrated in financial transactions, including a whole set of mature business system such as housing loan, money payment and capital supervision. Although the emergence of the Internet brokerage companies has brought a certain change to the current market in 2016, the brokerage companies still rely on the strategy of the low commission to attract

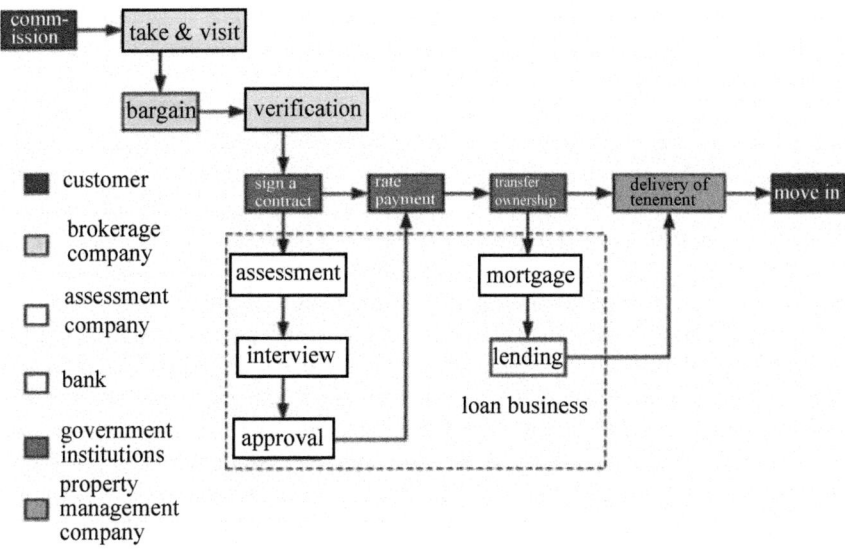

Fig. 5 The flow chart of second-hand houses transactions

more potential customers. The Internet has shaped the channel of attracting more potential customers; yet it has little influence on the transaction procedures. The traditional Off-line business model continues without any change.

We believe that the core transformation of the future transaction procedures is based on big data and big data analysis, the upgrade of online transaction, the formation of closed-loop optimization management. This will improve transaction efficiency. The detailed steps are listed as follows:

First, standardization. It is needed to split the transaction process and materialize a professional division of labor, namely a labor division between the buyer brokers and seller brokers. The details include assigning professional teams to perform onsite housing investigation, maintenance, data recording and other related tasks, in order to reduce the monopoly of housing resource information caused by over-lapping business operations. For example, the traditional brokers do not have the motivation to record the housing information; hence a designated, specialized personal responsible for data recording will help reducing the monopoly of housing information caused by vicious competition between housing brokers. The sharing of housing resources will, therefore, be possible.

Second, the creation of big data. The media has static information and only these companies in charge of real transactions have access to dynamic information. It is possible to make offline transaction data into measurable, comparable online data, hence to judge the customers' real intention, to analyze the reason for transaction failure, and offer targeted improvement measures accordingly.

Third, the data optimization and improvement. Based on data analysis of customer communication, onsite house visit, and customer evaluation among many other data, the system will be able to provide customers rating, locate key potential customers, improve service quality, focus on important potential customers, and improve user experience.

In general, the expansion of the information dimension, the Internet change of organizational relationship and the reshaping of the transaction process will finally bring a radical change to the cost structure of the brokerage industry and realize the ultimate unity of large scale economy effects and network economy effects. In an offline brokerage company dominated era, the key to success for a company lies in its large scale effects; while in an online Internet era, the key to success for a brokerage company depends on a perfect combination of the Internet effects and scale effects. From this point of view, the combination presents itself as the key bottleneck for almost all brokerage industry participants. For some Internet companies enjoying certain Internet benefits, they have not yet proved their offline capacities and hence suffered in the offline mud. For some other companies who enjoy certain offline scale effects, they are making efforts in establishing their own Internet capacity. Although the final structure is still somewhat uncertain, there is one thing for sure, i.e., in the process during which the mobile Internet reshapes the traditional brokerage industry, we can achieve large-scale effects in the house transaction procedures and Internet effects via information exchange and brokers' interaction. The online-offline dual effects superimposed together will have a strong positive feedback to bring fundamental changes to the entire industry. Only based on these, the user experience will promise a radical change.

Chapter 6
Supervision System

- The role of legal regulation is to define five relationships. First, it determines whether the relationship between the realtor and client is agent or intermediary. Second, it sets an industry admittance threshold. Third, it defines broker practice guidelines. Fourth, it constructs a mechanism for industry complaints and penalties. Fifth, it provides a protection mechanism for realtors.
- A professional industry association can play three roles. The first is to promote exchanges, coordination, and communication within the industry when it serves as an effective bridge between the government and enterprises. The second is to set up industry standards and code of conducts. The third is to coordinate disputes among members or between members and non-members, and discipline organizations or individuals with wrong doings within the scope of its power.

The supervision system of the real estate brokerage industry includes legal constraints, industrial self-discipline and management mechanism. The core demand for industrial supervision is to avoid the present ternary dilemma. First is to eliminate information asymmetry, to expand the breadth, depth and speed of the disclosure of housing information. Second is to solve "free riding" within the industry, to protect the interest of source information producers. Third is to safeguard practitioners against moral or ethical risks. In addition, industrial supervision also plays a role in enhancing safety, efficiency and consumer experience during transaction.

1 Legal Constraints

The significance of legal constraints lies in the top-level design, setting bottom line, criterion and judging standards for the industry, which lays the foundation for effective and healthy operation of the industry. The brokerage industry in the United States, Japan, China's Hong Kong and Taiwan has all established a supervision

© Xiamen University Press and Springer Nature Singapore Pte Ltd. 2018   125
S. Ba and X. Yang, *The Rise of New Brokerages and the Restructuring of Real Estate Value Chain*, https://doi.org/10.1007/978-981-10-7715-9_6

legal system covering the basic legal relationships of the industry, admittance, license system, and complaint and punishment and practice protection, dominated by the professional law and coordinated by other professional codes and rules. The current situation in China is hardly satisfactory as there may be many legal codes for the industry, but many are conflicting and improper. When a leading upper law has not been set in place, the mechanisms for supervision, enforcement and punishment are not sound.

1.1 Role: Legal Constraints Being the Bottom Line and Red Line

There are three roles that law plays on human behavior. The first one is guiding, by telling people what they can or cannot do and consequences of law breaking so as to affect people's behavior. The second is educating, turning people away from wrong doings through punishment. The third is value evaluation as law can provide criteria for judgment and measurement of right and wrong and standard for good and evil.

Legal constraints are the bottom line for brokerage institutions and practitioners. The name "bottom line" doesn't necessarily mean that standards are set low. On the contrary, high demands should be made. In the *Real Estate Licensing and Registration Act of USA*, the code of ethical integrity is written into law.

1.2 International Experience: Agent, High Entry Level, Professionalism, Severe Punishment, and Appropriate Protection

The legal regulations of the real estate brokerage industry in the United States, Japan, China's Taiwan and Hong Kong mainly include the following five aspects. First is to define whether the basic legal relationship between the broker and the client is agency or intermediary so as to lay the cornerstone of the system and innovation. Second is to set high industry admittance threshold. Third is to set up brokers' code of conduct, and constantly improve their professional quality. Fourth is to build a mechanism for complaints and punishment in the industry, deterring violations. Fifth is to create a broker practice protection mechanism to provide a safe working environment for brokers.

The five dimensions are mutually connected and supportive as the basic legal relationship between the broker and the client is determined and brokers' code of conduct is set. It clarifies illegal conducts and related punishment and supervision and risks practitioners may face as well as protection they need. High-level code of conduct cannot be implemented if there are no high-quality practitioners.

Complaints and penalties will be ineffective without a feasible and thorough code of conduct. Finally, without efficient complaint mechanism and strict penalties, the admittance system and practice requirements will exit in names only.

1.2.1 Defining the Basic Legal Relationship Between Broker and Client as Agent

In the United States, Japan and China's Taiwan and Hong Kong, broker-client relationship is defined as agent instead of intermediary. In the United States, for example, such legal relationship is reflected in the following aspects. First, the seller can authorize the broker to find buyers. Second, the buyer can hire a broker to find property management companies. Third, the broker can hire a salesperson to find buyers and property management companies. The broker is an agent to the client and a truster to the salesperson. As an agent, the broker for the seller or the buyer has fiduciary responsibilities to their employers, including striving for employers' best interest and disclosing information in full.

The institutional reason for defining the basic legal relationship between broker and client as agent rather than intermediary is mainly to avoid moral risks. It is natural that buyers always want to buy property at the lowest price, while sellers want the opposite, which comprises the fundamental interest conflict between the seller and the buyer. It is difficult for the intermediary to represent the interest of the two parties in a fair way and moral risks are inevitable. In the relationship of agency, however, the agent is dedicated to the interest of the authorizer, which in turn can effectively avoid moral hazard.

1.2.2 Setting High Industry Entry Threshold

Industry entry includes market admittance for brokers and for brokerage institutions. According to international experience, countries or regions set relatively strict entry threshold for brokers, including basic eligibility criteria, skill requirements, prohibiting conditions, etc. The US *Real Estate Licensing and Registration Act* demands that brokers must meet three requirements before practicing. In Japan and China's Taiwan, detailed forbidden conditions are listed. In China's Hong Kong, there is more concerned about the suitability of brokers' qualifications, which means that applicants will be approved only if the Estate Agents Authority considers them as "eligible". The standards of "suitability" mainly include ethics and integrity.

Entry for brokerage institutions in China's Hong Kong and the United States are relatively simple, requiring at least one sponsor or director to hold a valid license. In the United States, as long as the license is authentic, no registered capital is required for registration. However, entry threshold in Japan and China's Taiwan is relatively more stringent with a "double insurance", which not only requires a license, but also a deposit system to ensure that brokerage institutions are qualified professionally and secure financially.

From the institutional perspective, countries/regions set strict entry threshold and bottom line for brokers can ensure that practitioners have relatively high expertise. In reality, brokers in the US and Japan enjoy good reputation and respect due to the high entry demands, which has promoted the brokers' moral self-discipline.

1.2.3 Establishing High Business Code of Conduct

Practice guidelines for brokers in countries/regions are mainly about prohibitions, subordinated by permissions. According to *Code of Conduct* of Hong Kong SAR, brokers should strive to protect and promote the interest of customers and avoid any conflicts of interest and should not directly or indirectly harm the reputation of peers. Japan focuses on the protection of customer information, prohibiting the disclosure of customer's privacy. In China's Taiwan much emphasis is on the award of exemplary agents or outstanding behavior to safeguard the interests of customers. Jinzhong Medal is awarded to brokers with outstanding performances and standardized practice, in order to encourage practitioners to comply with ethical integrity required in business.

The United States has the most comprehensive code of conduct for brokers. The *Real Estate Licensing and Registration Act* sets out practice norms for practitioners in great detail. For example, when the interest of a broker is related to that of the title insurance company, the broker should not require the employer to obtain the property right insurance from the insurance company. Without the consent of both parties, the broker should not simultaneously represent the buyer and seller in the same transaction. The license of the broker shall be frozen when he/she is employed by the State Real Estate Commission. Before the expiration of the exclusive agent of other brokers, a broker should not maliciously induce the seller to change the broker, etc. Moreover, the *Real Estate Licensing and Registration Act* is modified every year, removing obsolete articles and adding new practice norms according to new problems and new demands.

From the institutional aspect, with MLS as the cornerstone, the information-sharing system in the US effectively solves the problem of asymmetric information and free-riding behavior, but it can't avoid moral hazard of agents. Detailed practice norms for practitioners aim to enhance professional quality of practitioners and overcome potential moral hazard. From the actual results, in order to avoid penalties, the US brokers will consciously abide by the practice guidelines, keeping guidelines as their habit. Therefore, American brokers tend to show a higher professional quality.

1.2.4 Constructing a Mechanism for Industry Complaints and Penalties

In terms of supervision and penalty mechanism, countries/regions vary greatly. In China's Hong Kong and Japan, the government is in charge of supervision and penalty. In Hong Kong, for example, under the authority of *Unexecuted Estate Agency Agreement,* the SAR government set up a department in charge of complaints and inspection and issued guidelines for complaints to specify the ways for clients to complain. In addition, a survey team was set up in the inspection system. Once illegal behavior is found, the government can directly exercise the right of penalty. On the contrary, in China's Taiwan, the industry associations are usually in charge of exercising rewards and penalties.

In the United States, supervision includes government supervision and industry supervision. Division of labor of government and industry association are as follows: government supervision is executed by the Commission of Inquiry, which can check the broker's business records at any time. Once it identifies problems, it promptly reports to the authorities to discuss the problems and then makes a decision on whether penalty is needed. Brokers with serious misconducts may be sued. Industry supervision is executed by the Industry Association, which mainly relies on three subordinate commissions to deal with complaints in a timely manner. They are the Grievance Committee, Professional Standards Committee and the Arbitration Hearing Office. The difference between the two lies in that the government has the right to revoke the license, while the association can impose a fine on the member or persuade him/her to leave the association but does not have the right to revoke the license.

The United States sets severe penalties for the misconducts of practitioners. In the brokerage industry, for cases including false statements, fraud, false advertising, offering agency service for several parties and false commitment which caused damage to interests of customers, practitioners will be punished by the regulatory authorities. The punishment includes fine, suspension of business, suspension of licenses, revocation of licenses, dismissal, etc. Practitioners with severe misconducts will be sued. In reality, the mechanism for complaints and penalties in the US has a huge deterrent effect on brokers. It is not easy for brokers to get away from punishment should violations be found (Fig. 1).

1.2.5 Creating a Proper Protection Mechanism

In the realtor's work, there are potential threats of being sued or compensated out of integrity of buyers and sellers or the realtor's negligence artwork. In order to help practitioners to avoid or minimize the losses caused by such threats, some countries

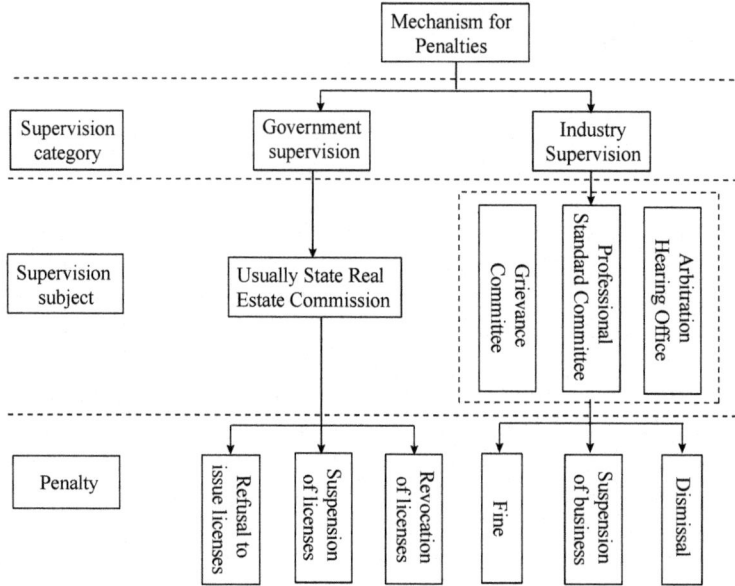

Fig. 1 Mechanism for complaints and penalties in the US. *Source* Lianjia Research Institute

and regions created proper protection mechanisms. For example, security deposit is required in China's Taiwan and in Japan, which can be paid to the victim should compensations be required due to violations to customers' interest. There is not a such a protective system in China's Hong Kong, but professional insurance covers the risks.

The United States has set up a comprehensive protection mechanism for practitioners, including: individual credit protection system, property insurance system, housing quality professional appraisal, broker fault insurance system, a model text of contract provided by industry association and the provision that brokers shall not provide legal services, etc.

From the institutional perspective, individual credit protection system, property insurance system and housing quality professional appraisal are mainly to overcome the problem of information asymmetry and to help brokers avoid potential liability. Broker fault insurance system, a model text of contract provided by industry association and the provision that brokers should not provide legal services can reduce potential risks caused by negligence or unprofessional conduct of brokers. In reality, a good protection mechanism is essential for creating a safe environment for practitioners (Fig. 2).

Fig. 2 Broker protection
mechanism in the US. *Source*
NAR; Lianjia Research
Institute

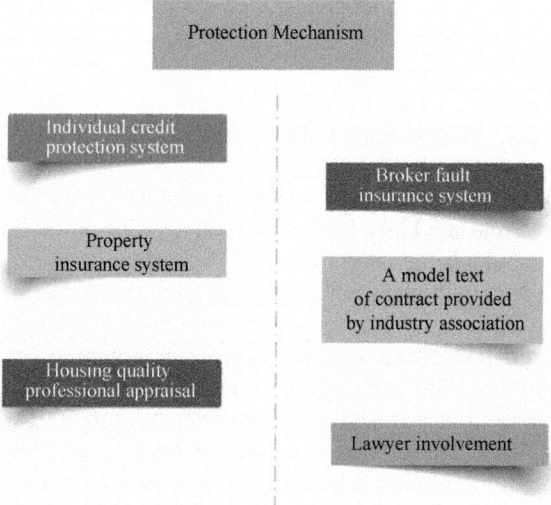

1.3   China: Lack of Upper-Level Legislation and Suitable Regulations; Ineffective Supervision, Execution and Punishment

A real estate market dominated by second-hand homes is accelerating in China, yet related laws and regulations concerning real estate brokerage industry have not been perfected. Supervision, implementation and punishment on illegal conducts of brokers are still weak.

1.3.1   Lack of Upper-Level Legislation

A *Real Estate Brokerage Law* is not yet set for China's brokerage industry to standardize its development, which is the root of problems and confusion in the market.

China has already issued related laws and regulations including *the Urban Real Estate Administration Law of the People's Republic of China, Provisions on the Administration of Urban Real Estate Intermediary Services, Interim Provisions on Professional Eligibility System for Real Estate Brokers, Implementation Measures for the Professional Eligibility Examination for Real Estate Brokers* and *Administrative Measures for Real Estate Brokers*. However, without an upper-level legislation, laws and regulations of the industry will encounter three major difficulties. First, different rules and regulations developed by various departments and local governments are not coordinated with each other, leaving many normative documents useless. Second, most regulations are quite detached from the reality, leading to the laissez-faire regulation or arbitrary intervention of supervision and enforcement. Third, good systems and regulations may fail to play their roles due to the absence of effective enforcement, supervision and punishment mechanisms.

1.3.2 Improvements Desirable in Existing Laws and Regulations

There are many problems in the existing laws and regulations.

From the basic legal relationship between the broker and the customer, China still adopts the intermediary system, resulting in inherent problems of the industry including information asymmetry, free riding and moral hazards.

On business entry requirement, China lacks strict qualification review, qualification examination, and license registration access mechanism. As for the business threshold for brokerage institutions, they only need to meet conditions of establishment of a general company, which means that the bar is set very low.

There are relevant provisions on brokers' code of conduct in China, but they are often too general and not professional enough. The contents are often vague, outdated and detached from the reality. In the United States, the code of conduct is specific enough with details like *"before the expiration of the exclusive agent of other brokers, a broker should not maliciously induce the owner to change the broker"*. The regulation in China only provides that *"improper conducts like luring, cheating, threatening or malicious collusion are not allowed in conducting real estate brokerage business"*. The reason lies in that the legal framework of the US real estate brokerage system is very clear, with very specific derivate problems. Therefore, practice regulations can be established in a specific and targeted way. In contrast, the legal system of China's brokerage industry does not have a clear framework. Therefore, practice standards can only be established in a generalized way as it's hard to be refined. Such vague codes without substantive contents can't effectively regulate practitioners and have a limited restraint on practitioners' ethics.

From the aspect of complaint and punishment mechanism, *Administrative Measures for Real Estate Brokers* and *Interim Provisions on Professional Eligibility System for Real Estate Brokers* have provisions that brokers who violated code of ethics or industry regulations would be fined and their qualifications would be evoked. However, China hasn't established an industry complaint channel like that in the US, nor any special survey commission or review and self-criticism system.

Broker protection mechanism hasn't been established yet. In reality, brokers' protection is mainly covered by brokerage institutions. But usually, once a broker commits a major violation or error, the brokerage institution will directly punish the broker, leaving the broker with no safeguard measures.

1.3.3 Ineffective Law Enforcement

Although relevant laws and regulations have made specific penalty measures on illegal behavior, conducts that violated regulations, false information, cheating customers, in reality, ineffective enforcement is prominent due to three reasons. First, there isn't a leading organization. When a number of departments jointly share the power of punishment, it is difficult to find and resolve problems effectively. Second, no proactive inspection or surveillance mechanism has been established and the complaint channel is not perfect, which leaves the government in a very passive position when dealing with illegal conducts. Third, law enforcement lacks coverage and depth. For example, when some small and medium-sized brokerage companies distributed false information and made cheating transaction on certain portal websites, they haven't been investigated or punished timely. Discipline on brokerage institutions and brokers are even weaker, which does little good to curbing the severe problems in the industry.

2 Industry Self-discipline

Industry association plays an irreplaceable role in brokerage industry management. According to international experience, on one hand, under the authority of the government, the association uploads and releases related information and implements laws and regulations to manage the industry in a legal way; on the other hand, more importantly, through effective self-discipline, the association can constrain brokerage institutions and brokers more strictly and promote the industry to develop in an orderly, healthy and standardized way with its rights of supervision and punishment. The main problems in the brokerage industry's self-discipline in China include lack of specialized associations, unclear responsibility of existing associations, lack of supervision and punishment mechanism, limited financial resources, and lack of substantial self-discipline.

2.1 Role: Self-discipline for Checking Market Failure and Government Mistakes

Industry self-discipline refers to the industry's self-regulation and constraints. Without the base of industry associations, industry self-discipline is empty talk.

Industry self-discipline is the inevitable outcome of market economy. Under the condition of market economy, administrative intervention is the "visible hand" and market regulation is the "invisible hand". While the former can mend the faults of the latter, it is often inadequate due to information asymmetry and lack of administrative resources. With the accelerated transformation of government functions, many management functions and public services of the government have been allocated to the society and the market. Thus, industry associations gradually emerge to be another major adjustment measure of correcting the market failure and government mistakes.

Compared with market regulation and administrative intervention, industry association has some inherent advantages in microeconomic management. First, industry associations have comprehensive and detailed industry information, which can reduce decision-making mistakes caused by the information asymmetry. Second, the standards developed by industry associations are based on actual needs and are negotiated by members on an equal footing, so they are recognized and consciously adhered to by members. However, it should be pointed out that there is no natural boundary between market regulation, administrative intervention and industry self-discipline. For the industry self-discipline to be effective, it needs to comply with boundary set by the state laws and regulations to separate it from administrative intervention.

A real estate brokerage industry association generally has the following roles. The first role is to promote industry exchanges, coordination and communication. As the bridge of effective communication between the government and enterprises, the government's request and guidance can be passed through the association to enterprises and brokers. On the other hand, enterprises and brokers can give suggestions on present policies and regulations and recommendations about their own demands through the association. Its second role is to set the industry standards such as code of ethics, information disclosure standards, data statistics and reporting standards. Its third role is to coordinate disputes between members, members and non-members, and punish institutions and practitioners who break rules within its scope of authority.

2.2 International Experience: Improving Association Functions According to Industrial Needs

Industry association is the product of continuous evolution of the market, but the way of production, functional orientation and organizational structure of national and regional trade associations vary a lot.

2.2.1 Birth and Growth of Industry Association Due to the Growth of Industry Scale and Professionalization

Industry associations were born along with the expansion of the market scale and professionalization. Although they were born in different ways, they came from the need to solve the problems during the industry's development and upgrading of its professionalism.

In the US, brokers formed the industry association from the bottom level to the upper levels spontaneously. Its growth and improvement are mainly based on the development need of MLS system. There are two main conditions for the spontaneous generation of an association. First, as the scale of market transactions

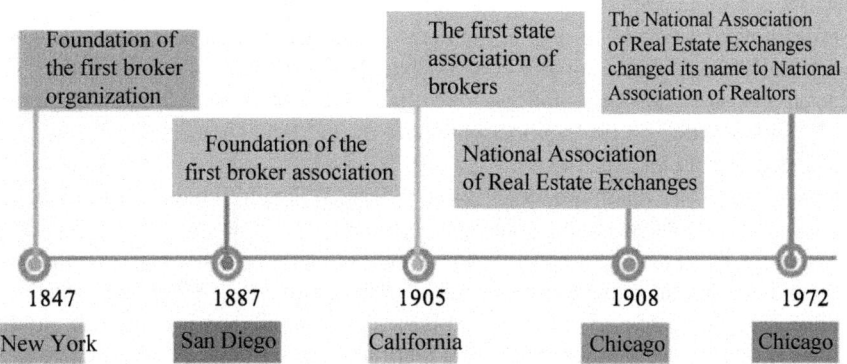

Fig. 3 Establishment process of NAR. *Source* Lianjia Research Institute

continues to expand, a large number of brokers enter into the industry. Second, as the transaction complexity continues to rise, more and more professional brokerage institutions are established. Based on needs of business exchange, disputes resolving and information-sharing, etc., these institutions started to have informal meetings frequently, which is the embryonic form of early industry associations. Under this background, the first American industry organization was established in New York in 1847. In 1887, the first brokerage association was founded in San Diego. As more and more regional associations were set up, a higher level self-disciplinary association was needed. In 1905, the first state association of brokers of USA was founded in California. In 1908, the first American real estate exchange association was set up in Chicago and was renamed the National Association of Realtors (NAR) in 1972 (Fig. 3).

In China's Taiwan, industry association was jointly founded by large brokerage institutions. In the late 1970s, high yields attracted a large number of small and medium companies to brokerage industry and caused severe problems such as irregular operation and vicious competition. To properly regulate the industry,, Chinese Taiwan Association of Real Estate Brokers was set up by 12 major real estate brokerage institutions in August 1981.

The Real Estate Companies Association of Japan was set up according to the *Real Estate Law* of 1952. The improvement and marketization of the association is mainly around introduction and management of REINS.

2.2.2 Different Organizational Structures and Responsibilities but Same Focus on Setting Standards, Executing Supervision, Educating and Training

The US industry associations operate on three levels, including a nationwide National Association of Realtors (NAR), 50 statewide associations of realtors, and 1800 regional associations of realtors. They are connected through a network, without a relationship of leading one another. Among the network, the National Association of Realtors (NAR) is the core. According to its organizational structure, the highest governing body is the board of directors, whose members are elected by state or regional associations. The Board of Directors consists of 14 departments, 36 professional committees and nine chapters, each bearing corresponding duties (Fig. 4).

There are three main functions. First is legal obligation, managing brokerage firms and brokers and offering services to them, which includes managing MLS system, checking compliance situation of standards of integrity, developing relevant regulations and rules, offering brokers services like education and information services, training courses, professional assessment, and public relations, etc. Second is the political function. Responsible for government lobbying among brokers, industry associations can affect government in terms of decision-making. Third is to influence legislation. According to a large number of first-hand information, when associations discover problems in the development of the industry they can report them and offer timely solutions, as well as promote effective rules of the industry to laws (Fig. 5).

Japan's industry association mainly includes the Association of Real Estate Agents of Japan (FRK), Association of Housing Exchanges, Association of Realtors of Japan and their affiliated subordinate local associations. FRK members are mainly large companies, while the other associations are mainly comprised of small companies. Among them, Association of Realtors of Japan was the earliest. It has the greatest number of members and is the most representative. According to its organizational structure, the highest governing body is the council, which consists of 11 committees such as special committee, rewarding committee, committee of laws and tax system, qualification examination committee, etc. All these committees have different responsibilities. Japan's industry association mainly plays a role of supporting management, which includes the following main functions: being a supporting institute of REINS (brokers and brokerage institutions can only be linked to REINS by joining in an association first); exchanges among members; collecting and publishing domestic and overseas information and research

Fig. 4 Organizational structure of National Association of Realtors. *Source* Lianjia Research Institute

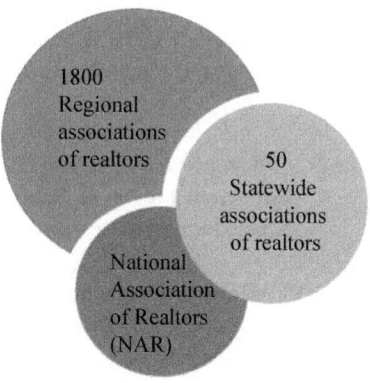

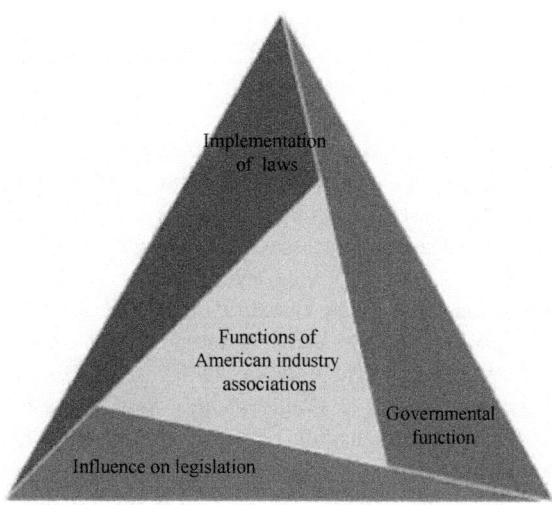

Fig. 5 Main functions of realtors' associations in the US. *Source* Lianjia Research Institute

achievement; training practitioners and publicizing knowledge among the public; holding meetings and conferences; supporting the weak and so on (Fig. 6).

Industry associations in China's Taiwan mainly include Chinese Association of Real Estate Brokers and its 20 subordinate branches in cities and towns. According to its organizational structure, the highest authority is representative congress,

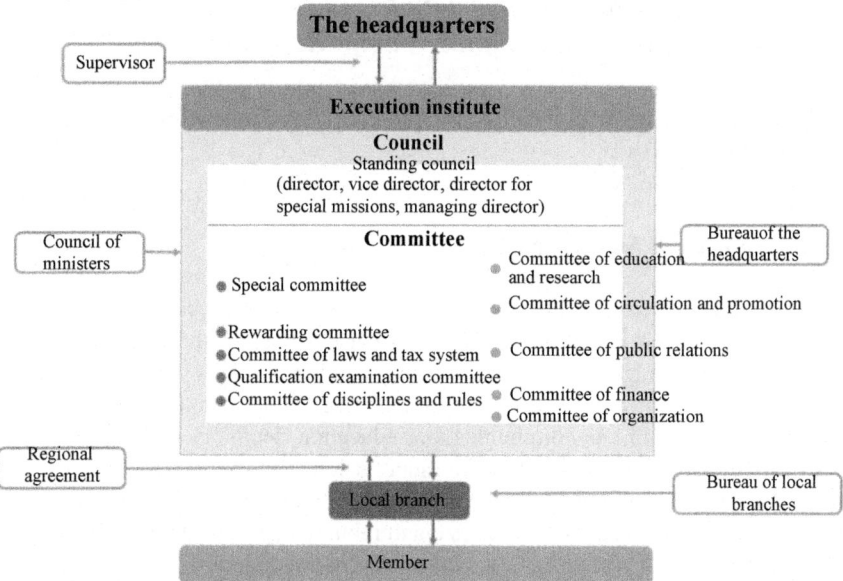

Fig. 6 Organizational structure of Japanese Real Estate Brokerage Associations. *Source* Lianjia Research Institute

which elects the council and the board of supervisors. The main governing body is the council, which consists of 7 committees (committee of long-term development, committee of laws, committee of education, committee of international affairs, committee of cross-strait affairs, committee of public welfare and committee of market information) for different responsibilities. The board of supervisors is responsible for supervision. General administrative matters are duties of the Secretary-General and other secretaries, officers and specialists.

Brokerage industry associations in China's Taiwan play a leading role in the management of industry with great power. According to 16 major functions set by *Constitution of Taiwan (China) brokerage industry associations*, its functions can be summarized into three aspects. First is legislation and law enforcement. The only special law of real estate brokerage industry in China's Taiwan is *Articles of Management of Real Estate Brokerage Industry*, which is not drafted by the managing departments, but by the industry association. Also, the organization and enforcement of the law is carried out by the head association and its subordinate associations. Second is supervision and punishment, like managing and supervising deposit of brokerage institutions, investigating and punishing brokers who violated laws and regulations and establishing code of conduct for brokers. Third is education and training, including organizing training and qualification examinations of practitioners and promoting exchanges within the industry and international communication and cooperation, etc.

2.3   China: Absence of Associations, Lack of Independent Management and Finance, Vague Responsibilities

At present, there are many regulatory problems in China's brokerage industry management (Fig. 7).

2.3.1   Absence of Association

In 2015, second-hand housing market in China reached nearly 4 trillion Yuan, which is expected to expand even further in the future. There are thousands of brokerage institutions and nearly a million brokers serving the industry but there isn't an industry self-discipline association. At present, the main function of industry self-discipline is communication, education, learning, research and other academic functions, the function of supervision and implementation is very weak. Based on the needs of the development of the industry and functions of the association, it is necessary to reorganize and rebuild a specialized association dedicated to the self-management of the real estate brokerage industry.

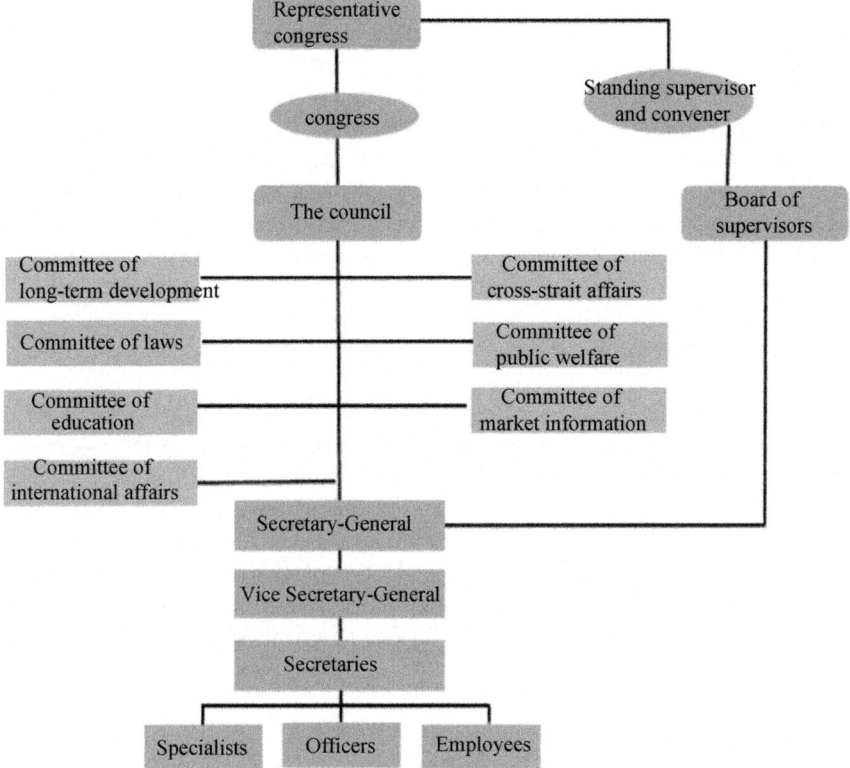

Fig. 7 Organizational structure of Association of Real Estate Brokers in China's Taiwan. *Source* collected by Lianjia Research Institute

2.3.2 Lack of Independent Management

According to the common practice of developed countries and regions, industry associations are self-regulatory organizations, which are independent in their functions and are not subordinate to any government units. Although the Chinese brokerage association has considerable self-regulatory authority, it does not have the independent right of management. The current China Real Estate Industry Association is basically under government supervision or guidance, which means that it is difficult for industry associations to play an independent self-regulatory role.

2.3.3 Lack of Independent Financial Rights

From the international experience, the industry association's income is independent, which mainly comes from the membership fee. Therefore, the income will mainly be used to serve the members. However, China's real estate industry association only has little income, mainly from government funding and donation, while the membership fee only takes up a small portion. Therefore, its financial rights cannot be independent. Due to financial difficulties, many of the authority of industry associations are limited, which means that the association can't play its management roles independently. Especially under the background that the industry is accelerating its pace of transformation, the pressure of industry regulation has become increasingly large. An association without financial and human resources can hardly be expected to establish a scientific and efficient governance mechanism.

2.3.4 Vague Responsibilities

What's more critical, laws and regulations haven't set a clear boundary of responsibilities for the government and the association. Although the association will assist the government with managing the industry, it hasn't obtained a clear management authority. Although industry regulations provide that the association can set norms on business management of brokers, detailed ways of implementation are not provided. Moreover, examination right, supervision right and punishment right for brokers and brokerage institutions, which are very critical to industry self-discipline, are all implemented by the government, severely weakening the management authority of the association.

3   Management Mechanism

An efficient management mechanism can help government and associations operate effectively and collaborate smoothly.

3.1 Role: An Efficient Mechanism for the Full Play of the Management Body

A management mechanism refers to the organizational structure and operational mechanism of management.

Management mechanism of real estate brokerage industry is divided into two levels. The first level refers to management mechanisms of the government, associations and enterprises. Take associations as an example, the management mechanism includes organizational structure and operational mechanism of associations at all levels such as classification of associations and institutional settings of each level, relationship of associations at all levels (whether it is a superior-subordinate relationship or a parallel network), how to cooperate with the government to develop industry policy, and how to deal with customer complaints, etc. Second level is the management mechanism among the government, associations and enterprises, such as institutional and mechanism settings of docking between the government and associations, and associations and enterprises, authorized functions of associations by the government, and arrangement of related institutions, supervision and reporting mechanisms and etc.

Industry management mechanism is important because it clarifies the division of roles of the government, associations and enterprises. Forming a management mechanism is based on laws and industry self-discipline, but laws and industry self-discipline could not play their roles effectively without a highly efficient management mechanism. If laws are considered as "skeleton", industry self-discipline the "muscle", then management mechanism is like the "nervous system" which commands and coordinates "skeleton" and "muscle". Only under coordination and command of a sound "nervous system" can "skeleton" and "muscle" exert their power.

3.2   International Experience: "Small Government, Big Association" Being the Best Practice

US real estate brokerage management mechanism is a typical "small government, big association" pattern, which is easier to promote collaboration and mutual support between the government and associations. The mechanism of China's Taiwan is a typical association-dominating pattern, in which the government only executes limited and indirect management. In Japan and China's Hong Kong, the government takes charge of the main part, while associations can only play a minor role.

3.2.1   The US Model: Big Association, Small Government

The US implements a management mechanism that the government and industry self-discipline are in parallel. The state government sets real estate commissions or real estate bureaus to manage real estate brokerage institutions and brokers. Based on the *Real Estate Licensing and Registration Act of USA*, the commissions and bureaus are mainly responsible for implementing laws of real estate brokerage and executing duties under the authority of the law, which mainly includes real estate brokerage qualifications access, management rulemaking, inspection penalties, complaint handling of real estate transactions from customers, review of licensing examination and etc.

Industry associations play a more important role in practice. They are stronger in terms of the degree and extent of managing real estate brokerage than the government and play a more direct role in promoting the standardization and progress of the industry. Therefore, the management mechanism of American real estate brokerage industry is a pattern of "big association, small government" (Fig. 8).

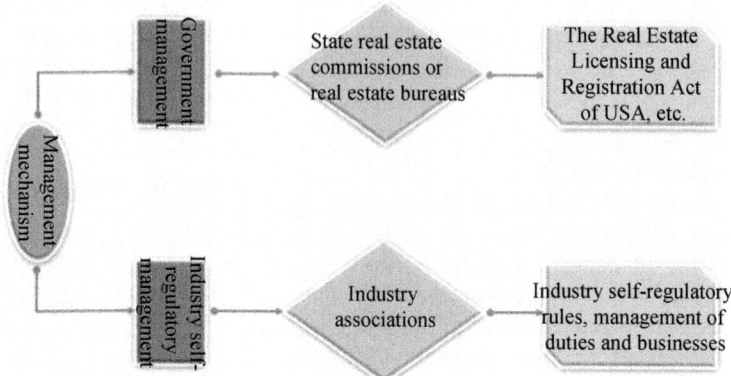

Fig. 8 US brokerage management mechanism. *Source* Lianjia Research Institute

3.2.2 Japanese Pattern: Law First, Government-Leading and Association-Subordinating

In 1952, when the real estate brokerage industry just emerged, Japan enacted a special law of the industry, the *Real Estate Law*, and thereafter continuously refined and improved it. Government plays a leading role in management of the industry under the direction and authority of relevant laws. Mainly executed by Ministry of Land, Infrastructure, Transport and Tourism, specific government duties include three aspects. First is implementation of the law including issuing decrees and supervising the industry. Second is management and supervision of information, which includes to managing the information-sharing and distribution system of real estate brokerage industry REINS through specific circulation institutions and supervising the truth of information by setting Fairy Competition Commission of Real Estate Industry. Third is management of licenses. Local governors are responsible for examining qualifications of real estate brokers and minister of Ministry of Land, Infrastructure, Transport and Tourism shall examine licenses of real estate brokerage institutions with no defined operating areas. The major function of industry associations is to assist the government management with duties including training, education and international communications and etc.

3.2.3 Pattern of China's Taiwan: Government Authorization, Association Leading

In China's Taiwan, government manages the industry in an indirect way with limited authority. The market access is fully liberalized, which means that companies do not have to meet any special requirements of setting up, and no direct supervision and inspection are set on operation of business activities. The main functions of industry management lie in the industry association, including license

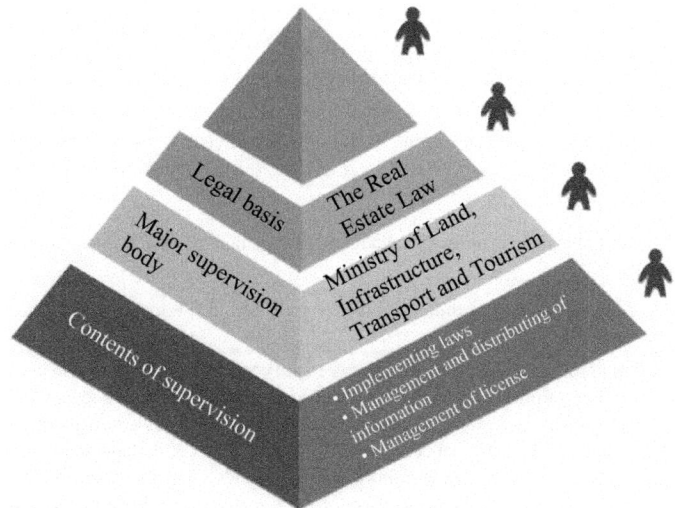

Fig. 9 Japanese brokerage management mechanism. *Source* Lianjia Research Institute

management, deposit management and etc. Under this pattern, associations not only need to execute self-management, but also need to help the government carry out direct supervision of the industry (Fig. 9).

3.2.4 Pattern of China's Hong Kong: Strong Administration, Weak Associations

Industry associations in China's Hong Kong play a minor role, mainly covering academic exchanges, education and training, performance evaluation and so on. Based on *Real Estate Agent Articles*, in November 1997, Hong Kong established the Estate Agents Authority as the regulatory authority of the real estate brokerage industry. Its members are appointed by the Chief Executive of the SAR, with a chairman, a vice-chairman and not-more-than-18 ordinary members. All members of the Authority and employees of administrative departments are considered as public servants. In the form of commission, Estate Agents Authority manages the brokerage industry in terms of industry access, statute, complaints, education, rewarding and punishment, etc.

3.3 China: Irrational Management Mechanism

International experience shows that orderly and standardized operation of the brokerage industry relies on effective integration of government administration and industry self-discipline. The key is to make a clear definition of power boundary between the government and industry associations (Table 1).

Managing authorities face a large and complex market with new problems emerging every day. When they are understaffed, it is challenging for them to cope with everything in detail or treat every case on time. It is not possible for

Table 1 Real estate brokerage industry management mechanism of US, Japan, China's Taiwan and Hong Kong

Region/ Country	Management mechanism	Functions of the government	Functions of associations
The US	Big association, small government	Government is mainly in charge of law making, and establishing duties of supervision and complaints. Associations promote other specific work	Government lobbying, to influence legislation, to develop industry guidelines and standards of integrity, management of MLS system, to check the implementation of standards of integrity and to implement punishment; to issue broker's licenses; to set regulatory rules and regulations; to provide services, including education, information, training, evaluation, as well as a large number of public relations work, etc.
Japan	Government leading and association subordinating	Legislation, law enforcement, supervisory control REINS, licensing, broker examination, punishment on false information, etc.	Deposit, research, information collection and publishing, workshops guidance, knowledge publicizing, conference and forums, support for the weak, exchanges among members, etc.
Taiwan	Government authorizing, association leading	Implementing indirect supervision by the law. Associations manage other duties	Drafting of laws, industry rules, agreements, deposit management, examinations arrangement, training, communication, licenses issuing, rewarding and punishing, etc.
HongKong	Strong administration weak associations	Regulation, statute, practice norms, execution, examination, education, licenses, rewards and punishments, review and etc.	Exchanges, meetings, training, etc.

Source Lianjia Research Institute

government officials to respond quickly to problems because there are considerations and coordination involved. As a result, conducts that violate or harm the industry cannot be quickly stopped.

At present, the main functions of China's industry self-discipline include organizing research and communication, setting and implementing standards of practice and rules, helping administrative authority organize and implement qualification examinations; applying for qualification registration; business training, continuing education; establishing credit files of brokerage institutions and conducting credit evaluation; providing related advice and technical support services; organizing international exchange activities; reflecting the views, suggestions and requests of members, supporting members practicing law, safeguarding the legitimate rights and interests of members and so on. Many functions are similar with that of advanced countries and regions. However, the problem is that many critical functions such as the implementation of practice guidelines and setting credit files, which are direct management ways for brokerage institutions and brokers, do not have legal protection. Unlike practice in some advanced countries, laws and regulations in China do not authorize associations with rights of inspection and standardization, supervising standards of integrity and punishing illegal conducts.

4 Summary and Suggestions

In the supervision system of the industry, legal constraint, industry self-discipline and management mechanism are three aspects with distinctive roles, which can't be replaced by one another. The three aspects can play the fullest roles by carrying out their duties respectively, supplementing and supporting one another.

To this end, we propose the following suggestions.

4.1 Constructing a Comprehensive System of Industry Laws and Regulations

A sound legal system needs to be established, modifying laws and forming upper-level legislation, i.e., *Real Estate Brokerage Administration Law*. Administrative laws and regulations related with real estate brokerage industry include *Provisions on the Administration of Urban Real Estate Intermediary Services, Implementation Measures for the Professional Eligibility Examination for Real Estate Brokers* and *Administrative Measures for Real Estate Brokers*. These laws and regulations need to be sorted comprehensively, deleting unnecessary contents and adding new provisions based on development characteristics of the industry and international experiences to form upper-level legislation, *Real Estate Brokerage Administration Law* and then apply for deliberation of the Standing Committee of the National People's Congress.

The new *Real Estate Brokerage Administration Law* should include the following aspects.

Content: Reconstructing a basic legal system requiring "agent, high entry, quality upgrading, strict punishment and proper protection" to establish the legal cornerstone of the brokerage industry management. The laws and regulations related to real estate brokerage industry need to be sorted comprehensively, deleting unnecessary contents and adding new provisions based on development characteristics of the industry and international experiences to form a comprehensive, systematic and unified system of regulations and rules. Five basic legal systems including basic relation between brokers and customers, industry entry, broker practice standards, complaints and penalty mechanism and broker practice protection should be especially emphasized when reconstructing the legal system. In terms of specific provisions, international experience should be combined with China's reality, so that provisions could be specific, detailed and workable.

Scope: Laws and regulations should cover the entire real estate brokerage serving area, including traditional brokerage institutions involved in real estate transactions, agencies, Internet companies, third-party payment, banks and insurance companies. In accordance with the trading process, a comprehensive supervision regime should be established, which should especially strengthen the supervision on non-traditional intermediaries of housing transactions like Internet companies.

Management: The reality of multiple party management and lack of unified standards needs to be changed by streamlining industry management relations and implementing unified management mechanism. At present, in China, there isn't a specific unit or department authorized by law to lead real estate brokerage industry, leading to multiple management and lack of unified standards. According to international experience, effective implementation of the laws and regulations of the brokerage industry depends on the establishment of a relatively unified management body. On one hand, it can greatly enhance the efficiency of management as many industry issues can be solved without coordination among different departments. On the other hand, it can effectively conduct evaluation and supervision. This is the way for the government to manage the industry effectively.

Implementation: Authorities, such as MOHURD (Ministry of Housing and Urban-Rural Department of the People's Republic of China) can set departments of complaints and department of dispute-processing and set a unified national complaint hotline to timely detect illegal or irregular problems of the industry. Problems will then be handed over to the subordinate departments or industry associations or brokerage institutions accordingly. For problems within its own jurisdiction, administrative penalties could be given directly. In practice, relevant laws and regulations should be constantly adjusted, refined and revised to gradually promote the industry standardization.

4.2 Establishing Industry Associations and Improving Their Functions

The brokerage industry should be singled out from existing associations, reconstructing and reorganizing specialized brokerage industry associations for brokerage industry. Learning from the system that "employees must be part of a related enterprise and enterprises must be part of a related association" of the USA and China's Taiwan, it can be required that real estate brokers join in a brokerage institution to conduct business and brokerage institutions must join in the association and accept self-regulatory management of industry associations. In terms of setting levels, reasonable levels and the division of functions can be established based on industrial needs, professional needs, development needs and revolution needs to gradually form a system of real estate broker association with three levels (national, provincial, city and county levels). In terms of organizational functions, international experience could be learned and then combined with real management and business needs to identify the internal functions of associations. Professional work would be dealt with through a special panel.

Enriching the functions of industry associations can be mainly reflected in three aspects.

First is to grant power to associations through laws. The revised *Real Estate Brokerage Administration Law* directly divides roles of government and associations in terms of industry management, so that industry associations may have legal legitimacy, legality and rationality.

Second is to establish a restraint mechanism of industry associations for brokers and brokerage institutions. Three basic systems need to be established. First is the entry mechanism for brokerage institutions. It's essential to enhance the industry entry threshold, using strict license management or deposit system to ensure professionalism, appropriateness, reliability and effectiveness of responsibility of brokerage institutions. Second is the broker qualification exam. According to development of the industry and professional practical needs, the industry association should determine the contents of the examination and report it to the government to set it as a fixed examination system. The examination system is run by the industry association and its affiliated associations. Third is the control of critical nodes of the practice. Codes of conduct for practitioners which are practical, detailed, normative, operational and easy to supervise should be established.

Third is to give full play to industry associations in terms of self-monitoring, self-management and self-regulation and to grant associations with punishment rights to illegal conducts. Industry associations should be granted by laws to establish mechanisms for complaints, disputes and settlements. For example, brokerage institutions that break rules can be fined and even cancelled the membership, while brokers who break rules can lose qualifications, be fined or cleared out of the industry or suspended. It's very important because without strict implementation of effective supervision, timely and effective punishment, all regulations will be useless and powerless.

4.3   Promoting a Mechanism of "Small Government, Big Association"

The pattern of "small government, big association" fits the management situation of China's real estate industry due to the following reasons. According to international experience, compared with patterns in Japan and China's Hong Kong, the pattern of "small government, big association" in the US and China's Taiwan exerts much higher efficiency. Second, according to China's reality, relevant government departments have to deal with many businesses with a small number of staff. Because they are not professionals in this industry, it is a great challenge for them to manage such a large number of institutions and practitioners. Third, against the backdrop of central government's requirement of streamlining administration and delegating power, the pattern of "small government, big association" fits the trends of administrative reform in China.

Government will still be present even though its functions become fewer and limited. It should follow the principle of "*do what it should, and don't do what it should not*". "*Do what it should*" means that the government should conduct the top-level design well. "*Don't do what it should not*" means that by streamlining administration and delegating power, the government should grant more power to associations to promote the industry development in terms of self-management, self-serving and self-improvement.

Chapter 7
Professional Brokers

- The basic meaning of professionalism is the ability and quality of using specialized knowledge to transform resources into results.
- Low professionalism in China's brokerage industry is caused by the absence of industry entry regulation, lack of protection of the exclusive right of information, and lack of a cooperation mechanism, together with the unscientific commission allocation system and the transaction-oriented rather than customer-oriented incentive mechanism.
- A "triple entry system" and a "five key link control system" have been implemented in developed countries such as the US and Japan. Brokers' professionalism is enhanced through strict entry and whole life cycle control.

Professional brokers are the core pillar to the healthy development of the brokerage industry. With the expansion of the house stock market in China, it is expected that there will be more than one million full-time brokers to serve the country's 250 million urban households and 150 trillion RMB of housing assets. The call for the brokers' professionalism is more urgent today than ever before.

Compared with successful international mainstream market, China should learn and speed up its brokers' professionalization. Measures include setting the bottom line from the system level, establishing and improving the broker industry entry and prohibition mechanism, providing a favorable career-long learning system, and constantly improving brokers' professionalism and morality. Once brokers' self images and social recognitions are well established, brokerage will become a well-respected profession worthy of lifelong pursuit.

© Xiamen University Press and Springer Nature Singapore Pte Ltd. 2018   149
S. Ba and X. Yang, *The Rise of New Brokerages and the Restructuring of Real Estate Value Chain*, https://doi.org/10.1007/978-981-10-7715-9_7

1   The Definition, Connotation and Importance of Brokers' Professionalization

Professionalism is essentially a kind of ability and quality. It can be measured from six aspects, including professional qualification, ethical conduct, image and disposition, self-recognition, industrial recognition, and social recognition.

1.1   Definition and Connotation

Professionalism refers to the ability and quality of using professional knowledge to transfer resources into results.

In terms of connotation, professionalism = professionalization + value recognition.

Professionalization contains three aspects:

A. Professional qualification, such as qualification review, qualification examination, license, certificate, permission, follow-up education etc.

B. Ethical conduct, such as code of conduct, integrity and ethics.

C. Image and disposition, including external appearances such as dress, hairstyle and logo as well as manners and temperaments.

Value recognition also contains three aspects:

A. Self-recognition, referring to the broker's approval of work, measurable through one's sense of accomplishment, honor and self-realization.

B. Professional recognition, referring to the broker's recognition of brokerage industry, which can be measured by a sense of professional belonging.

C. Social recognition, referring to the social recognition of brokers and the brokerage industry, which can be measured by the general impression, reputation and respect for the profession.

1.2   The Necessity for Professionalism

Lack of professionalism is one of the root causes of the chaos of the real estate brokerage industry, which harms customer's interest, brokers' career development and the management of the brokerage institutes.

1.2.1   Low Consumer Experience Caused by Low Professionalism

Low-level professionals directly victimize consumers. Painful experiences include endless harassment calls, false housing information all over the Internet, being tricked into signing contract or buying a problematic house. Due to the lack of proper broker supervision, victimized customers do not have a channel to complain or claim compensation. Trust between home buyers and brokers is further damaged by exaggerated accounts of bad intermediary agents, leading to poor consumer experience as one has to be vigilant and worried at all times.

1.2.2 Brokers' Low Sense of Accomplishments

The main population of the brokers engaged in China's real estate brokerage industry age in their twenties. Experienced brokers do not stay long as it is hard for them to develop a sense of belonging while working in an unfriendly environment. The dilemma is further complicated because low professionalization does little good to winning social respect.

For a long time, China's real estate brokerage industry lacks the necessary entry restrictions, leading to the existence of unprofessional and unethical dealings, such as false information, false promises, deliberate deception, secret contract, and violent battling for housing resources and customer resources. While both buyers and sellers suffer from these frequent misconducts, the image of the industry is greatly harmed. Brokers cannot win social respect and recognition and qualified and respectable people are not attracted to join in the industry.

In contrast, brokers are highly professionalized in the United States, where realtors enjoy the same status as lawyers and dentists and are widely respected by the community. This explains why brokerage is a lifelong career in the US.

1.2.3 Hindering Enterprise and Industry Development

In general, an employee's work value = personal ability × degree of professionalism. For enterprises, the professionalism can effectively improve employees' work value.

The level of professionalism is closely related to the development of a company, because low quality staff will lead to increased management and communication costs, and problems will accelerate with the growth of the number of brokers, which will be a barrier to the sustainable development of the company. In recent years, some brokerage companies have taken the lead in the internal reform; the level of professionalism has been enhanced from various aspects such as the employment criteria, vocational training, system construction, and corporate culture. Such reform has helped enterprises to lay a good foundation for expansion. Taking the whole industry in view, its overall professionalism is still low and not favorable to the establishment and development of brokerage companies with a scale economy.

Only by constantly improving professionalism in the brokerage industry can practitioners' knowledge, skills, concepts, thoughts, attitudes, mentality and ethics reach a higher level and more secure and efficient transactions be made possible that deliver quality consumer experience. Only in this way can the brokerage industry take off the reputation of bad intermediary agent and gain a standardized and healthy development.

2 Status Quo and Problems of Broker Professionalization

Under the present institutional mechanism, it is difficult for China's brokerage industry to achieve professionalization as advanced as that of the United States and Japan.

2.1 The Status Quo in China

Compared with the United States, China's real estate brokerage industry has a lower degree of professionalism. The main population of the brokers engaged in China's real estate brokerage industry age in their twenties. The entry bar is set low and accumulation of work experience is not encouraged. The professional recognition is low and its social reputation is poor (Fig. 1).

2.1.1 Low Level of Education

The majority of American brokers hold a university bachelor's or master's degree while their counterparts in China are mostly graduates from high school, secondary or tertiary technical colleges. Statistically speaking, more than 61% American

Fig. 1 Connotation of professionalism *Source* Lianjia Research Institute

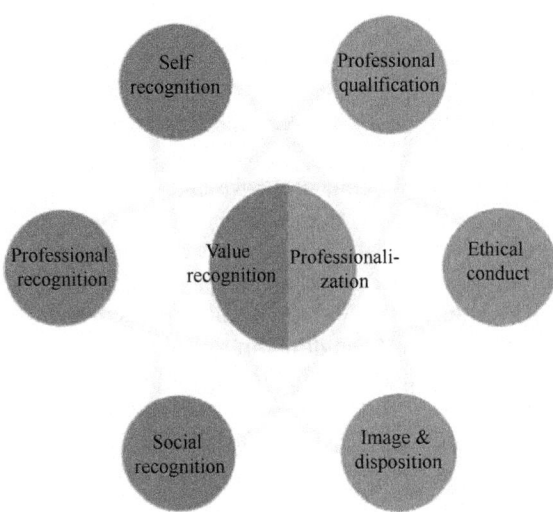

brokers hold a bachelor's or a higher degree while in China the number is only 15.07%. About 20% American brokers hold a master's degree, while the number is 0.07% in China. It is obvious that brokerage has successfully attracted many high quality talents in the US while it has failed to do the same in China. Figure 2 provides a comparison of the distribution of degree holders among brokers in China and the US. Figure 3 provides the distribution of education level of Chinese brokers' with more than 10 years' work experience.

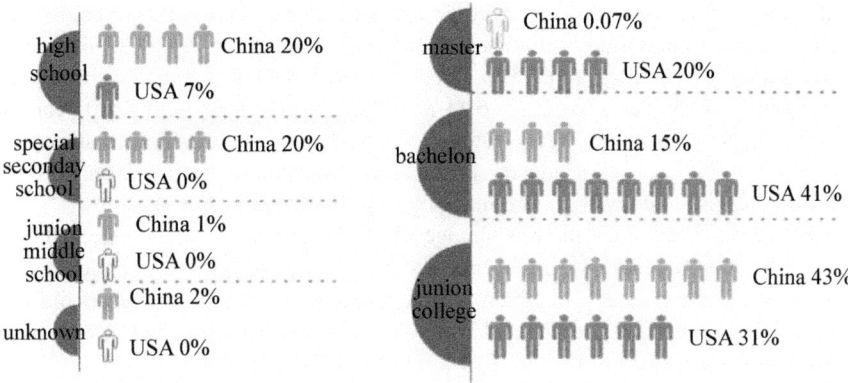

Fig. 2 Distribution of Chinese and American brokers' education background *Source* Survey of a Chinese Agency, NAR and Lianjia Research Institute

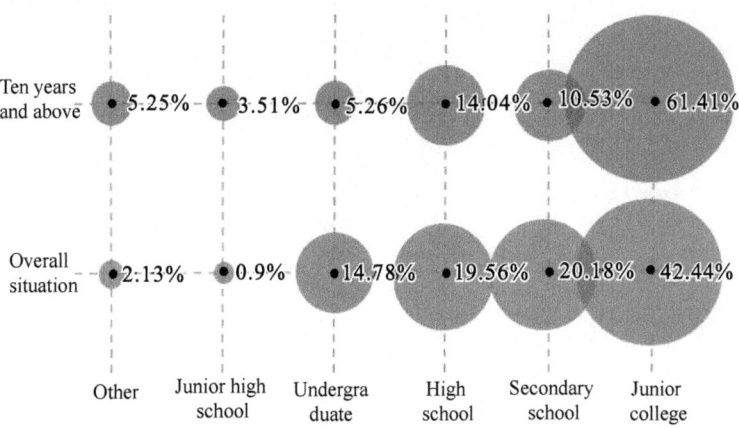

Fig. 3 Distribution of China's brokers' education background with more than 10 years' experience in brokerage industry *Source* Survey of a Chinese Agency, Lianjia Research Institute

2.1.2 High Employee Loss Rate

The number of American brokers who have worked in brokerage for 14 years or more accounts for 40.6% of the total, among whom more than 4% have worked in brokerage for more than 40 years. In China, 67.67% of brokers are under 30. It is almost impossible to find a broker who has worked over 12 years in China. The average service time for American brokers is 12 years, while it is less than 2 years in China.

Brokers in the US have accumulated rich working experience, while it is virtually impossible for China's brokerage industry tokeep experienced agents. The claim is further supported by two sets of data. First, retention rate of China's new brokers after a year is less than 30%. Second, brokers with 6–8 years' of brokerage experience in China accounted for 6.61 and 3.22% for brokers with 8–10 years of working experience in brokerage market, which may mean that more than half of the brokers will leave the industry in the next few years even if they have been working in this industry for more than 6 years, as shown in Fig. 4.

The survey shows that the median age of US brokers is 57 years old. 37.8% of them are over 60 years old, taking the highest proportion. 77% brokers treat brokerage as a lifetime career. In China, the median age of brokers is 28 years old. Up to 67.67% are under 30. Less than 4% are over 43. Few people regard brokerage as a lifetime career (Figs. 5, 6, 7, 8, 9, 10, 11, 12, 13, 14, 15).

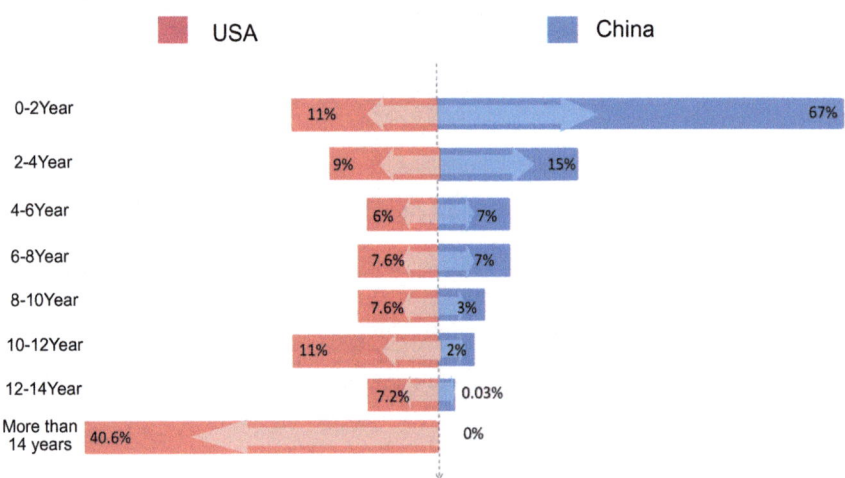

Fig. 4 Comparison of service years between Chinese and American brokers *Source* Survey of a Chinese Agency, NAR and Lianjia Research Institute

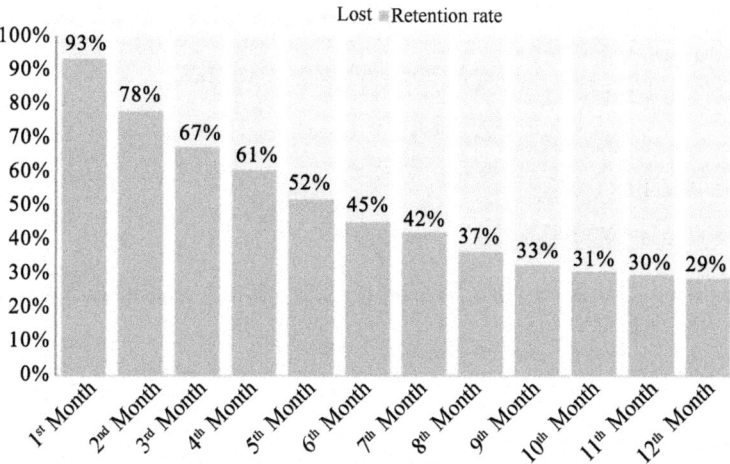

Fig. 5 Chinese brokers retained in the industry within one year *Source* Survey of a Chinese Agency, NAR and Lianjia Research Institute

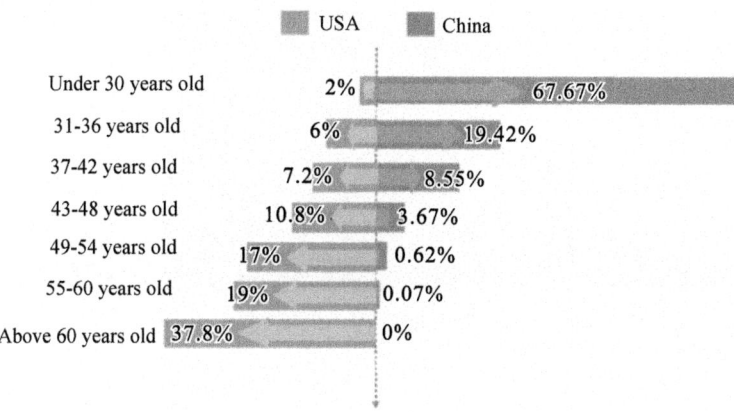

Fig. 6 Age distribution of brokers in China and the US *Source* Survey of a Chinese Agency, NAR and Lianjia Research Institute

2.1.3 Low Industry Recognition

In the United States, only 5% of the brokers entered brokerage as their first job. The vast majorities joined the profession halfway through their career. About 19% of them had a job in management, business, or finance related occupations prior to entering brokerage. About 6% worked in education, 3% in computer or math and 2% in the legal industry. It proves that both individual and social recognition of the occupation in the US is high. Brokerage has a competitive edge in the market against demanding professions in management, business, finance, law or computer.

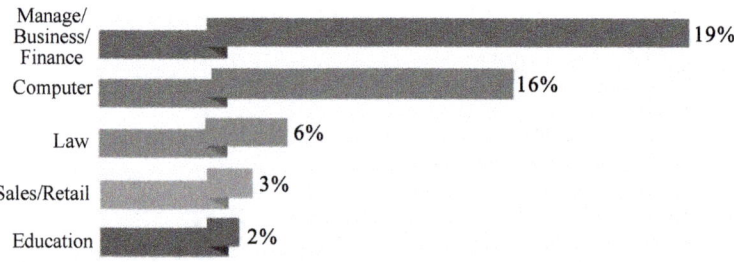

Fig. 7 Previous full-time job of brokers in the US *Source* NAR; Lianjia Research Institute

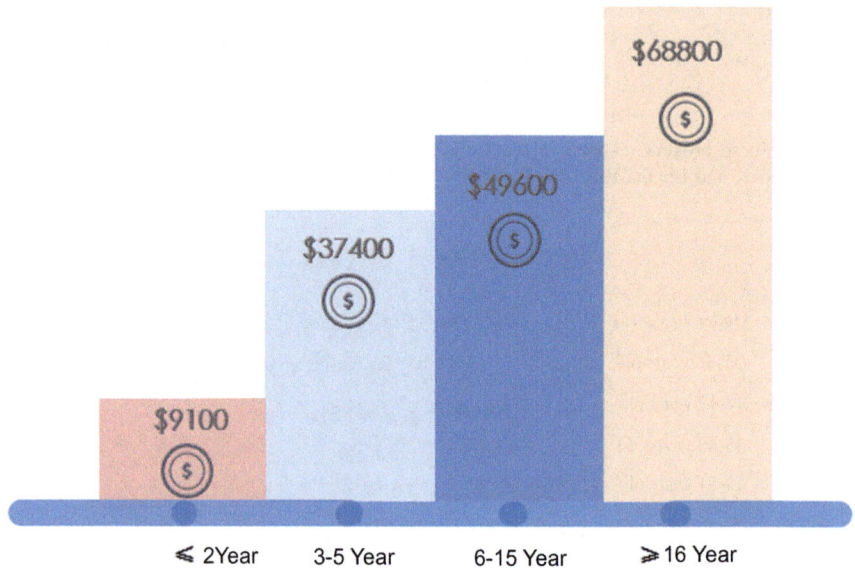

Fig. 8 US brokers' service years and median income *Source* NAR, Lianjia Research Institute

In China, the majority of brokers had brokerage as their very first job, mostly under the pressure of making a living. Those who transferred to the real estate business are usually from non-competitive and low profile occupations. Many would run away after they have accumulated certain experience and capital. Low individual and social recognition remains the biggest challenge for brokerage industry in China.

2.1.4   Wage Growth not in Pace with Experience

American brokers enjoy higher salaries for longer service years. They can expect higher pay through accumulating effective work experience.

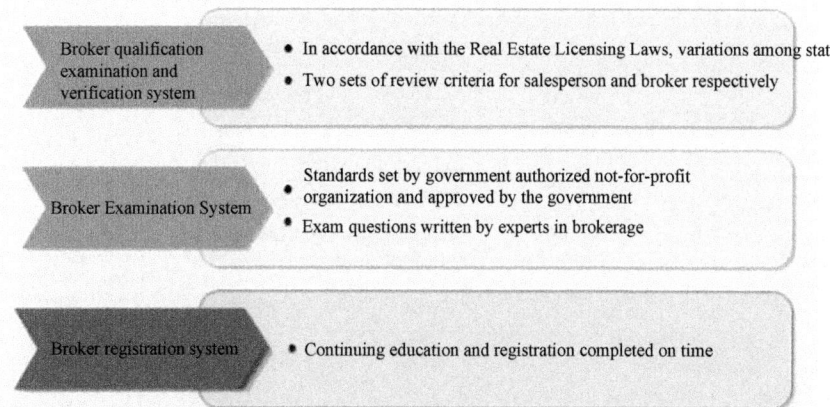

Fig. 9 US Triple entry mechanism *Source* NAR, Lianjia Research Institute

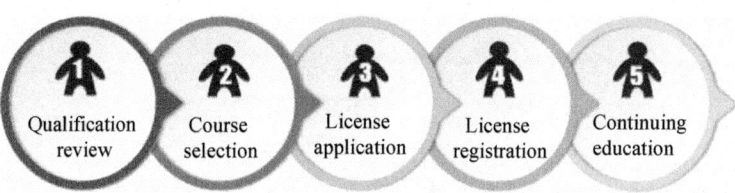

Fig. 10 Five key link control *Source* NAR, Lianjia Research Institute

In China, most brokers stay around 0–2 years. There is little correlation between one's salary and the number of service years after one has stayed in brokerage for more than two years. Real estate brokerage favors young people. Accumulation of experience does not lead to one's competitiveness.

2.2 Roots of the Problems

The following section provides explanations on low professionalism among brokers in China.

2.2.1 Absence of an Industry Entry Regulation

It is stipulated in China's *Administrative Measures for Real Estate Brokers* (1995) and *Provisions on the Administration of Urban Real Estate Intermediary Services*

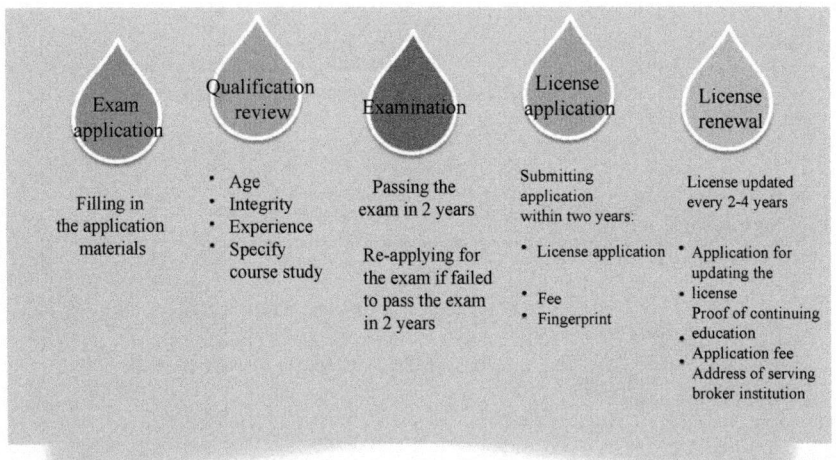

Fig. 11 The process of obtaining realtors' license in the US *Source* NAR, Lianjia Research Institute

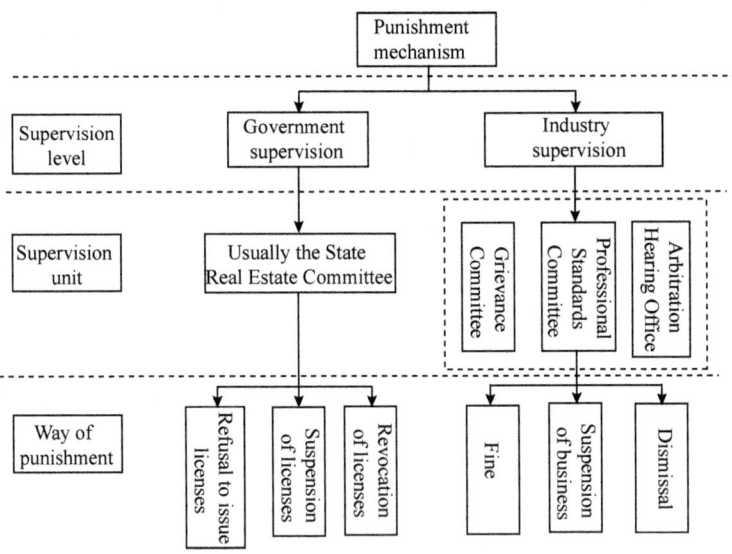

Fig. 12 US broker penalty management chart *Source* NAR, Lianjia Research Institute

(1996) that brokers must pass examinations and obtain a qualification certificate before they engage in real estate brokerage business.

In reality, supervision for China's real estate brokerage industry entry does not exist. Certain requirements on broker's qualification, examination, license or

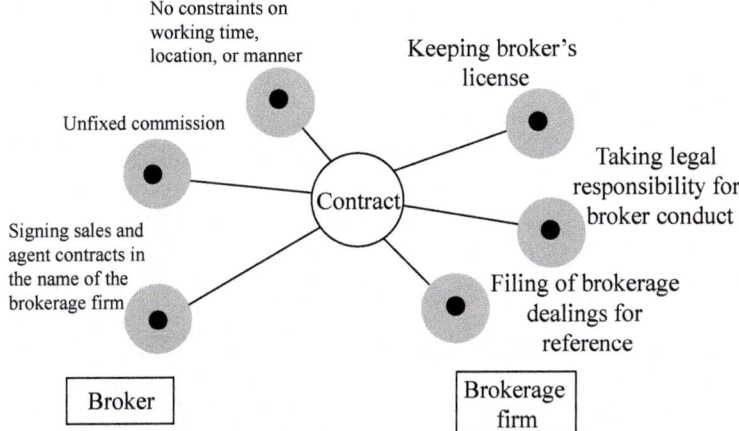

Fig. 13 Relationship between brokerage firms and brokers *Source* Lianjia Research Institute

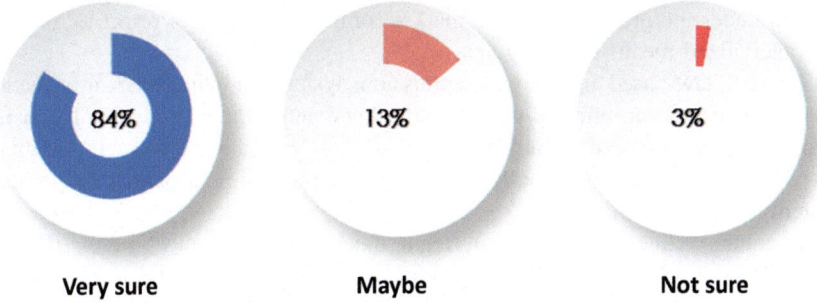

Fig. 14 Survey results on "whether continue to stay in the real estate industry in the next two years" *Source* NAR, Lianjia Research Institute

permission are not strictly followed. Practical and realistic code of conduct or ethical standards is not yet available. There is not a way to guarantee that the broker has the basic professional quality, nor a way to discipline brokers through cancellation of licenses. The lack of entry regulations and effective supervision and implementation mechanism has turned China's brokerage into a free entrance profession. This is one of the causes of chaos in China's brokerage industry.

2.2.2   Lack of Information Protection

Information protection has long been neglected in brokerage as there isn't a protection mechanism for keeping exclusive right of home sources and client sources.

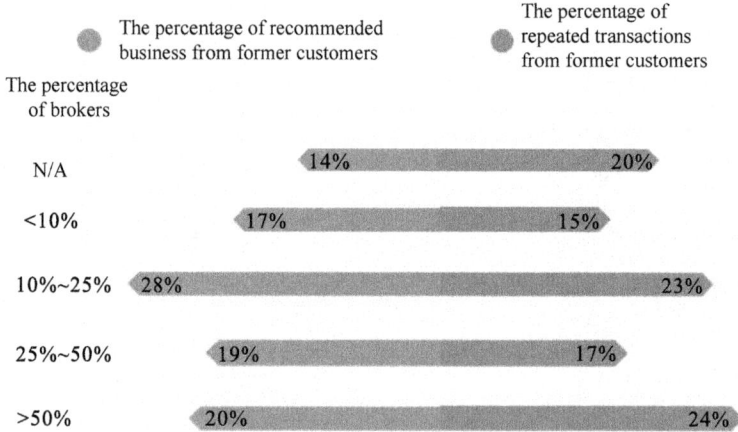

Fig. 15 Percentage of repeated transactions and recommended business by past consumer/clients
Source NAR; Lianjia Research Institute

Pushed under the pressure of fierce market competition, brokers resort to immoral and uncivilized means to seek gains.

The US law-based exclusive commission system and the MLS information sharing platform can effectively protect brokers' intellectual property of housing information. Brokers are willing to disclose for they get paid according to an agreed proportion no matter who finally settles the dealing. Thus, a broker cooperation system is put in place.

In contrast, due to the lack of legal mechanism of protection on housing information in China, in order to obtain housing information and to prevent the deception of information by other brokerage firms and brokers, the brokers are forced to either hide the housing information or provide false information, thus generating a large amount of false information, which greatly hinders the broker's professional development.

2.2.3 Lack of a Cooperation Mechanism

The game rules established by US MLS have oriented brokers to cooperation since it brings greater earnings than competition does. But in China, all transactions are based on competition. There is no cooperation between companies. Since there isn't a cooperation commission division mechanism, only the final transaction can bring brokers any profit. Without effective cooperation, there is no professional division of labor and efficient teamwork. It is also impossible for brokers to accumulate professional knowledge and experience.

2.2.4   Lack of a Scientific Commission Division Mechanism

With the same commission rate, the commission division mechanism to a certain extent determines the broker's income and the broker's value orientation. The level of income also directly affects the broker's degree of professionalism. The higher the wages, the higher value of the broker's recognition of the work will be, and the more satisfaction and sense of accomplishment will be got from the job. In return, when more and more talented people are attracted to enter the profession, the level of expertise and moral standards of the industry will be enhanced.

In the United States, the relationship between brokers and brokerage firms is based on an equal contract system instead of employment. Brokerage firms and brokers divide the commission in accordance with the agreed proportion of brokers' commission ratio to be up to 70–80%. Brokers are not required to pay from the commission to the company apart from a fixed fee and venue fee. In China, the relationship between brokers and brokerage firms is employment. For a long time, the broker's commission rate remains lower than half that of the US, and a broker's salary is low and unstable. Substantial increase in brokers' commission ratio and design of the sharing mechanism based on cooperation and experience is beneficial in reducing staff turnover rate and improving staff quality. This has been testified effective in related enterprise practice.

2.2.5   Transaction-Oriented Rather Than Customer-Oriented

In the United States, the broker's commission rate is fixed. Most states require brokers not to provide rebates to customers, forcing the brokers to win customers through the service competition rather than price competition. In China, the brokerage industry commission rate is as low as 0.5–3%. The commission rate can be negotiable within the same brokerage firm. Brokers often make commission return promises to customers. Inter-firm, inter-broker competition is based on price, which not only harms the broker's income level, but also damages the customer's service experience. When customers seek a lower commission rate, brokers may turn to unethical conducts. When the brokerage industry has long been caught in the quagmire of price competition, it is difficult to guide the industry evolution from transaction-oriented price level to the customer-oriented service level.

3   International Experience of Broker Professionalization

Brokers' professionalism in the United States, Japan, China's Taiwan and Hong Kong is generally high. In terms of specialization, all countries and regions are trying to enhance the broker's professionalism through means such as strict entry mechanism and the whole life cycle control mechanism. The promotion of professional quality naturally increases the broker's "value recognition". As for the mature market, the broker's self-recognition, industry recognition and social recognition are also high.

3.1 International Experience of Broker Specialization

Specialization is the basis of professionalism. In the United States, Japan, China's Taiwan and Hong Kong, brokers' professionalism are obtained through a series of entry and process control including professional course learning, strict examination system, and continuing education.

3.1.1 Strict Entry and Full cycle Control

The entry system and supervision system in the United States, Japan, China's Taiwan and Hong Kong are quite similar with certain differences in details.

In the United States, a broker's journey from qualification application to acquiring business permission is regulated by "triple qualification entry" and "five key link control".

"Triple qualification entry" means that:

First, applicants who do not meet the requirements of age, education, integrity, experience and necessary courses cannot pass the real estate brokerage qualification examination.

Second, candidates who fail to pass the real estate broker qualification examination will not be issued with real estate brokerage license.

Third, licensed brokers must first sign up with a brokerage institution and attend the internship work for a period of time before getting the registration permission from the certificate issuing department.

"Five key link control" refers to:

First, applicants' qualification review should be strictly carried out.

Second, courses in preparation for real estate brokerage exam should be carefully selected and learning outcome supervised.

Third, after passing the real estate broker qualification examination, the candidate has to pass the qualification review before the license can be issued. If candidates do not apply in time, the exam result expires in one year. If the review result is negative, the candidate is forbidden to get a license in two years and must apply again and go through the whole process a second time.

Fourth, the brokerage license is valid only after registration. The broker's license needs be regularly updated. If not, the license will be cancelled automatically and the broker should stop business immediately.

Fifth, licensed brokers are required to participate in continuing education. If they fail in continuing education, they can still lose their licenses.

Japan's entry mechanism is relatively loose. Its major legal constraint is on *real estate notary*, requiring a minimum of 20% of the staff holding the qualification and the brokerage firm can review ordinary brokers' qualification.

In China's Hong Kong and Taiwan, brokerage entry administration is similar to that of the US, but it is relatively lenient in the registration process. After passing the exam, the broker can obtain a broker's license. In Hong Kong eligibility criteria are set to review candidates' financial stability and mental stability. Whether candidates have filed bankruptcy will also be informed during entry application.

The key link control on brokers in the United States, Japan, and China's Hong Kong and Taiwan include:

- **The first link control: qualification review**

Real estate broker qualification examination system is required by the *Real Estate Licensing Laws*. Although the provisions are different among states, the differences are small. All states require that applicants reach the required legal age and education without any records of misconducts. The moral census is strict. Candidates with a criminal record or other record of misconducts are prohibited to participate in the follow-up examinations. Based on the real estate license hierarchical management mechanism, the requirements on real estate brokers are more stringent than those on the salespeople.

Salespeople's qualification requirements

A. over 18 years of age;

B. being honest and reliable, clean of any criminal or misconduct record;

C. completing up to three courses, including 2 compulsory courses: *Real Estate Principles* and *Real Estate Practice*, and one from the twelve elective courses: *Business Law, Common Interest Development, Computer Applications in Real Estate, Escrow, General Accounting, Real Estate Law, Mortgage Management, Asset Management, Real Estate Appraisal, Real Estate Economics, Real Estate Finance, Real Estate Office Administration*;

D. Completing up to three semesters' study or finish at least 3/4 of the learning contents.

Broker qualification requirements for license examination application

A. over 18 years of age;

B. being honest and reliable, clean of any criminal or misconduct record;

C. at least two years' full-time work experience as a real estate salesperson in the last five years; holding a university degree (real estate major graduates may be exempt from the two-year full-time sales work requirement);

D. completing up to eight required courses, including 5 compulsory courses: *Real Estate Law, Real Estate Appraisal, Real Estate Economics* or *General Accounting, Real Estate Finance,* and *Real Estate Practice*; plus three elective courses in *Advanced Legal Aspects of Real Estate, Advanced Real Estate Appraisal, Advanced Real Estate Finance, Business Law, Common Interest Development, Computer Applications in Real Estate, Escrow, Mortgage Law, Asset Management, Real Estate Management,* and *Real Estate Principles*;

E. completing up to 3 semesters' learning at institutions designated by the state real estate committee.

There is no distinction between salesperson and broker qualification in China's Hong Kong. Applicant's integrity and ethical review is emphasized and brokers' integrity and law abiding required. Candidates are required to have completed the fifth grade secondary or equivalent education. No course learning is required.

Japanese qualification examination and verification does not involve morality. The minimum education requirement is a secondary education diploma. Anyone who has worked in the real estate brokerage industry for 2 years or completed the practical courses can participate in the real estate notary exam.

- **The second link control: license examination**

In the United States, the real estate agent qualification exam is the most important threshold for real estate brokerage career. Real estate brokers and salespersons are required to pass the qualification exam in order to obtain the appropriate license. There are big differences between the two. Brokers can register with brokerage firms and engage in independent brokerage business. They can employ sales staff and have a management responsibility for sales staff. Salespeople cannot operate business independently. Their job is to assist brokers. They do not have the right to sign contract. Demands and surveillance on brokers concerning quality verification, examination and licensing are more stringent than those on the sales staff.

Specific examination process and form are as follows:

① After passing the qualification review, the applicant may choose the examination time and place according to the official website of the State Housing Authority. The exam cycle and time are different in each state. In California, broker exams are held 2–3 times per month, while sales staff exams are held 10–15 times per month.

②Brokers' exam takes up the morning and the afternoon. There are 200 multiple choice questions, 100 in the morning and 100 in the afternoon; lasting 150 min each. The passing score requires 75% correct answers. Salespersons' examination lasts for 3 h and 15 min. There are 150 multiple choice questions. The passing line is 70% correct answers. The passing rate for brokers' examination is normally around 20%.

③The examination is composed of computer-based testing and paper testing. Results of computer-based testing will be informed after the completion of the examination. The results of paper testing take 5–7 working days after examination and are announced by the local real estate management bureau.

④One can retake the exams as many times as necessary within 2 years if one fails the exams the first time and has paid makeup exam fees. However, if one cannot pass the exams within the two years, the application becomes invalid and one is required to re-apply for it.

Japan's qualification exam is more professional and difficult than that of the US. The contents of the examination are set up by the Ministry of Land, Infrastructure, Transportation, the Ministry of Agriculture, Forestry and Fisheries, the Ministry of

Finance, the Ministry of Internal Affairs and Communications and the Consumption Office. The passing rate is between 15 and 18%. The passing rate for first time examinees is only 1–2%.

In China's Hong Kong, brokers and sales staff take different exams. Work experience in real estate is not required. As long as candidates pass the examination, they will obtain the license. The brokers' passing rate is about 20%, but the salespersons' passing rate is about 60%. Broker training courses in China's Taiwan include the legal articles, real estate related contracts, and brokerage practice.

- **The third link control: obtaining the license**

In the United States, after the applicants pass the qualification exam, within one year the State Property Administration will send the license application to the applicant. Applicants are required to submit the license application (which covers personal social security number, tax ID, etc.), application fee and fingerprint card within two years. Once approved by the real estate authority, they will obtain a broker's license or salesperson's license.

The practice in China's Hong Kong is similar with that in the US. It is simpler in China's Taiwan where the one can obtain a license once passing the examination. In order to ensure effective learning, Japan requires the candidates to apply for the qualification within one year after passing the exam. After one year they need to be re-trained. The qualification is updated every five years, and each time they need to re-take the required courses.

- **The fourth link control: license registration**

In the United States, real estate brokers are not approved for operation once licensed. They must first sign with a brokerage agency, and participate in a period of internship work. Only after registration by the license issuing department can they start business. License renewal is also required after the practice of regular registration, usually once in 2–4 years. During the registration period they need to continue to participate in continuing education, and take the exam. Those who do pass the follow-up examination and un-registered real estate brokers will have their licenses revoked by the government.

License is not required upon real estate entry in Japan and China's Taiwan. It is more easily done in China's Hong Kong than in the US. Candidates are required to provide materials according to the requirements of the Authority. Registration can be completed after the review.

- **The fifth link control: continuing education**

Continuing education mechanism is an important means to ensure that brokers can enhance the professional skills. It is also an internal driving force for brokers to continue to learn. In the United States, brokers licenses must be renewed every four years and are required to attend an annual continuing education and need to complete the established course within a given time. Some states require a follow-up exam, but it is usually easier than the first one (Table 1).

Table 1 Comparison of brokerage industry entry control process in different countries and regions

Country/ Region	Agent classification	Entry requirements	Exam pass rate	License acquisition	Renewal time	Continuing education
The United States	Salespeople, brokers	Education, integrity, work experience	Around 20%	Registration system	2– 4 years	✓
China's Taiwan	Sales assistants, brokers	Education, work experience	–	–	4 years	✓
China's Hong Kong	Sales assistants, broker	Education, integrity	20% for brokers, 60% for salespeople	Registration system	4 years	✓
Japan	General agent, real estate notary	Education, work experience	15–18%	–	5 years	✓
China's Mainland	General agent	–	–	–	–	–

Source Lianjia Research Institute

3.1.2 Restraint and Punishment Mechanism

The Punishment Mechanism

"Triple qualification entry" system and "five key link control" system have helped maintain high standards and high professionalism in brokerage industry. The value of a punishment mechanism lies in its effectiveness in circumventing the broker's misconducts. False promises, false advertising and other types of cheating by brokers in the United States are strictly regulated. Both government and industry exercise supervision over brokers' conducts. Punishment may include refusal of licensing, detaining the license, revoking the license, fines, suspending business, or dismissal.

The Constraints on Brokers by brokerage Firms

In the United States, brokerage firms and brokers are in independent contractual relationship. The constraints on brokers are relatively weak. A brokerage firm has legal responsibility for its brokers. In many states it is required by law that broker's license must be kept by the brokerage firm; therefore, the firm shall bear full legal responsibility for the broker's business conducts. Brokers must sign the sales and purchase contracts in the name of the brokerage firm. The firm collects the commission and pays the fines for the broker before paying the broker commissions according to the specific circumstances or getting compensation from the broker for the paid fines.

In China's Taiwan, brokers and brokerage firms are in contractual relationships. In China's Hong Kong and Japan, brokers and brokerage firms are in the relation of employment. Their management mechanism is basically the same with that in China's mainland.

3.2 The International Experience of Value Recognition

Value recognition can reflect the brokers' professionalism as well. In the United States, brokers have high regards for their work and the brokerage industry. Brokers and the industry also enjoy very high social recognition.

3.2.1 Selfrecognition

The most direct manifestation of self-recognition is that brokers are willing to continue to work in the industry and treat it as a lifetime career.

According to a research of the US National Association of Realtors, 77% brokers take brokerage as a lifetime career and 84% brokers hold that they will remain in the real estate brokerage industry in the next two years, which fully reveals that American brokers attach great importance to the work and have a very positive sense of belonging.

3.2.2 Industry Recognition

Industry recognition can be measured by two factors. The first is possessing a large proportion of high quality professionals in the industry. The second indicator is that employees in other sectors (especially in high demand and high salary professions) are attracted to work in the real estate brokerage industry.

In the United States, 61% of the brokers hold a university bachelor's or higher degree. Up to 20% hold a master's degree. The vast majority of real estate brokers came from other industries. About 19% of these people worked previously in positions related to management, business, or finance. The job transition proves the attraction of the brokerage industry and serves as an indication of practitioners' recognition of the industry.

3.2.3 Social Recognition

In the United States, the customer satisfaction with brokers is overs 70%. Clients choose their brokers mostly based on their social reputation. Most of the brokers' transactions are repetitive and referral deals. According to a survey of the National Association of Realtors, in 2014 in the United States, up to 80% brokers have repeating dealings, and 86% of brokers have business recommended. 24% of the brokers have more than half of their business from repeated transactions. About 20% of the brokers have more than half of their business from former clients' recommendation. The numbers show that in the US brokers enjoy a good reputation and high social recognition.

4   Summary and Suggestions

Without brokers' professionalization, there will be no rise of good brokers. Since the professionalization of brokers is no easy task, we propose the following suggestions.

4.1   Implementation of Real-Name Practice, Establishment of Qualification Files, and Establishment of Examination System

4.1.1   Implementation of Real-Name Practice System, Establishment of Brokers' Integrity File

There are close to one million employees working in China's real estate brokerage. It is not realistic to require all practitioners to take and pass the qualification examination before giving them work permission all within a short time. It is more feasible to set a transitional period by implementing the real-name practice system in place before a full-scale implementation of qualification examination and license system. Real name is required in releasing home information. Severe punishment should be given to false information providers. Supervision department may set up a broker file system, keeping a record of the basic personal information and performance of each broker, as well as rewards and punishment. The file should be updated on a regular basis by the broker's firm and reported to the authority for reference. On top of the broker's personal file, an open public search platform can provide broker's integrity profile and enable public supervision of a broker's work.

4.1.2   Establishment of a Broker Qualification Review System, Providing Learning Courses to Lay a Good Foundation for the Promotion of the Brokerage Registration System

A brokers' qualification review system should be first implemented to set the basic entry threshold covering age, education, integrity records and criminal records. It is necessary to provide professional courses for brokers who have passed the qualification review. The brokerage firms may take the responsibility to oversee their brokers to complete the courses. Different levels can be applied to include titles such as associate brokers and brokers, corresponding to different responsibilities and rights in the promotion of broker license system we can be set up a longer time interval. It may take a longer time to implement the license system. But it can be required that practitioners pass the qualification review in order to conduct business. At the same time practitioners should be encouraged to take the license examination so that there will be more and more licensees in the brokerage industry.

4.1.3 Speeding up the Broker Qualification Examination and Enhancing Its Value Through Careful Course Design

It is imperative to start the broker qualification examination in China as soon as possible. The qualification examination in the US may well provide references concerning exam contents. Since most of the practitioners in China are from a lower educational background, the initial curriculum may include courses such as the *Real Estate Practices* and *Real Estate Laws and Regulations*. Practical courses may include *Real Estate Appraisal, Real Estate Taxation and Estate Transaction Process*.

4.2 Implementation of Qualification Examinations, Establishment of a Dynamic Evaluation System, Strengthening Professional Ethics, and Improving Broker Evaluation System

4.2.1 Full-Scale Implementation of the Broker Qualification Examination

After the implementation of the broker's qualification review, it is important to stress the importance of the broker's qualification examination. For example, a five-year transition period may be set. Within five years, practitioners who have not yet passed the qualification examination can still work in the industry. However, after 5 years, only license holders will be allowed to stay in brokerage business. This is a measure to encourage more practitioners to participate in professional qualification examination.

4.2.2 Establishment of Broker's Ethical Standards

Industry associations may take the lead to introduce a fair, enforceable and supervisory brokerage code of conduct, requiring brokers to exercise higher moral awareness and safeguard the reputation of the industry.

4.2.3 Establishment of a Dynamic Online Broker Evaluation System

The low frequency of real estate transactions has made it very difficult for brokers to establish a good personal reputation. A dynamic broker evaluation system can effectively reduce moral hazard. The industry association can be responsible for setting up a dynamic public evaluation platform to guide the consumers to evaluate the services provided by brokers and brokerage firms, rewarding the well-evaluated brokers, and imposing warnings or penalties on brokers who are poorly rated or complained.

4.3 Full Implementation of the Licensing System and Gradual Implementation of a Lifelong Learning System

4.3.1 Full Implementation of the Broker License Management System

Broker license management system can be implemented on the basis of completing the broker qualification review and qualification examination system. Comparable to acquiring a driver's license bypassing the driving test, a broker's license management system that covers measures such as refusal, detention, revocation, fines, suspension of business and expulsion should be the ultimate choice for brokerage qualification management. It is suggested that after a considerable number of brokers have passed the qualification examination, the license management system should be comprehensively implemented. A sophisticated broker bottom line management system is made possible through strict implementation of the management system with specific articles.

4.3.2 Strengthening Professional Education for Establishment of Life Long Learning System

Professional knowledge is the inner driving force of broker's specialization. Measures to improve brokers' professionalism may include the following. First, improve brokers' knowledge system construction. Additional courses should include *Real Estate Finance, Real Estate Mortgage and Loan* so as to expand brokers' scope of professional knowledge on top of the required curriculum. Second, brokers' personal image should be enhanced through standardizing work procedure and manners. Third, brokers may be required to study psychology and marketing to enhance their communication skills. Associations and brokerage institutions should organize communication and training to brokers to help them keep pace with the market development.

Chapter 8
Policy Checklist

- Short-term goal: to set up industry bottom lines, including market admittance, authentic information and capital security to counteract problems in transaction security.
- Mid-term goal: to set up industry standard, including institutional construction, the establishment of a legal supervision system and a code of conduct covering practitioners within the industry, reforming and improving the transaction process so as to turn the brokerage industry into an industry which adds values to the community, consumers and practitioners.
- Long-term goal: to initiate industry transformation, including speeding up the use of the internet and financial tools, promoting brokers' professionalization to steer brokerage industry to be more professional and provide better services.

A decade after the establishment of China's real estate brokerage industry, it still faces serious challenges and problems. In view of industrial supervision, the root of these problems lies in the lack of a basic framework for industry operation. Other factors include the absence of a good legal system, the lack of clarified duties for the supervision subjects, insufficient coverage of supervision, limited enforcement, and the lack of basic constraints on agents and brokers' actions. In addition, as today's brokerage industry is rapidly growing into a fusion of financial, information technology and other areas, the present supervision system can hardly cover new market changes and adapt to them. Therefore, the key to achieving the transformation of the industry and establishing "six pillars" for a healthy and standardized real estate brokerage industry is to improve the market supervision subject, to improve the legal system, to establish a constraining mechanism covering multiple subjects, to regulate behaviors and operational processes of brokerage firms and brokers, to constantly improve the quality of employees and to solve new problems in the brokerage industry in a dynamic and continuous way.

© Xiamen University Press and Springer Nature Singapore Pte Ltd. 2018   171
S. Ba and X. Yang, *The Rise of New Brokerages and the Restructuring of Real Estate Value Chain*, https://doi.org/10.1007/978-981-10-7715-9_8

Based on the current situation and feasibility of policies, a "three-step" strategy is proposed. The short-term goal is to set up bottom lines; the mid-term goal is to establish industry standards; and the long-term goal is to realize industry transformation.

1 Step One: Setting the Bottom Lines for Brokerage Operation

There are three prominent problems in the present brokerage industry, namely, low professionalism among brokers, false housing information and lack of financial security. In the short term, the brokerage industry should establish the bottom lines regulating market admittance, information authenticity and capital security so as to ensure smooth and safe transactions.

1.1 To Promote the Broker Admittance System Step by Step, and Set the Bottom Line for Market-Oriented Industry Admittance

1.1.1 Implementing a Real-Name System for Practice; Establishing Credit Files for Brokers

Before full implementation of qualification examination and licensing system, a real-name system for practice should be used as a transitional alternative. Brokerage firms will record information including basic information of in-service brokers and reward and punishment information to the real-name file for brokers, regularly update the file, and report to the authority for the record. On this basis, the authority can establish an integrity file for brokers, open inquiry platform to the public so that each broker conducts practice under the public supervision.

1.1.2 Setting up a Qualification System for Brokers; Laying the Foundation for the Full-Scale Implementation of Broker Licensing Admittance System

Basic thresholds should be set up by the industrial association from aspects including educational background, integrity records, criminal records, etc. to examine the qualifications of brokers. In the short term, brokers will not be able to practice until passing the qualification examination. Also, brokers will be encouraged to actively participate in the qualification examination so that the number of licensed brokers will gradually increase.

1.1.3 Accelerating the Establishment of Qualification Examination and Providing Training Courses for Brokers

It is necessary to speed up the broker qualification examination program. Considering that the majority of current brokers in China do not hold higher education diplomas, the brokerage curriculum should be combined with the practice of brokerage business, laws and regulations, such as real estate related laws, housing valuation inspection, tax calculation, transaction process and other practical contents. The association should provide relevant courses to brokers who have passed the qualification examination, and the brokerage firms should encourage brokers to complete the courses.

1.2 Standardizing the Process of Information Generation and Distribution and Establishing the Bottom Line for Authentic Housing Information

Nowadays, with the diversified development of the brokerage industry, some Internet companies are engaging in housing information dissemination services and some offline intermediaries are transforming to Internet-based ones. The trend will continue for a period in the future. Because of a regulatory gap in this area, authentic housing information can't be guaranteed. Therefore, it is imperative to establish a cross-departmental supervision mechanism by MOHURD (Ministry of Housing and Urban-Rural Development of the People's Republic of China), MIIT (Ministry of Industry and Information Technology of the People's Republic of China) and SAIC (State Administration for Industry and Commerce of the People's Republic of China). The housing information provider should abide by the principle of "whoever distributes the information shall hold responsibility" and a standardized housing information distribution regulation that can cover multiple market main bodies should be established.

1.2.1 Setting Unified Criteria for Authentic Housing Sources

It is recommended that together with industrial association and other departments, MOHURD should set unified criteria for real housing sources, requiring that real housing sources must meet the requirements of "authentic existence, authentic commission, authentic price and authentic pictures". "Authentic existence" means that the house exists physically. If the same house is sold out or revoked, related information should be revised within 24 h. "Authentic commission" means that the owners are selling houses out of their own willingness by commissioning the certain brokerage firm. "Authentic price" means that the price is released based on the owner's real intention. If the owner changes the price, real estate brokerage institution should revise related information accordingly within 24 h after the owner's adjustment. "Authentic pictures" means that pictures of the house (exterior and interior design included) should be taken in the real locations on site. Administrative departments of real estate industry at all levels, industry associations, real estate brokerage firms and institutions which provide information distribution services should standardize and examine information of housing sources according to definition and criteria released by MOHURD.

1.2.2   Enforcing Full and Compulsory Written House Commission System

For the houses which are commissioned for sale, the seller should form a relationship with the real estate brokerage institution with written documents, and take records of basic situation of the house, commissioned selling conditions, commissioned price, form of commission, and etc. If the seller refuses to provide information, or the provided information does not conform to the reality, or the seller refuses to sign the written commission, the real estate brokerage institution should not accept the commission and should not provide information distribution service for the houses without written acknowledgement.

1.2.3   Enforcing Full Implementation of the System of *Description of Houses*

In accordance with Article 22 of *Administrative Measures for Real Estate Brokerage*, real estate brokerage institutions and real estate brokers should use *Description of Houses* to describe house situation and key information of transaction in written form. Real estate brokerage institutions and real estate brokers should provide *Description of Houses* to customers when releasing information of houses and introducing houses to customers. To set a unified standard, it is recommended that the MOHURD and CIREA (China Institute of Real Estate Appraisers and Agents) set a unified template of *Description of Houses* for the country for signing uses.

1.2.4   Enforcing Real-Name Release System

Housing information should be released by real estate brokers in real names. False ownership is not allowed. For real estate brokerage institutions and non-real-name brokers who haven't been filed in the real estate administrative department, the Internet platform that provides information distribution services shall not provide them with services. As for releasing individual housing information, registering information online in real name is also required.

1.2.5 Establishing a Deposit System for Real House Sources

Real estate brokerage institutions and Internet platforms which provide housing information distributions services are required to pay deposit for real house sources to industry association, while the association answers to informants from the society. If the released information is not accorded with requirement of "authentic existence, authentic commission, authentic price and authentic pictures", the industry association has the right to place penalty from the deposit and reward the informer. Real estate intermediaries who have not paid the deposit will not have access to housing information distribution services provided by related institutions.

1.2.6 Establishing a Blacklist System for False House Sources

Real estate brokers who have released a large number of false house sources will be publicized on the blacklist. In addition to publicizing the blacklist, platforms with information distribution services are not allowed to provide information distribution services for brokers on the blacklist for a certain period of time. Internet platforms with information distribution services must strengthen the verification of authenticity of house sources, and establish a channel for exposure and complaints on false housing information. Moreover, consumers can report false information to information administrative departments including Reporting Center for Illegal and Harmful Internet Information of the People's Republic of China so that the conduct to release false information would be investigated severely.

1.3 Full Implementation of Capital Supervision System; Establishment of a Bottom Line for Secure Transaction

Follow the mode of "led by government, guided by association and operated by enterprises". Establish regulations and standardsfor capital supervision. Promote the participation of qualified third-party payment companies and other professional organizations to provide diversified financial supervision.

1.3.1 Identifying the Process, Rules and Regulatory Body of Capital Supervision

Process of capital supervision should be jointly established by MOHURD, the central bank and other departments to clarify types of capital supervision, time-point for conducting capital supervision and specific requirements for unfreezing capitals and a list of materials which buyers, sellers and brokers need to provide. For the time being, diversified ways including quartet supervision, government supervision and third-party supervision can be made available and consumers can be guided to choose a most suitable way.

1.3.2 Establishing Information Submitting and Verification System of Capital Supervision

The capital supervision institution should report the newly-added capital supervision business and completed unfrozen capitals which have been to the authorities on a monthly basis with specific and sum statistics. With an automated verification mechanism based on IT system, capital supervision information submitted by capital supervision institutions should be cross compared with ownership transfer registration information of governmental departments and trade information submitted by brokerage institutions. In this way, each transaction capital can be delivered safely according to capital supervision standards.

1.3.3 Encouraging Qualified Professional Institutions to Provide Diversified Financial Supervision

As multiple supervision methods coexisted, the role of real estate management institutions are gradually transferring from participants of capital supervision to supervisors, which is mainly responsible for the establishment and supervision of the system. Encouraging professional institutions like qualified banks or third-party payment institutions to carry out capital supervision with a market-oriented way can improve the efficiency and experience of supervision on the basis of transaction safety.

2 Step Two: Establishing the Code of Conduct and Standard Business Process for Practitioners

In the next three to five years, the reform and development of the brokerage industry should strive to solve the prominent problems in business dealings and focus on its institutionalization and standardization, establishing a legal supervision system covering multiple market subjects to standardize conducts of practitioners and improve efficiency and transparency of the transaction process, On the basis that all outstanding business problems have been solved.

2.1   Improving Laws and Regulations of the Industry and Establishing a Supervision System Covering Multiple Subjects

2.1.1   Revising the *Law of the People's Republic of China on the Administration of the Urban Real Estate*

Based on suggestions from related departments and the market, regulations including *Provisions on the Administration of Urban Real Estate Intermediary Services, Interim Provisions on Practice System of Real Estate Brokers, Measures for Certificate of Practice Qualification of Real Estate Brokers and Measures for the Administration of Real Estate Brokers* should be reviewed and combined to establish *Law on the Administration of Real Estate Brokerage*. By adding it into the *Law of the People's Republic of China on the Administration of the Urban Real Estate, Law on the Administration of Real Estate Brokerage* can be seen as the higher law for real estate brokerage industry.

The newly revised *Law on the Administration of Real Estate Brokerage* should define the basic legal relationship of real estate brokerage, clarify the industry's admittance mechanism, establish the real housing information distribution system, stipulate the rights, obligations, prohibited acts and legal responsibilities of institutions and personnel, create a mechanism to handle complaints and protect practitioners and define the scope of official duties of supervision departments and brokerage institutions.

The newly revised *Law on the Administration of Real Estate Brokerage* should not be confined to the traditional brokerage industry. All the entities involved in housing transactions should be included in the supervision framework, including traditional brokerage institutions, agencies, Internet companies, third party payment institutions, banks and Insurance companies, and etc. In accordance with the transaction process, a supervision system with full coverage shall be established. In particular, complementary regulations shall be set on non-traditional intermediaries (such as the Internet platform) engaging in housing transactions to fill the gap of supervision.

2.1.2   Strengthening the Dominant Role of Market Regulation of Industry Association

First, it is time to establish China Real Estate Broker Association in accordance with the concept of "streamlining administration, delegating more powers to lower-level governments and society and improving regulation". As an independent social organization, it accepts organizational guidance from the Ministry of Civil Affairs and business guidance from MOHURD, but it is not subordinate to administrative departments. Funds of the association are mainly from its members. The core functions of the association include the implementation of industry self-discipline according to law, improvement of the professionalism of the industry, promotion of cooperation and competition, enhancement of quality of practitioners. Second, in accordance with the principle that "employees must join a related enterprise and enterprises must join a related association", real estate brokers must join brokerage institutions to practice, and real estate brokerage institutions must join the association to accept the self-discipline of the association. Third, the association shall be delegated the basic power of industry supervision, such as organizing examinations, qualification examination, license issuance, complaints and arbitration, supervision and punishment so that the association can become a real supervision institution, forming rigid constraining forces on brokerage institutions and brokers.

2.2 Establishing a Code of Conduct for Brokers and Improve the Overall Quality of Brokers

2.2.1 Promoting Phased Broker Business Licensing System

On the basis of perfecting the qualification exam and qualification review of brokers, broker admittance system should be implemented in different stages. The broker must pass the qualification exam and obtain the license for practice. A five-year transition period can be set, during which time, brokers who haven't passed the qualification exam but passed the qualification review may remain in business. When the five-year transitional period is over, only those who have passed the exam (including primary broker associate examinations or official broker exams) and obtained license can stay in business.

2.2.2 Setting Ethical Standards of Brokers

Industry association should set fair and enforceable ethical standards for brokers which are under supervision. The standards should require brokers to set a code of conduct of higher moral level, and to jointly safeguard the reputation of the industry. Industry association and brokerage institutions should take measures such as issuing warnings, conducting disciplinary talks, or disqualifying licenses for ethical violations.

2.2.3 Establishing an Online Dynamic Evaluation System for Brokers

Because of the low frequency of characteristics of real estate transactions, it is rather difficult for brokers to establish personal reputation. Dynamic evaluation system is conducive to overcoming moral risks. On the basis of real name practice of brokers, it is feasible to establish a dynamic public evaluation platform at the association level, guiding consumers to evaluate services provided by brokers and brokerage institutions. Well-evaluated brokers shall be rewarded while brokers with poor evaluation or complaints shall be given warnings.

2.3   Implementing a Verification System of Housing Property Rights to Reduce Transaction Risks

2.3.1   Establishing a Compulsory Verification System of Housing Property Rights

Verification of property rights should be required nationwide, taking property rights verification as a compulsory session during transaction so as to reduce the risk of property rights. Real estate administrative departments at all levels should speed up collecting housing property rights information to promote the national housing property rights information network. Public service platform of housing property rights inquiry should be improved to shorten the time of inquiry feedback as well as the processing cycle. The property intermediaries should provide property survey report to clients in written forms after the inquiry.

2.3.2   Establishing an Online Information Inquiry Platform

Online information inquiry platform should offer inquiry services to real estate brokerage institutions with records and licensed real estate brokers, allowing institutions inquire housing property rights or property information through the online service platform. After inquiry, real estate intermediaries should provide written reports to clients.

2.3.3   Offering Real Time Changes of Property Information During Transaction

For new information such as housing mortgage or seizure after online contracts, online service platform should offer dynamic notifications to real estate brokerage institutions and consumers by online reminders or SMS reminders.

3   Step Three: Promoting Professionalization and Transformation of the Brokerage Industry

Under integrated stimulation of the Internet and financial industries, brokerage industry will manifest its value in terms of professionalization and participation in the future. Brokerage industry should take the initiative to use the Internet technology to optimize the whole process, use the liquidity of the financial system to promote innovation of its transaction system, and promote the professional transformation of brokers for the prosperity and development of the brokerage industry.

3.1   Introducing "Internet +" Technology to Enhance Intelligent Experience of Transaction

3.1.1   Establishing a Decision-Making Information System for Consumers Based on Big Data

In order to make consumers participate in decision-making of transactions more rationally and more efficiently, a market information disclosure system should be strengthened, and market information transparency should be improved. In addition to publicizing the commission contract and information of *Description of Houses*, real dynamic selling information should also be made available to consumers, including the historical transaction prices of the house, the number of times the house is seen, the seller's offer adjustment record, transaction prices of houses within a community, and comparison of the prices of house sources in the same period. In this way, consumers can take the initiative to determine the market status and value range of houses with publicized information in a rational way.

3.1.2   Upgrading "Internet Plus" for Transaction Process

Qualified professional organizations should be encouraged to use Internet and mobile Internet technology to transform trading patterns and trading processes, so that procedures could be simplified through Internet for buyers and sellers. Buyers and sellers can upload documents required for transaction and confirmed by means of messages. Consumers are provided with information inquiry services including the Internet, mobile phone Apps, customer service calls, text messages and etc. Meanwhile, integration of business information flow and capital flow can be achieved to reduce the time cost of consumers as well as on-site office pressure of government departments for service visibility, supervision transparency, transaction efficiency, and transaction security.

3.2   Exploring the Liquidity of the Financial System Framework to Promote the Innovation of Transaction System

3.2.1   Acknowledging the Lubricant Role of Financial Liquidity in Second-Hand Housing Transactions

Second-hand housing liquidity finance has an important role in smoothening transaction process and improving transaction security and efficiency. For this kind of short-term cash flow innovation with smooth transaction, clear distinction and support should be offered to build a favorable of policy-related public environment.

3.2.2   Encouraging Innovation and Exploration of the Liquidity of Finance

It is recommended that departments like MOHURD, the central bank, the CBRC, should carry out specific researches on financial business arisen from for the second-hand housing transactions and arrange relevant brokerage institutions to be research members. During setting the research project, brokerage institutions involved in the research may be chosen as pilot and experimental objects to explore the operation details and the process specification of the financial business.

3.2.3   Gradually Allowing Qualified Brokerage Institutions to Provide Financial Services to Second-Hand Housing Transactions

On the basis of fully understanding the advantages and disadvantages of second-hand housing financial products and forming a standardized system, qualified brokerage institutions should be gradually allowed to provide financial services to second-hand housing transactions. Brokerage institutions can apply for operating qualifications to MOHURD, which will get approval and recorded by MOHURD and relevant departments. Intermediaries should report regularly to the designated authorities and present risk disclosures at the same time.

4   Improving Broker Quality for Long-Term Development and Professional Transformation

In the long run, the value of brokers lies in providing more meticulous offline services.

4.1   Fully Implementing the Broker's License Management System

The license management system should be fully implemented once the number of brokers passing the qualification examination reaches a certain percentage. The regulatory system should cover refusal, detention, revocation, penalty, suspension of the business operation and expulsion. The license management system should be fully enforced and an all round broker management system should be established.

4.2   Strengthening Professional Training and Gradually Establishing Brokers' Life Cycle Learning System

Professional knowledge is the internal driving force for brokers' professionalization. Their professional abilities should be improved from the following aspects. First, the knowledge system of brokers should be improved by taking related subjects, including real estate finance, mortgage loan and so on, apart from the basic courses, aiming to enhance the professionalism of brokers. Second, the appellation and etiquette used in the process of transaction should be standardized. Establishing standardized operating procedures is required to constantly improve the image of brokers. Third, learning programs of sales skills including psychology, marketing should be provided to enhance brokers' communication skills. Industry associations and brokerage firms can provide regular communication and training opportunities to organize brokers to study, for improving the synchronous development of brokers' knowledge system at the same pace of market development.

Printed by Printforce, the Netherlands